Monday, May 12, 2008 – 1:33 P.M.
Borders book store Café – Wolf Rd.
Albany, New York

D1481812

Monday, May 12, 2008 – 1:33 P.M.
Borders book store Café – Wolf Rd.
Albany, New York

CLASSICAL WORLD

CLASSICAL WORLD

DR. IAN BARNES

CARTOGRAPHICA

A CARTOGRAPHICA BOOK

This book is produced by
Cartographica Press
6 Blundell Street
London N7 9BH

ISBN: 978-1-84573-326-1

QUMCLWO

Printed in Singapore by
Star Standard Industries Pte Ltd

CONTENTS

INTRODUCTION

THE CLASSICAL WORLD AND THE GROWTH OF CIVILIZATION

*T*hroughout history different civilizations have risen and fallen, and although sometimes it has been possible to predict this fall, it has usually been impossible to stop it. Some civilizations have been extremely successful and have lasted for hundreds, if not thousands, of years, while some have been more transitory.

Often completely unconnected civilizations have shared success at the same time in different parts of the world.

A feature of all civilizations is that they do not last for ever. History has shown that a catastrophic change in circumstances can cause the most powerful and established civilization to collapse almost overnight.

This might have been as the result of military invasion, as in the case of the Incas of South America. After 4000 years the Incas had virtually no enemies and were free to develop their civilization; then the Spanish arrived and the old order collapsed within a year or two.

Sometimes mother nature has been to blame, as in the case of the ancient civilization that grew up along the banks of the Indus River in India. It was successful for hundreds of years and then the river changed its course and that was the end.

Perhaps we are currently heading for a similar catastrophe. If, as predicted, global warming causes the polar ice caps to melt, sea levels worldwide could rise by up to 30 feet, submerging vast areas of land and key cities worldwide. London, New York, Miami, Mumbai, Calcutta, Sydney, Shanghai, Lagos, and Tokyo would be among those largely submerged by such a rise.

PREHISTORIC CULTURE
Stonehenge, in Wiltshire, England, is one of the best known prehistoric monuments in the world. It is believed that the huge standing stones were erected around 2200 BC— about a century before the start of the Bronze Age in Britain— and the surrounding circular earth bank and ditch, which constitute the earliest phase of the monument, have been dated to about 3100 BC. The monument dates back to a pre-civilized England, which consisted of regional tribes, and although they were not nearly as advanced as the Ancient Egyptians, the challenges of transporting and erecting the massive stones indicates a high level of technological sophistication and social organization. The monument almost certainly played some kind of ritualistic role, most likely connected to burial of the dead.

THE NEOLITHIC AGE (STONE AGE)

True civilization began in Neolithic times, spreading from the savannas of East Africa. Neolithic man was noted for his invention of food production methods, grinding grain with stones and making pottery. Such techniques introduced a rapid transformation in lifestyle. The nomadic hunter-gatherer existence ended for many, as people began to cultivate wild cereals. Living in one place to tend to crops meant that people began to congregate in mud-brick villages. A guaranteed food supply and the ability to store it for later use meant that a bad growing season could be survived. Populations increased and moved to open lands, rich with alluvial soil. Very similar societies grew with politico-religious hierarchies. Parallel developments led to proto-civilizations being born in the river valleys of the Tigris–Euphrates, the Nile, the Yellow River, and the Indus.

Farming communities now had the opportunity of producing food surpluses, allowing some of the population to become potters or other craftsmen, priests, and chiefs. The idea of leisure and the acquisition of possessions eventually led to trade and the concept of the market place. With the domestication of donkeys and horses, commercial caravans were possible and villages began to trade with one another. Specialization was the norm, with pottery, textile production, metallurgy, and the manufacture of weapons all sought after skills.

These revolutionary techniques that so changed life did not happen simultaneously in time and space. The Mesolithic period (middle Stone Age) saw stone-grinding and the first domestication of cereals before pottery was invented. In the Near East, pre-pottery cultures have been unearthed in the southwest corner of Iran, through northern Mesopotamia, and Syria into the Jordan Valley in Palestine.

By 6000 BC, Neolithic pottery had spread around the Aegean, to southern Anatolia and western Iran. Thus, culture surged outward. Asia, Africa, and Europe followed these patterns, but they were insignificant in the Americas.

Chinese civilisations also began to develop soon after, following Near Eastern examples. While agricultural societies matured, some populations remained nomadic, inhabiting parts of North Africa, Arabia, and the vast steppe-lands of Eurasia. The latter region would witness incursions as marauding nomads burst through mountain ranges into China, the Iranian plateau, and Mesopotamia. This led to the building of protective walls around villages, with some settlements growing into city-states, especially in Mesopotamia.

THE BRONZE AGE

In parts of Eurasia, copper began to be used as a material for weapons and tools; Cyprus was an island rich in copper and it actually gets its name from the Greek word for copper. Eventually, bronze replaced copper because it took a harder edge and was thus more durable.

In order to make bronze, small amounts of tin were needed to add to the copper to make an alloy. Tin was only found in a few areas, so Neolithic economies were forced to give up self-sufficiency and begin international trading in order to secure the desired minerals. This search was made easier by the expansion of city-states into larger political units, which effectively were early empires.

The resultant Bronze Age varied considerably in time and duration in Eurasia. The earliest evidence of copper usage was in Mesopotamia and Egypt from around 3000 BC onward, with bronze produced some five or six hundred years later. The Bronze Age in Europe did not begin until after 2000 BC and began later still in parts of Asia, most of Africa, and all of Oceania.

In China, the Neolithic Yang-shao culture, which existed around 3950 to 1700 BC, developed in Shaanxi and Shanxi and was gradually succeeded by the Lung-shan culture with its permanent villages and domesticated animals, between 2000 and 1850 BC. By the time of the feudal Shang dynasty, lasting from around 1500 to 1000 BC, there is evidence of bronze funerary objects at royal tombs in An-yang.

Throughout the Bronze Age, migrations of peoples took place as steppe culture developed. The use of horse, cart, and wagon allowed the easy movement of populations into Central Asia, east of the Caspian Sea into India and Anatolia and north of the Black Sea into the Balkans.

One of these mobile groups was related, and they are now known as the Indo-Europeans. As the group split up geographically in their journeys, their earlier language also split and developed into Sanskrit, Persian, and other Near Eastern languages. Most European tongues also evolved from this stock. Some of these peoples drifted into Bronze Age regions and blended with settled peoples, while others apparently acted violently, as in the case of the collapse of the Dravidian-speaking Indus Valley civilization.

THE FIRST CIVILIZATIONS

True cities had begun to develop in Neolithic times. An important example of an early city is Çatal Hüyük in southern Anatolia. This, with Jericho, was one of the two most important Neolithic sites in the Near East. Occupied from 6500 to 5400 BC, its 32-acre mound comprised tightly packed houses, for approximately 6000 people, with access to the houses through the roof. The interiors were sometimes decorated with murals

BRONZE WEAPONRY
There is no consensus as to exactly when and where bronze was first discovered, and indeed it is likely that it was invented independently in different areas around the world. The earliest known tin bronzes are from what is now Iran and Iraq and date to the late 4th millennium BC, but some experts suggest that bronze was used in Thailand a thousand years earlier than this. One of the most significant uses for bronze was in the production of weaponry. Sword production in China is attested from the Bronze Age Shang Dynasty. Bronze was also used for weaponry production in Europe, and the illustration shows a collection of bronze weaponry found in modern-day Romania. It was a much more durable material than copper, allowing the production of more deadly weapons.

depicting animals, humans, landscapes, and geometric patterns. Cult items included figurines of a seated mother goddess, which is thought to have represented childbirth.

Subsistence agriculture produced cereals and legumes, high quality woollen textiles, and linen. The town traded Syrian flint and Turkish obsidian, which sometimes reached southern Palestine. Other goods included turquoise, jewelry crafted from seashells, and copper.

Early Eurasian cities survived by building fortifications, designing new weaponry, perfecting archery, and by expansion. Small and weaker states were simply absorbed. Ever more complex bureaucracies were required to regulate trade and administration of their kingdoms. Literacy was needed for accurate records. Sophisticated rulers, priests, and generals all required accounts and laws.

Early Mesopotamia developed a form of wedge-shaped cuneiform writing on clay. This system was employed by Sumerians, Akkadians, Babylonians, Assyrians, Canaanites, Hittites, and Hurrians and therefore spread through the Semitic, non-Semitic and Indo-European languages. Pictographs were adopted in the Indus Valley while the Chinese independently produced pictograms that were etched into animal shoulder blades to form oracle bones. Many of these have been found in Shang archaeological digs. Over the course of time early pictographic scripts with symbols representing individual words and concepts were replaced by symbols representing sounds.

Religion, the economy, and astronomy all demanded the study of chronology. The construction of a calendar was essential for organizing civil society and ritual observances. Lunar and solar calendars were both used, the first working calendar being designed in Egypt. Time reckoning, according to Mesopotamian clay tablets, commenced as early as the 27th century BC. Different states used different methods of measuring time. Regnal years were generally used in Babylonia where years began at the beginning of a king's reign.

Lunar calendars were linked to farming and its various activities. Interest payments and loans could also be calculated. Calendars also made it possible to hire servants for a fixed time period. As one state expanded at the expense of others, the victor's calendar would be imposed on the vanquished, as happened after the Persian conquest of Babylonia in 539 BC.

In India, the Indus Valley civilization flourished, where the interesting housing featured rooms grouped around a courtyard or single room huts. Some houses possessed bathrooms and toilets linked to covered street drains. Artisans produced goods that were traded with the peoples of Persia and Afghanistan.

In China, the Neolithic Yang-shao culture in Shaanxi and Shanxi involved a slash and burn agriculture with farmers not only growing millet and raising pigs, but hunting and fishing for alternative sources of protein. The succeeding Lung-shan culture was characterized by permanent settlements with herds of cattle, sheep, goats, and pigs.

The most important center for human development was Mesopotamia with subsistence based upon the rich soils deposited by the Tigris and Euphrates rivers. This allowed cities to expand to 10,000 inhabitants or more. Their highly decorated temples were also academic centers of excellence with priests, teachers, mathematicians, and astronomers. These institutions were also frequently used as food distribution centers.

Clay tablets, commonly used for recording commercial activities, were also used for recording literature, particularly the Epic of Gilgamesh.

The country collapsed under the impact of the Akkadian tribes united by Sargon, whose empire stretched from the Persian Gulf to the Mediterranean.

This opening up of the area allowed trade to flourish. Commercial sailing voyages visited Bahrain and the Indus Valley, exporting grain in return for copper, carnelian, timber and ivory. Lapis lazuli came from Afghanistan, while tin was an important internal commodity and copper was imported from Cyprus. Overland routes entered the Balkans and Arabia. Baltic amber found its way to Bronze Age Greece and Egyptian pearls from Fayum ended up in England, showing the extent of trade at this time.

CRADLE OF CIVILIZATION
The highly fertile soils deposited by the rivers Tigris and Euphrates allowed civilization in Mesopotamia to flourish, with the rich agricultural land supporting large sedentary populations. These larger settlements fostered developments in housing, social organization, and intellectual pursuits such as mathematics and astronomy.

CIVILIZATION IN EGYPT AND THE NEAR EAST

There followed a period of steady development of civilization, with a number of largely isolated civilizations all progressing at approximately the same pace.

Civilization in Egypt would never have happened if it hadn't been for the Nile. Every year floodwaters deposited alluvial soil, essential for successful agriculture, while the river also provided water for irrigation and transport. During the Old Kingdom, from 3100 to 2023 BC, came the unification of Upper and Lower Egypt, the creation of a sophisticated state bureaucracy, the first writing, and the construction of the Great Pyramids of Giza. The capital, Memphis, as well as being the power center of the Pharaohs, was also the center of international trade with the Levant, Sinai, and Nubia, as well as the base for mining expeditions to Sinai. After 2181 BC, Egypt disintegrated into independent provinces.

Mesopotamia also flourished due to alluvium from the Tigris and Euphrates rivers, giving birth to a number of city-states which competed for more land as their populations grew. Cities such as Kish, Ur, and Umma confederated under Lugalzagessi (Umma) but their wealth attracted the Semitic Akkadians, united by Sargon, who ruled from around 2334 to 2279 BC and who conquered the lands of Sumer.

Akkadian control stretched to the Mediterranean but collapsed under Gutian (the Guti were a nomadic Mesopotamian tribe) attacks in 2000 BC. By 1894 BC, the Amorites of the small Babylonian kingdom expanded their lands, especially under Hammurabi, who ruled from around 1792 to 1750 BC. Some 20,000 clay tablets from Mari have been discovered that describe this age. Hammurabi is best remembered for his Code of Laws, detailing legal procedures and punishments; laws of property, finances and family; plus compensation for personal injury. The Hittites destroyed Babylon in about 1531 BC, leaving a broken state at the mercy of the Kassites.

The Egyptian Middle Kingdom, between 2025 and 1550 BC, saw the country reunified under Mentuhotep of Thebes. Trade followed with Syria and Palestine while Nubia paid tribute. Despite pyramid building, architecture, and literary masterpieces, the kingdom once again declined, with the invading Hyksos capturing most of Egypt while leaving the south to pay tribute. The New Kingdom, between 1550 and 1069 BC, commenced with the expulsion of the Hyksos by Ahmose, who ruled between 1550 and 1525 BC. Expansion followed into Palestine, Syria, and Nubia to provide buffers against potential attacks from Asia and Kush. Conflicts with the Mitanni, rebellion in Palestine and an expanding Hittite state once again weakened Egypt, as did a religious revolution under Akhenaton.

Pharoah Ramesses II battled the Hittites at Kadesh in about 1275 BC, but the result was a military stalemate that ended in a peace treaty, affirmed by an inter-dynastic marriage. Egyptian energies were next used to combat migrating Libyans, the raids of the Sea People, and the rising power of Assyria.

Throughout Egyptian history, relations with Nubia, or Kush, were important. Forts were maintained on the border with long-term Egyptian garrisons serving as bases for raids. Amenophis I, ruling from 1575 to 1504 BC, pushed the border south to the Second Cataract of the Nile at Semna. He maintained close control over Nubian governors and the walled towns with Egyptian temples he built symbolized pharaonic control. Thus, Nubian economic resources, such as copper, ivory, ebony, and skins, could be extracted.

Tuthmosis II, ruling from 1512 to 1504 BC, extended his southern border to the Fourth Cataract, appointing a viceroy over Nubia. The region was fully Egyptianized and its army was used for Egypt's benefit as more goods were acquired: grain, oil, cattle, minerals, luxury items, slaves, and gold from the Nile, Wadi Allaqi and Gabgada. However, by 1000 BC, Egypt lost control of Nubia.

Confronting the New Kingdom had been the Indo-European Hittites who had invaded Anatolia in the 2nd millennium BC. Labarnas I founded the kingdom in around 1600 BC and his successor, Mursilis I, sacked Babylon, destroying its first dynasty. Although its borders did not remain constant, the empire developed under Suppiluliumos from 1380 to 1346 BC. He destroyed the Mitanni and seized some cities as dependencies, notably Carchemish. In Anatolia, Arzawa was seized but the Kaskians in the north retained a hard-fought independence. Conflict with Egypt ended after the Battle of Kadesh.

After 1200 BC, the Hittite state collapsed under pressure from the Sea Peoples and Phrygians, yet some city-states survived, and these retained a Hittite identity.

Assyria was the new power threatening the Hittites and Egypt. After an early power surge between 1356 and 1117 BC, there was a decline until, in 935 BC, the Assyrian Empire saw a new resurgence which lasted until 609 BC. Under Shalameneser III (859 to 825 BC) and Tiglath-pileser III (745 to 728 BC) new territories were added, but these rebelled constantly. The Empire reached its greatest extent under Ashurbanipal, when it extended into Egypt. In spite of military aid from Egypt, the Empire's final rapid demise in 609 BC came about as a result of aggression by the combined military strength of a new Babylonian state and the Medes.

The new Babylonian Empire, sometimes known as the Chaldean Empire, lasted for 87 years from 626 to 539 BC.

THE WONDERS OF ANCIENT EGYPT
The Great Pyramid of Giza is believed to have been built as a tomb for Fourth dynasty Egyptian pharaoh Khufu. The construction of this vast edifice —which was the tallest man-made structure on Earth for over 3,000 years—is believed to have been constructed over a 20 year period, completed around 2560 BC.

The Great Sphinx of Giza is a large half-human, half-lion statue that is commonly accepted by Egyptologists to represent the likeness of King Khafra, who is also believed to have built it during his reign. If this is true, it would place the time of construction somewhere between 2520 BC and 2494 BC.

Its formation was the result of a rebellion against its Assyrian masters, leading to the effective capture of the entire Empire.

Nebucadezzer II, the Great, who ruled from 605 to 561 BC, was a leading figure who defeated Pharoah Necho of Egypt at Carchemish in 605 BC and destroyed the Hebrew Kingdom of Judah in 597 BC. The Empire finally fell in 539 BC as a result of an onslaught by a united army of Medes and Persians under Cyrus the Great.

GREECE AND THE AEGEAN CIVILIZATIONS

The Minoan culture of Crete had a major influence on Bronze Age Aegean civilization. As Cretan ships traded with Sicily, Cyprus, and Egypt, they established colonies on Cythera, Rhodes, and the Anatolian coast. Renowned for the palace at Knossos, with its columns, magnificent frescoes, and bronze figurines of bull-jumpers, this culture developed the Linear B script, a way of writing that predated Greek script by several centuries. Although Knossos was destroyed in the late 14th century BC this did not herald the complete end of Minoan society, since other palaces and towns survived until 1200 BC.

Mainland Greece witnessed the Mycenaean civilization, which was notable for its many fortified cities such as Mycenae, Tiryns, Pylos, and Thebes, designed as much to overawe as for strategic reasons, being statements of power rather than warfare. Mycenaean sites spread all around the Aegean Sea and there is much evidence of colonization and trade, with Mycenaean pottery being found as far away as the Sudan and western Asia.

The Mycenaean world suddenly collapsed in about 1100 BC, but there has never been any specific explanation why.

It was at around this time that the Bronze Age came to an end, when mounted warriors armed with iron weapons invaded from the north. They moved south into Greece, the Peloponnesus, Crete, the Dodecanese and southwest Anatolia. This Dorian incursion was accompanied by waves of northwestern Greeks, causing Aeolic and Ionic Greeks to migrate to Anatolia, the Cyclades, Euboea, and Chalcidice.

The iron weapons of these invaders were far superior to the softer bronze weapons that had been used up until then. The new Greeks established city-states in valleys and on promontories. This was a time of great thinkers with new political ideas and a growth of mathematics, while at the same time a whole range of gods were worshipped.

These city-states actively pursued colonial policies. In some cases people moved on as populations rose, in other cases they moved because of political unrest, but the main reason was probably the result of developing maritime trade. Trading cities were established at al-Mina in Syria and Naukratis in Egypt as

well as throughout the Black Sea, Cyprus, Cyrene, Sicily, Campania, southern Anatolia, and southern France at Massilia (Marseilles). A base in Etruria enabled exploitation of the northern tin route, but further expansion into the eastern Mediterranean hinterland was prevented by Phoenician competition and a number of growing empires. The Black Sea grain trade became increasingly important to Athens.

The wealth gained by all this trade, together with the importation of Egyptian, Mesopotamian, and Indian ideas enriched Greek culture, leading to the development of a literature of drama, comedy, history, and philosophy.

The widening Greek world was eventually confronted by events in the Near East. Cyrus the Great, ruler of the Medes and Persians, founded the Persian Empire, which ultimately acquired Mesopotamia, Egypt, and Anatolia, but the Greek Ionian cities were allowed to keep their independence provided they paid taxes and sent soldiers to fight in the Persian army.

In 512 BC Darius I, who ruled Persia from 521 to 486 BC, invaded Thrace to fight the Scythians. Darius then decided to invade Greece after an Athenian fleet aided the fruitless defense by the Scythians. In 490 BC, a Persian fleet sacked Naxos and parts of Euboea before landing near Marathon where the Athenians and their Plataean allies thoroughly defeated the Persians. Darius's son, Xerxes, invaded Greece in 480 BC, subjugating Thessaly, but he was obstructed by Leonidas and his Spartans at Thermopylae. The Greeks won a naval battle at Salamis and finally defeated a Persian army at Plataea in 479 BC, leaving mainland Greece free.

Spartan strength, which had been so important in the Persian wars, conflicted with Athenian imperialism, which had suffered from rebellions and failed foreign adventures. The resultant Peloponnesian Wars, lasting from 478 to 404 BC, saw fighting on land and sea with battles at Syracuse, in Chalcidice, Anatolia, and the Peloponnesus itself. Athens was finally starved into surrender and was ruled in 404 BC by a Spartan-organized oligarchy, the Thirty Tyrants. In the following year, however, exiled Athenians liberated the city, restored democracy, and negotiated a settlement with Sparta.

A new power emerged in Macedonia in 356 BC after Philip II seized the throne from his nephew. While he had been a hostage in Thebes, he had studied the military tactics of the Greek general and statesman Epaminondas, and on his return he reorganized his army into a mixture of cavalry, archers, javelin throwers, and an infantry phalanx armed with pikes (sarissa). Intervening in Greek affairs and crushing Theban and Athenian forces at Chaeronea in 358 BC, Philip expanded his state and became master and arbiter of Greece.

GREEK WARFARE
This sculpture is believed to depict the Spartan king Leonidas, who died holding the pass at the Battle of Thermopylae in central Greece. The battle, which took place in 480 BC, saw an alliance of Greek city-states fighting the invading Persian Empire led by King Xerxes I. Vastly outnumbered, Leonidas's men were able to delay the Persians long enough for Athens to plan a decisive naval attack. Greek military training, tactics, and weaponry were to prove decisive in countless battles against its enemies.

After Philip was murdered in 336 BC, his son Alexander, later known as Alexander the Great, assumed power. Greece at that time was divided into a number of independent states maintaining their status by war. Thessaly, Epirus, and Illyria were at odds with the southern Boiotian League. The decline of Athens and an emergent Macedonia placed Persia under threat. The Persian Archaemenid dynasty founded by Cyrus the Great ruled lands from Anatolia to the River Indus. The imperial provinces (satrapies), were governed by Persians who collected annual tribute from subject peoples. Innovations were a canal dug from the Red Sea to the Nile, a great system of roads allowing a royal courier to travel from Susa to Sardis (1700 miles) in a week, a postal system, and a mint. Most subject peoples fought loyally for Darius III, the Persian leader, against Alexander.

Alexander ruthlessly eradicated all rivals and opposition, hammered the Danubian Getae and crushed revolts in Thebes, Athens, Arcadia, Elis, and Aetolia. Thebes was razed and its inhabitants all killed or enslaved.

After other states submitted, Alexander crossed the Hellespont in 334 BC into Asia Minor. Persian satraps (regional governers) were defeated at the Battle of the Granicus and Darius was defeated at Issus, after which all coastal cities capable of supplying the Persian fleet were captured. 332 BC witnessed the seizure of Egypt and the foundation of the city of Alexandria.

After defeating the Persians again at Gaugamela in 331 BC, Alexander won the Persian Empire following the murder of Darius. He then campaigned into Uzbekistan and Afghanistan, invaded the Punjab before, on his troops' request, returning westward, only to die of fever in Babylon aged 33 years in 332 BC.

After Alexander died, his Empire disintegrated. Twenty years of warfare then followed before the former Empire was finally divided among his generals. Ptolemy acquired Egypt, Kassandros Macedon, Lysimachos Thrace, Seleucis Persia, and Antigonus Anatolia and Syria. Further warfare saw Antigonus' death and the redistribution of his lands.

The Seleucid Empire, the largest successor state, eventually conflicted with Rome. Egypt lost much of its identity as the Ptolemaic dynasty introduced Greek administration and Greek officials into Egyptian administration. Cleopatra, who was born in Alexandria in 69 BC was the last of the Ptolemy line and was allegedly the first Ptolemy to learn Egyptian.

THE ROMAN EMPIRE

At a time when Rome was little more than a village, the Etruscans were building the first civilization in Western Europe. For 500 years, from around 900 to 400 BC, it is thought that the Etruscans existed as an elite group that ruled the local inhabitants. Settled north of the River Tiber, Etruscan wealth depended upon minerals and the Etruscans extended the power of their twelve fortified cities into the Po Valley, Latium, and Campania, but their major cities, despite having common economic and political interests, never managed to coordinate policy.

Rome, which was founded in 735 BC, came within the Etruscan sphere of influence because it was located at the lowest crossing point of the Tiber, and was therefore important in linking Etruria to Campania.

Eventually, in 510 BC, Rome threw off Etruscan rule, declaring itself a republic. In 506 BC, with help from Latin League allies, it achieved full independence after victory over the Etruscans at Aricia. By the end of the 5th century, Rome was a notable city and in 396 BC the Romans sacked the Etruscan city of Veii.

A major problem faced by the Romans and other communities in Italy at that time was an incursion by the La Tène Celts into northern Italy. The Celtic intention was to Populate the fertile river valleys, and Etruscan towns were fought and destroyed, while Rome itself was sacked in 390 BC.

The Romans recovered and Marcus Furius Camillus, who drove off the Celts or bought them off, began a political expansion involving the waging of four wars against the Celts.

ROMAN ENTERTAINMENT
The classic Roman town of Thysdrus (now knon as El Jem) in Tunisia boasts an immense amphitheater, dating from the 3rd century AD. The elliptical theater had room for 35,000 spectators, making it the second largest Roman ampitheater after the Colosseum in Rome. Public entertainment was central to Roman culture, and these great theters would have hosted a range of events. As well as the traditional gladiatorial games, there would have been mock sea battles, animal hunts, executions, reenactments of famous battles, and dramas based on Classical mythology.

At the same time the Hernici and the rebellious Latin cities were coerced back into the Latin League. Three Samnite Wars, 243 to 341 BC, 326 to 304 BC, and 298 to 290 BC, reduced a combined Lucanian, Celtic, northern Etruscan, and Samnite threat and thereby established Roman supremacy in central Italy. The defeat of Pyhruss of Epirus, an ally of enemy Tarentum, secured Roman lands, and by 266 BC Rome controlled all of Italy south of the River Rubicon.

In 264 BC Rome was invited to intervene in the politics of Messana in Sicily, which was in direct conflict to the interests of the North African empire of Carthage. This resulted in three Punic Wars: 264 to 241 BC, 218 to 201 BC, and 149 to 146 BC. This hundred years of conflict eventually resulted in the complete destruction of Carthage.

Rome's gains from these geographically widespread wars were eastern Spain, Corsica, Sicily, Sardinia, and Tunisia. Simultaneously, in 191 BC, the Romans conquered Cisalpine Gaul in northern Italy. By now the Romans had developed an effective navy and so possessed the means of establishing a wider empire by both land and sea.

When Rome defeated Italian enemies, their land was redistributed to Roman citizens by establishing semiautonomous colonies or individual land-holdings. Some defeated cities became "Roman" or were forced into an alliance. Rome's acquisitions during the Punic Wars became provinces ruled by magistrates sent by the Roman Senate to administer and collect tribute.

But Rome's ambitions stretched further than Carthage. During the 2nd Punic War, Philip V of Macedon allied with Hannibal. Two wars, in 214 and 200 BC, crushed Macedon, and a third in 168 BC saw Macedon reduced to the status of Roman province, as was the remainder of Greece in 146 BC.

Rome also supported Pergamum against the Seleucids, soundly defeating Antiochus III. In 133 BC, Pergamum was bequeathed to Rome, becoming the province of Asia, soon to be joined by Cilicia in 101 BC while attempting to eliminate piracy from its waters.

During the last century BC the Roman Republic moved increasingly toward dictatorship. The generals Marius and Sulla became over-powerful, the latter becoming dictator after defeating Mithridates of Pontus who had invaded Asia. When he retired, Gnaeus Pompeius Magnus (Pompey) emerged, crushing Cilician piracy and finally breaking Mithradates and gaining the submission of the Armenians. He imposed a settlement on the Near East in 64 BC, making the remnants of the Seleucid state the Roman Province of Syria, and the Judaean Kingdom became a dependency.

Gaul also suffered the weight of Rome. The province of Gallia Narbonensis was created in 121 BC. After Julius Caesar was appointed Governor of the two Gaullish provinces in 59 BC, he decided to go on and conquer all of Gaul. By 53 BC Gaul was subjugated until Vercingetorix rebelled, but was then defeated at Alesia. In a sideshow, Caesar had invaded Britain in 55 BC, defeating Cassivelaunus, King of the Catuvellauni, and effectively ending British aid to the Gauls.

Caesar's Gallic victories persuaded him to cross the Rubicon into Italy with an army. This was an illegal act and he faced opposition from some of the senators and from Pompey, whose army he defeated at Pharsalus in Greece in 48 BC. Pompey fled to Egypt, but was murdered and Caesar invaded, defeated the King, and placed Cleopatra in charge. Pompey's sons were defeated in Spain.

44 BC saw Caesar declaring himself perpetual dictator, prompting a number of Senators to arrange his assassination on the Ides of March. There followed a period of civil war as Octavian, his heir, and Mark Antony defeated Brutus and Cassius, two of Caesar's assassains, at Philippi in 42 BC.

Mark Antony fell under Cleopatra's spell, but by then he had fallen out with Octavian. The lovers were defeated at Actium in 31 BC by Octavian's army and committed suicide in 27 BC, giving Egypt to Rome. Octavian changed his name to Augustus and became the first Roman Emperor.

Under Augustus, the Roman border was pushed north of the Alps and Balkans, but Roman legions were slaughtered in the Teutoburg Forest when they crossed the Rhine. The Roman frontier was therefore pulled back to the river. Meanwhile, the Empire was divided into Imperial and Senatorial provinces with client kingdoms acting as buffer states.

Following Augustus, Emperor Claudius, who reigned from AD 41 to 54, was a weak man who needed a victory to quell discontent in Rome. The invasion of Britain at Richborough in AD 43 saw the start of a steady conquest of southern England and Wales. Native leader Caratacus was beaten in AD 51 as was Boudicca's Icenian revolt in 60 and 61. By 69, the Brigantes (a British Celtic tribe) were controlled and Roman General Gnaeus Julius Agricola later attempted the conquest of Scotland, but events on the River Danube meant that troops had to be pulled back and his gains were abandoned.

Elsewhere, Roman misgovernment in Judaea incited a revolt between 66 and 70, and this was ruthlessly put down by future Emperor Vespasian and his son, Titus, in a bitter conflict with the Zealots. The revolt was essentially ended by the siege of Jerusalem. Some Zealots fortified the city of Masada and rather than face capture 960 people committed suicide. A second Jewish revolt erupted in 132 led by Simeon bar Kokhba, with the main concentration of rebels being in the Judaean Desert.

AD 135 saw bar Kokhba killed at Bether. The revolts took an enormous toll on both sides and Emperor Hadrian was forced to report severe manpower losses to the Roman Senate.

The Parthian and Sassanian states were constant problems for Roman foreign policy. The Parthians were rebellious Seleucid subjects whose leader, Mithridates I, conquered Babylonia and Media, later adding Elam, Persia, and parts of Bactria to his Empire. When attacked by Tocharians and Yuezhi, a weakened Parthian state made a treaty with Rome in 92 BC. Later, a Parthian victory at Carrhae in 53 BC held Rome but Trajan's successful attack between 113 and 117 won land as far as the Tigris, the expansion stopping due only to revolts elsewhere.

In AD 165 and 197 Roman armies attacked Parthia but Artabanus V (213 to 222) drove them back. His sudden death caused a dynastic change when the future Sassanian King Ardashir I, 224 to 240, acquired the crown. Sassanian rule eventually stretched from the Tigris to the Indus Valley and from the Aral and Caspian Seas to the Persian Gulf.

Four centuries of Sassanian rule (224–651) saw constant war with Rome, with each side experiencing changing fortunes. Emperor Valerian was held captive by Sharpur I, the only Roman Emperor ever to be captured. He was subsequently tortured to death.

The reign of Khusrau II (591–628) saw Sassanian armies gaining the eastern provinces of the Byzantine Empire—the Eastern Roman Empire—before being defeated by Arab armies in 651.

The years 250–271 witnessed a number of foreign invasions into the Roman Empire. The Germanic Goths attacked the Balkans and Anatolia; Dacia was lost; Athens was sacked and Emperor Decius was killed. The Parthians ravaged Antioch.

By about 260 the Arab state of Palmyra, under Odenathus and Zenobia, filled a power vacuum and expanded throughout the Levant and Anatolia before they were defeated in AD 272.

A more insidious foe for the Romans was the spread of Christianity. Originally regarded as an Oriental cult like Mithraism, the faith spread first amongst the widely distributed Jewish population and then the non-Jews. Nero scapegoated Christians for the Great Fire of Rome in AD 64.

Serious persecution commenced in the 3rd century, especially under Emperor Decius (249–251), followed by Galerius in 303. Fortunes only changed in 312 when Emperor Constantine made Christianity the state religion, the Emperor being baptised on his deathbed in 337.

Returning to Trajan, who was the first Roman ruler to conquer new territories for the Empire, his wars against Dacia and Parthia are worthy of note. Dacia lay across the Danube in modern Romania and two wars, one between 101 and 102 and the other in 105, were required to subjugate the kingdom and turn it into a province.

In the war with Parthia in 114, Trajan acquired Armenia as a province, as had happened with Mesopotamia. He advanced to the Persian Gulf, but then retreated and abandoned southern Mesopotamia by 117.

Gaul fell into the hands of Postumus, an alternative Emperor. This Gallic Empire of Postumus lasted from 260 to 273 and comprised Gaul (much of present-day France) and two German provinces, with Spain and Britain joining later. These western provinces had a distinct identity and prosperity. Between 270 and 275 Emperor Aurelian reunited the Empire and rebuilt its borders.

The problems faced by Aurelian were taken in hand by Diocletian on his accession in 284. He divided the Empire into a system of four regional Empires with himself as *primus inter pares* (first among equals). Civil and military power was separated, with army commands organized across provincial boundaries to eradicate any potential rebellions by powerful civilian governors. A uniform coinage was minted to aid the economy. His reforms were so successful that Diocletian decided to abdicate in 305.

Once he had gone, Diocletian's collegiate system rapidly collapsed. Maxentius promptly seized Italy and North Africa, but Constantine made himself western emperor, and soon invaded Italy and defeated Maxentius. Then, in 316, he turned on Licinius, the eastern Emperor, and grabbed Greece and the Balkans. He renewed his campaigns in 324, finally defeating Licinius and reuniting the Roman Empire.

TRAJAN'S COLUMN
Trajan's Column in Rome was built in honor of the Roman emperor Trajan, whose reputation as a great Roman leader is perhaps bettered only by Augustus. Trajan reigned from AD 98 until his death in 117, and although he was a successful domestic leader, it was in battle that he secured his greatest achievements. Following victory over Dacia (present-day Romania and Moldova, as well as parts of Hungary, Bulgaria, and Ukraine) in 105, Trajan pushed further east, and in 107 conquered Nabatea (in present-day Jordan), gaining the short-lived province of Arabia Petraea. He launched his final campaign in 113 against Parthia (situated in northeast Iran), advancing as far as the city of Susa in 116 and expanding the Roman Empire to it greatest extent.

Diocletian's and Constantine's reforms strengthened the Empire. This was crucial considering Germanic threats on the Rhine–Danube border and Persia in the east. Emperor Julian fought the Franks and Alemanni and died fighting the Persians in 363. Visigoths rampaged through the Balkans in 376, but were contained and settled inside the borders as allies. When Emperor Theodosius died in 395, the Empire was divided between his sons, Honorius in the west and Arcadius in the east, but the western Empire was already collapsing.

The Barbarian tribes had been suffering from mounting demographic pressure and attacks from the fierce, nomadic Huns from Central Asia. Germanic tribes had been given land in the Empire in return for guarding the borders, but in 406 Gaul was overrun by Vandals, Alans, Suevi, and Burgundians. The Vandals moved through France and Spain to North Africa while the Visigoths moved into Italy and then into Spain.

The Germanic peoples formed their own states, even fighting in concert with Rome against Attila at Châlons in 451. The Ostrogoths settled in Italy, western Hungary, and much of the northern Balkans. A Burgundian Kingdom extended from near Lake Geneva down the Rhône Valley until conquered by the Franks in 534.

When the Merovingian Frankish King Clovis I converted to Christianity he established a special bond between the Frankish Kings and the Papacy. Clovis founded the Church of the Holy Apostles (Ste. Geneviève) at Paris and was made an honorary consul by eastern Emperor Anastasius, which technically brought the Franks into the Empire.

The Eastern Empire, with its capital at Constantinople, faced increasing problems from the Sassanians. Emperor Justinian, who ruled what was now the Byzantine Empire, had a dream of restoring a Christian Roman Empire to its former lands. During his reign from 527 to 565, he waged a successful war against the North African Vandals and obtained a foothold in Spain. Italy was retaken, a stalemate established with the Persians, but the Balkans continued to be threatened by Bulgars, Avars, and Slavs.

The Byzantine comeback was short-lived and the Lombards soon acquired most of Italy except for Ravenna, Rome, and Naples. The Avars raided the Balkans, while the Persians devastated Syria and, by 619, had conquered Palestine and Egypt. The Visigoths expelled the Byzantines from southern Spain. The rise of Islam and its explosive advance out of Arabia saw the Byzantine Empire stripped of its assets except for its Balkan and Anatolian possessions. After more than 1300 years the Roman Empire had finally run its course and the Arabs began to spread along North Africa and into Spain.

THE GUPTA EMPIRE
This coin was the product of the Gupta Empire, which was one of the largest political and military empires in the world. It lasted from 320 to 600 and covered most of Northern India, the region presently in the nation of Pakistan and what is now western India and Bangladesh. The peace and prosperity created under the leadership of the Gupta Dynasty allowed learning and culture to flourish, and the period of Gupta rule is often referred to as the Golden Age of Indian science, mathematics, astronomy, religion, and philosophy.

CIVILIZATION IN INDIA

While Bronze Age Egypt and Crete were developing their civilizations, a similar civilization was flourishing along the banks of the Indus River. For a thousand years a rich culture developed, with sophisticated cities, all based on the wealth created by growing wheat and rice on the rich alluvial soil brought down by the river during its periods of regular but unpredictable flooding.

This Harappan Empire, as it was called, came to an abrupt end around the year 2000 BC when the river changed its course. Nearly two hundred known archaeological sites have been uncovered in the area. There were major cities at Mehenjo-Daro, Harappa, and Dholavira on Khadir Island near Kutch. These were built to a geometric grid pattern with walls and citadels. The first two were built with mud bricks but the latter was built of stone, and there were even stone reservoirs.

The growth of wealth led to industrial activity, and manufactured goods were traded in Persia, Mesopotamia, Afghanistan, and Central Asia for lapis lazuli, turquoise, gold, silver, and copper. Harappan seals record carvings of bullock carts and sailing vessels but the script is indecipherable. Some seals depict a prototype Siva while one at Dholavira displays a swastika, which was a Hindu symbol.

After the fall of the Harappan Empire, there were many centuries of invasions and counterinvasions but in the 3rd century BC attempts were made to unify India when Chandragupta, who ruled from around 321 to 297 BC, rebelled against his Magadha King and seized the Punjab from its Greek rulers. This united the Kingdoms of the Ganges Plain, forming the Mauryan Empire, which lasted from around 310 to 185 BC.

The Mauryans created an imperial silver and copper currency which spread beyond their borders. The King's grandson, Asoka, continued his predecessors' interest in religion. Chandragupta had converted to the religion of Jainism and ended up starving himself to death, while Asoka chose Buddhism and gave it official recognition. Asoka's Empire comprised two-thirds of the subcontinent, but after his death in 232 BC it was split up as it fell into the hands of the Yuezhi, Sakas, and a new local Sunga dynasty.

Between AD 30 to 350, the almost forgotten Kushan Empire flourished, but a power struggle saw its Indian lands eventually disintegrating into a series of small states. This power struggle was won by Chandragupta I, who ruled from 320 to 330, and his son Samudragupta, who ruled from 330 to 375. This Gupta dynasty conquered northern India, coerced tribute from kings in Assam, Nepal, and Bengal, penetrated western India, and married into the Vaakataka royal family. Although the Guptas were Buddhists, there was a heavy Hindu influence in the country that established the preeminent status of Hinduism and Sanskrit literature. The state eventually fragmented as a result of White Hun invasions.

After the Guptas, India's many states saw a whole series of dominant dynasties rise and fall, such as the Harsa, Calukya, and Pallavas. Meanwhile, Hinduism consolidated itself, despite a renewed upsurge in Buddhism, resulting in the unification of the many schools of Hindu philosophy.

Caste restrictions—a system of hereditary social stratification—were tightened, forbidding a girl to marry beneath her own caste but allowing her to rise in caste through marriage to a higher-caste man. This sometimes led to polygamy as high-caste men sought extra dowries.

The Calukyas built the Papnatha Siva temple at Pattadakal in the 8th century while the Pallavas raised several monuments such as the Arjuna Ratha at Mamallapuram.

India succumbed to Muslim rule in the 12th century when Muhammed of Ghur's mobile cavalry smashed the Hindu Rajputs at Tarori near Delhi. His Sultanate of Delhi eventually defeated two Mongol invasions in 1304 and 1306, exacted tribute, and seized Gujerat, Malwa, and the Deccan. Later, Muslim and Hindu rebellions weakened the state.

The end came in 1398 when the Mongol warlord Tamerlane, or Timur, invaded Delhi. According to his memoirs, in the course of one hour 10,000 Hindu prisoners were beheaded. The invasion smashed the Empire and left the Delhi Sultanate as just one more northern state.

In southern India Chalukya aid had enabled the Pallavas at Kanchi to be replaced by a Chola dynasty of Tamil Kings, who ruled from 888 to 1267. Invasions of Ceylon and Bengal had accrued wealth, and maritime power enabled tribute to be extracted from Pegi in Burma, Malaiyur in the Malaysian peninsula, and the Srivijaya Empire in the Indonesian islands. The Cholas appeared to resist Muslim encroachments but eventually fell under the pressure of new regional dynasties.

THE INSCRUTABLE CIVILIZATIONS OF CHINA

Bronze Age China grew on the Yellow, or Huang Ho, River plain in what are now the provinces of Henan, Hebei, and Shandong. The Shang civilization, with its capital at Anyang, was based upon warrior priest kings who used horses and chariots.

Peasant agriculture underpinned society and the ready source of peasant labour enabled the building of earth town walls such as Zhenghou's, which enclosed 3 square miles.

The Shang were displaced by the Chou in about 1111 BC, taking over the Shang realm as a going concern. Feudalism flourished, which helped to decentralize power. Non-Chinese in the north, such as the Yi, Mau, and Di were assimilated and their lands absorbed. Chou society is renowned for its ritually inscribed bronze ceremonial cauldrons.

When the Chou collapsed, feudal vassal states became powerful such as the Qi, Chu and Ch'in (also known as the Qin). Chaos ensued leading to the Spring and Autumn and Warring State periods, which lasted from the second half of the 8th century BC to the second half of the 3rd century BC. Some 100 states existed at that time but only fourteen were significant. Various states dominated at different times but eventually a balance of power developed between the Ch'in, Qi, Jin, and Chu.

The Ch'in reformed, basing its administration upon territorial lines by eradicating clan-based aristocratic rule. King Zheng of Ch'in destroyed many rival states and by 221 BC he was ruling all of China. Zheng was the first Chinese Emperor and he gave himself the title, Shi Huangdi. He ruled his centralized country in a despotic fashion and is chiefly remembered for building the 4,000-mile Great Wall of China and for his funeral terracotta army.

Unifying measures included the standardization of coinage, measures of length and volume, as well as characters in writing. Campaigns were led against the nomadic Xiongnu in the north and against Thai Khmers and Viets in the south.

When Shi Huangdi died in 209 BC, there were a series of revolts and a devastating civil war. China was unified in 202 BC under Liu Bang, Prince of Han, later known as Gaozu.

The Xiongnu were always a danger because they could obstruct the Silk Road through Xiangjiang. This 4,000-mile caravan trade route commenced at Linzi in Shandong and ended in the Roman Near East. It carried a two-way traffic, with silk flowing west and wool, gold, silver, and luxury items flowing toward the east. The road, which also had offshoots into India, also transmitted religions and philosophies, which was how Buddhism and Nestorian Christianity reached China.

Under the Han, between 140 to 87 BC, a series of campaigns against the Xiongnu resulted in the conquest of Xiangjiang and the extension of the Great Wall into the northwest.

The Han dynasty lasted for 400 years and asserted its control over large areas of Korea, southern, and southwestern China and Vietnam. The Ch'in method of administration was continued and state-sponsored military farming settlements were founded in border regions. Commerce remained as usual with the addition of sea-routes to Burma and India. The Silk Road was extended to Japan and the Han court received tribute in AD 57 and 107 from the Japanese Kingdom of Wo.

Trade was vigorous, with China importing cornelian, agate, glass, and amber. Han expansion was also based upon technological innovations. They mined salt, for instance, by

THE FIRST CHINESE EMPEROR

The Terracotta Army is a collection of 8,099 life-size Chinese terracotta figures of warriors and horses located near the Mausoleum of the First Ch'in (Qin) Emperor, Shi Huangdi, who, after destroying rival states, unified China. Shi Huangdi introduced a centralized bureaucracy and promoted standardized legal codes, writing forms, coinage, and scholarly practice. He is, even now, a controversial figure, largely down to his despotic rule of the country. As well as the Terracotta Army, his reign is best known for the construction of the Great Wall of China, a magnificent feat of engineering, but one that was achieved at the cost of many lives.

forcing water into the ground and then pumping out the resulting brine. The brine was then heated to form salt crystals.

An iron suspension bridge was constructed and the metal technology spread into Central Asia. Iron was even exported to Rome. The salt and iron industries were nationalized, the development of the ox-drawn plough aided agriculture, and horse stocks were improved by crossbreeding with Ferghana stallions.

Eventually the Han rulers became weak and were increasingly being controlled by rival generals. Cao Cao captured the last Han Emperor in AD 220, but was not strong enough to prevent China splitting into the states of Wei, Shu, and Wu, each of which claimed imperial status.

The Three Kingdoms period heralded a period of intense political disunity while 16 Kingdoms were established along the northern border areas by Xiongnu, Mongol, Di, and Tibetan peoples. Fragmentation and political retardation ended with the foundation of the Sui dynasty from 581 to 618.

Sui Emperor Wendi reunited the country and rebuilt the economy. Yangdi, the second Sui Emperor who ruled for four years from 604, indulged in vast construction projects which were financially damaging and onerous to the peasantry, as were the campaigns in Gansu, Champa, Formosa, and Korea.

This led to rebellions and a number of northern nomad raids. Yangdi's reign came to an end when he was strangled and a Sui official, Li Yuan, took the imperial title as Gaozu of the Tang dynasty.

Much Chinese culture was driven by Confucianism, a worldview that was concerned with humanism and developing a social and political code of ethics. Confucius studied ancient religious beliefs and rituals and ancestor worship. He generated a moral framework for political conduct in his writings. Confucianism developed the concept of the Mandate of Heaven where Heaven gave kingship to a virtuous ruler but could withdraw it from an evil, weak, or corrupt king. Hence, dynastic changes and rebellion could be legitimized by the Mandate to restore social and political harmony.

The Tang dynasty, between 618 and 906, introduced a single, unified Empire of cultural magnificence, territorial expansion, wealth, commerce, and a skilled Confucian-orientated administration. A legal code, land equalization, and a reduction in taxes benefited the population but left the state short of funds.

China began an expansion into Central Asia until its army was stopped by the Arabs at the Battle of Talas in 763. The Tang authority was weakening and its court became subject to intrigue and corruption. Peasant rebellions, Uighur and Tibetan occupation of Central Asia, and economic hardship weakened the Tang. Threats came in the form of the Khitan

Empire, established in Manchuria and Inner Mongolia, and the northeastern Xixia state. In 907 the Tang dynasty collapsed and China had to wait until 960 before it was once again reunified, this time by the Song.

In the 1200s the Song were invaded by a Mongol horde, under the leadership of Kublai Khan. The war lasted until 1279; the Jin Tatars were forced out of north China, the Tangut Xixia obliterated and south China was captured. Tibet, Annam, and Tonking were attacked along the way.

Kublai, the grandson of Genghis Khan, adopted Chinese ruling methods using Chinese officials. Buddhism was favored and China was reunified. Burma and Korea became tributary territories, but invasions of Japan in 1274 and 1281 failed disastrously.

Much of the information about Kublai Khan comes from Marco Polo, the Venetian traveler. He travelled to China in 1271 with his father and uncle. He entered Kublai Khan's diplomatic service and his memoirs, *Il Milione*, chronicled his time in China. He was amazed by Chinese innovations and especially admired paper currency, coal, the post roads, naval architecture, and the sheer volume of traffic on the River Yangzi.

THE MILITARIST CIVILIZATION OF JAPAN

The earliest accounts of Japan are recorded in Chinese histories of the 3rd century AD. Japan comprised a multiplicity of clan-based political units ruled by both men and women. Some of these units had relations with the Korean rival Kingdoms of Paekche, Korguryo, and Silla, while embassies to China existed between AD 57 and 266.

Originally, Japanese troops fought on foot but, around 400, an infantry army backing the Paekche against the Korguryo was defeated by cavalry and, before long, Japan was sending expeditions that included mounted warriors. This was all made possible by changes in Japan's political organizations.

The Yamato clan had fought to achieve political supremacy in Japan. The Yamatos ensured that a concerted effort was made to raise cavalry as the preferred military tool. In spite of this the imperial line was unable to retain the semiprotectorate over Paekche in the face of a rejuvenated regional domination of Silla.

Yamato control over Japan was in fact very loose and other clans also held dominant positions. Nevertheless, Chinese imports in terms of political philosophy led to imitation of the Chinese court, even to the extent of ministers conspiring to achieve the crown.

Tamato lands expanded, leading to political and economic reorganization. Buddhism arrived, supported by the powerful Soga clan. When Empress Suiko ascended the throne in 593 for her 35-year reign, Crown Prince Sh'toku established Chinese forms of government and founded Buddhist monasteries such as the Shiten'ji, H'k'ji, and H'ry'ji.

In 604, the Prince issued the Seventeen Article Constitution, a vague moral code providing political and philosophical legitimacy to centralized imperial government.

In 645, Soga dominance became so overwhelming that the future Emperor Tenchi and Nakatomi Kamatari, founder of a new Fujiwara clan, overthrew the Soga and initiated reforms.

The 646 Taika Reforms attempted to curtail the power of Japanese clans to ensure Yamato supremacy and they became known as the Taika Laws in 702. All laws were codified and a Domesday Book-style survey was implemented. Land was nationalized using the Chinese Tang system but, in a pragmatic fashion, the hereditary estates of clan chiefs were returned as a salary for official duties. A council of state was introduced with eight ministries and sub-departments but this reform failed through lack of revenue, the direct result of far too many tax-exempt aristocratically-owned estates.

The capital was moved from Asuka to Nara, which was designed after the Tang capital at Changan. The civilization surrounding Nara in the eighth century brought forth the Great Buddha of Todai-ji, a huge statue housed in a magnificent temple, and an enormous upsurge in Japanese literature, leading eventually to the formation of the Japanese state.

Despite laws, the authority of central government was dependent on local lords keeping order. They received commissions to wage war and, rather than levying peasant conscripts, raised elite warriors instead. These soldiers were horse-archers and proto-samurai, who were backed by tenants levied as infantry. Rebellions against centralized rule were rife and lawlessness abounded. Provincial governors acted alone and received rewards for keeping the peace, making them even richer and more powerful.

Eventually, landlords at court used their warriors or samurai (translated as "those who serve") as agents to run their estates. By the 11th century, the Taira and Minamoto clans were the most powerful and their rivalry was accentuated during the Högen rebellion of 1156, fought over the imperial succession.

In the Heiji rebellion in 1160, the Taira won and killed all the Minamoto except for some children. In 1180 these children, now adults, attacked the Taira and started the Gempei Wars, which lasted from 1180 to 1185 and which resulted in the thorough destruction of the Taira.

This conflict became an important reference point for skill at archery and swordsmanship, together with the Code of Bushido (analogous to the European concept of chivalry), with undying loyalty to one's lord and the use of ritual suicide. The Samurai ethos was established and reinforced by feudalism, especially after Minamoto Yoritomo acquired the title of shogun (military leader of Japan) to embellish his status as military dictator.

Another characteristic of Japanese warfare was the emergence of armed Buddhist monks, supporting rival Buddhist sects. Apart from internecine strife, the monks became useful military makeweights in the Gempei Wars.

THE MANY CIVILIZATIONS OF CENTRAL AND SOUTH AMERICA

South America has been home to a large number of civilizations in the Andes and the Columbia and Amazon Basins. The Middle Orinoco has produced ceramics dating from around 3600 BC, while Caral, with its platform mounds and plazas, was established in the Peruvian Supe Valley as early as 2600 BC.

Elsewhere in the eastern Andes are the temple ruins at Chavin de Huantar with its bas-reliefs depicting human and animal figures. The Moche culture, near today's Trujillo, produced a fishing and agricultural civilization whose funeral rites display grave finds of gold, silver, and precious stones. Murals show human sacrifice together with boats, fishermen, birds, shellfish, and animals. Prisoners of war were beheaded.

The Tihuanaco and Huari Empires dominated much of the central and southern Andes, as well as some coastal areas. Tihuanaco's Kalasaya temple has a famous Gateway of the Sun. Huari culture displayed good quality pottery decorated with human, bird and animal images. Archaeologists have found tapestry, shirts, hats, and belts.

EARLY ANDEAN CIVILIZATION Chavin de Huantar is an archaeological site dating back to around 900 BC and it is located 250 kilometres north of Lima, Peru. The Chavin people, much like all the Andean cultures, had no system of writing, bu their metallurgy, soldering, and temperature control methods were advanced for their time. They also had a knowledge of textiles that allowed them to revolutionize cloth production. Finds at Chavin de Huantar suggest that they developed a trade network and agricultural system, but between 500 and 300 BC it appears that the society was in decline. Large ceremonial sites were abandoned, some unfinished, and were replaced by villages and agricultural land.

RISE AND FALL OF THE MAYA CIVILIZATION
The Maya civilisation is notable for the only known fully developed written language of the pre-Columbian Americas, as well as its spectacular art, monumental architecture, and sophisticated mathematical and astronomical systems. Mayan roots were in the pre-Classical period, but it wasn't until the Classic Period (c. 250 to 900) that the civilization fully blossomed. For reasons that are still unestablished, the Maya civilization started to decline in the 9th and 10th centuries, with theories to explain this including foreign invasion, the collapse of trade routes, disease, and natural disaster. The civilization finally collapsed in the 16th century, when the Spanish invaded.

The Chimú Empire incorporated much of northern Peru and depended upon irrigated agriculture. The Empire expanded under careful administration and military endeavor. The Chimú managed a 100-mile canal carrying water from the upper Chicama Valley to fields in the Moche Valley. Later the Chimú were taken into the Empire of the Incas.

Central America also developed a variety of cultures, the first major civilization being the Olmec in the lowland jungles of the Mexican Gulf coast. Some archaeologists visualize Olmec as the Mother Culture influencing the Maya, Teotihuacan, Totonac, Zapotec, Toltec, Mixtec, and Aztec cultures. The Olmec used slash and burn agricultural techniques, traded for minerals, and possessed a society divided into priests, bureaucrats, merchants, craftsmen, and farmers. They are renowned for the carved basalt heads, some weighing as much as 20 tons.

The Mayan city-states lasted from about 1000 BC to AD 809, but remnants lingered on in spite of a Toltec invasion in AD 980. Their final demise only came when they were virtually wiped out by the Spanish Conquistadors in the 16th century. In spite of that, a number of Mayan traditions still linger to this day.

Each Mayan city was ruled by a king who was engaged in perpetual warfare to acquire prisoners to sacrifice to Mayan gods. Famous cities include Palenque, Tikal, and Copán. Technically and scientifically able, the Mayans developed secular and sacred calendars written on two interlocking, cogged wheels so that the calendars could work in concert. Hieroglyphic writing was decoded in the 1960s and Mayan records were carved on stelae and in bark paper books, most of which were destroyed by the Spaniards.

The early 10th century saw the dominance of the Toltec-Chichimeca peoples with Tula as their imperial capital. Their state spread from the Valley of Mexico to Yucatan, Guatemala, and Honduras, and was a model for the later Aztecs. The capital had pyramids, a ball court, sculptured figures, and chacmools (carved warriors lying on their backs with hollowed bowls on their chests to receive sacrificial offerings). The warlike Toltec were eventually conquered by the nomadic Chitimecs.

The Aztecs settled in the Valley of Mexico, first paying tribute to the Tepanec rulers, then overthrowing them. The Aztec culture required war captives as sacrificial victims to the sun and many city-states were conquered, but the Oaxaca and Tlaxcalans remained free. They later helped the Spaniards against the Aztecs.

The Aztec capital, Tenochtitlan, was an island surrounded by canals and raised garden beds. These chinanpas produced a wide variety of food to be eaten with turkey and domesticated dogs. The Aztecs, like other cultures, used a ball court. Trade was significant especially in luxury items such as green quetzal feathers. Tribute taxes could be in the form of food, cotton clothes, warriors' vestments and shields, and reed mats. The Aztec state depended on tribute, which could then be traded on. The Aztec Empire crumbled in April 1521 when Hernan Cortés and his Spanish army broke into Tenochtitlan.

Elsewhere, Spanish imperialism spelled the end for the Andean Incan Empire. The beginnings of the Inca Empire dated back to around 2500 BC, but in about AD 1000 they moved to the Cuzco Valley and began dominating neighboring tribes. Between 1438 and 1533 was the period of greatest Incan expansion. Incan society was hierarchical, with the Sapa Inca supreme.

The Empire was noteworthy for its irrigation and aqueducts, monumental stone architecture, and an amazing road network complete with suspension bridges. State records of food stores, population, troops, and taxes were kept by quipas, a set of color-coded cords with knots accounting for divisions.

The Empire grew many vegetables and cereals, examples being maize and quinoa, avocado, and beans. The medical profession was effective using herbal remedies, including quinine. Surgeons could amputate using coca leaves as an anaesthetic, and even blood transfusions were performed.

1532 witnessed the arrival of Francisco Pizarro and the Spanish Conquistadors; the Incas were rapidly over-run and the following year Pizarro ordered the execution of the Inca king, and the 4000-year history of the Incan Empire came to an undignified end.

NORTH AMERICAN CIVILIZED GROUPS

In North America from AD 75 until at least 1500, the Mississippian culture flourished throughout the Tennessee, Cumberland, and Mississippi River valleys. These societies possessed certain common features including a pottery style, maize agriculture, large flat-topped mounds near a town plaza, and a carefully constructed social hierarchy. The key cities were Cahokia, Moundville, Spiro, and Etowah, but these were surrounded by hundreds of palisaded villages, hamlets, and farms. The inhabitants tended their fields and supplemented their diet by hunting, fishing, and collecting wild plants.

The largest city, Cahokia, had a mound 100 feet high. The summit of this Monk's Mound once had a wooden building over 100 feet long by 45 feet wide, perhaps 48 feet high and was the home of the elite ruler, the Great Sun. However, the society's administration was supported by ever increasing demands on agricultural production.

By 1500, this city of the Sun was ruined and abandoned.

There are a number of possible explanations, but it is likely to have been a combination of soil depletion, over production, climatic change, warfare, and disease.

In the town at Moundville the strict social ranking is shown by grave finds. Elite graves of all ages and sexes show copper axes, gorgets, stone discs, and paints, suggesting a definite inherited status. Villager graves, on the other hand, contain pottery bowls with bone and flint tools. These goods are distributed by social position, gender, and age.

Mississippian houses have been reconstructed at Spiro. Walls were built around cedar posts set into the ground with cane and grasses woven between. This structure was daubed with clay, and small fires on each side of the wall hardened them. The roof was thatched with grass attached to rafters.

The various cities display religious cult features reminiscent of the Green Corn ritual, which is still used in the southwest of the United States. Sequences of rites were designed to generate social harmony, to respect the dead, and to appease natural forces and the sun.

Before European intervention there was a sophisticated system of trade running along a north–south axis of the Mississippi, supported by tributaries such as the Wisconsin, Illinois, and Ohio rivers from the east and the Minnesota, Missouri, and Arkansas rivers entering from the west. One major east–west route flowed down the St. Lawrence, through the Great Lakes to the Grand Portage and the Lake of the Woods.

Moving west, lake links existed via the Yellowstone and Missouri rivers, eventually reaching the Columbia River and the Pacific Ocean. Trails, especially the warriors' route, ran the length of the Appalachian Mountains from New York to Georgia while the St. Lawrence was tied to New York by Lake Champlain and the Hudson River.

In the southwest, Pueblo villages were key points near the Rio Grande River. Routes also followed the Red and Arkansas–Canadian rivers, passing through the Sangria Mountains to reach the head of the Rio Grande and then Mexico. As trade routes criss-crossed, nodal trade points became important, such as Santa Fé, Taos, Yucca, Montréal, Mobile, and The Dalles in the sorthwest coastal region. Before European contact, the Wasco-Wishrams dominated The Dalles.

Trade goods included dried fish and fresh salmon, animal pelts, dried plants, slaves, pearls, copper, hematite, silver, chert, galena, mica, flint, soapstone pipes, quartz, obsidian, bear, shark and alligator teeth, shell beads, turtle shells, and pottery.

Within a generation of Columbus's arrival in 1492 European diseases had made their way along the trade routes. Particularly devastating was the smallpox epidemic that reached inland.

The expedition of the Spanish explorer De Soto in 1540 to 1541 caused further catastrophe to the region. Many societies were destroyed, either as a result of fighting with the Spanish, but more often as a result of catching yet more diseases that the Spanish had brought with them.

The result was that the Mississippians were so decimated that survival depended on victims and refugees confederating. Descendants of these people are the Creeks, Cherokee, Chickasaw, and the Choctaw, who still consider the mound at Nanih Waiya to be the Great Mother in their creation myth.

CIVILIZATION IN AFRICA

In North Africa, the Carthaginian Empire evolved out of earlier Phoenician colonization. Encompassing the North African coast, together with islands in the western Mediterranean and parts of Spain, the Empire resisted Greek encroachments in Sicily and a Carthaginian-Etruscan fleet repelled the Phocaean Greeks off Corsica.

The Carthaginian navy traveled all over the Mediterranean and ventured along the African Atlantic coast, as well as going up into Britanny in the search for tin. Mercantile wealth was based on a virtual monopoly of lead, tin, silver, and gold. Carthage exported salted Atlantic fish, textiles, furniture, beds, weapons, and various luxury items.

Its wealth allowed Carthage to raise large mercenary armies, comprised mainly of Libyans, Numidians, and Spanish Celts, to fight against Greek colonies in Sicily and eventually against Rome.

The three Punic Wars occurred after Roman and Carthaginian interests conflicted in Sicily over Messana. Carthage suffered major defeats at Trasimene in 217 BC and Cannae in 216 BC, but was finally shattered at Zama in 202 BC and their city was finally destroyed in 146 BC, with its population either killed or enslaved.

Ancient Cushite Kingdoms existed at Kerma, Napata, and Meroë, located along the River Nile in an area of Nubia spreading from southern Egypt to northern Sudan. A first Kingdom broke into an Egypt weakened by the Hyksos in around 1650 BC, but ultimately Amenhotep I, ruling from 1514 to 1493 BC, conquered Kerma, destroying the state, while Thutmose I extended Egyptian power upstream of the Nile's Fourth Cataract to exploit the region's gold. When Egyptian occupation ended, a new Cushite Kingdom emerged under Piye who seized Upper Egypt.

A later King, Shabaka, conquered all of Egypt and this Cushite 25th Dynasty backed Hebrew King Hezekiah's rebellion against Assyria. The Cushite King Taharqa was defeated by Assyria, whose Saite Prince clients regained Upper

***JEFFERSON AND THE
CLASSICAL INHERITANCE***
Thomas Jefferson had a
particular affinity for Greece.
Republicanism and democracy,
the two ideas at the core of the
foundation of the United
States, both had their roots in
Classical Greece.

Egypt. When Napata was sacked, the Cushite capital moved to Meroë. The previously Egyptianized Cushite culture became more Africanized after Cush's isolation from the north.

A rival Kingdom, Aksum, emerged in the northern Ethiopian highlands, its King, Aeizanes, despatching an expedition which destroyed Meroë in AD 350.

A later African Empire was the Songhai in West Africa, located on the River Niger in today's central Mali. Originally, Songhai was ruled by Mali, its geopolitical importance providing access to Timbuktu and Gao. The Songhai nobility eventually rebelled against Malian rule, with independence finally being achieved in about 1464 with the rise to power of Sonni Ali, ruling from 1464 to 1492. He defeated Mali and crushed revolts amongst his Mande people, while fighting against Tuareg, Mossi, the Fulani, and the Dogon tribes of the Bandiagara hills.

Sonni displaced the Tuareg from Timbuktu. Apart from military skill, Sonni reconciled the differences between his animist pastoral subjects and the urban Muslim communities. His heir was deposed by Mohammed I Askia Ture (1493–1528). He captured Diara, Fouta-Toro in Senegal and made Air, the Hausa states, and Bornu-Kanem tributaries. The Tuareg were dominated and the borders were pushed north to the salt deposits at Taghaza close to the Moroccan border.

Muhammad's control of the trade routes and his complex state bureaucracy and army garrisons strengthened the state. Salt was precious and the slave trade prospered, while Songhai became the middleman for gold mined in the Akan states in Guinea. Eventually, Morocco moved on the Taghaza salt deposits. The Moroccan forces, with their early firearms, invaded Songhai, defeating its forces at Tondibi, Timbuktu, and Gao, and seized all the administrative centers, leaving the pastoralist Songhai to fruitless guerrilla war.

THE LEGACY OF THE CLASSICAL AGE

The two most significant political legacies of the classical era are the republican vision of US President Thomas Jefferson and the dream of the Italian Duce, Benito Mussolini to retore the Roman Empire.

The American vision of government as expressed by Jefferson and John Adams viewed all citizens as equally subject to the law, with their individual liberty residing in an empire of state-republics whose acquisitions of territory, such as the Louisiana Purchase, would provide the opportunity to create new state-republics equal to the old, with political power, in contrast to European empires, diffused and decentralized.

A decentralized union of free republics would prevent evil concentrations of power and would be defended by the citizen, in the form of a virtuous citizen militia for national defense rather than a standing army. This vision of republicanism claims that citizens have inalienable rights that cannot be voted away at the whim of poitical leaders.

In return, agreeing with Greek and Roman ideas of private and public virtue, the citizen owes a duty to his republic. A property-based civic, patriotic, idealistic citizenry, neo-classical in political philosophy, needed to understand the past before making its own history. Jefferson's idealistic views of a limited property-owning democracy envisaged an agricultural nation of yeoman farmers rather than Alexander Hamilton's commercial and manufacturing ethos, seen as too open to corrupt temptations of self-interest.

This republican dream, elitist in spirit, dreamt that the perfected citizen would expand the republican empire into the West, a new garden to be tilled by the citizen-soldier-farmer.

In Italy, Prime Minister Mussolini, from 1922, eulogized religion, the patria (rule by men), and Rome's mission in the world. His political rhetoric, couched in historical terms, presented a "Roman passion," an exalted Romanità, in order to legitimize his dreams. He portrayed himself as the heir or reincarnation of Caesar Augustus and claimed he would lead Italy to its deserved greatness.

Roman symbols and festivals were introduced. New roads reinvented a Roman tradition, the drained Pontine-marsh villages became new colonia, while the fascist militia was divided and sub-divided into legions, cohorts, centuries, and maniples, reminiscent of the Roman past.

Labor Day was celebrated on the anniversary of the foundation of Rome while the eagle and the wolf became icons. A new man, homo fascista, was the model of the regime, the ideal representing the virtuous citizen of ancient Rome. With the images in place, the dream could become an adventure.

Italy was unified by road and rail, as well as by propaganda victories, such as the Battles of the Marshes, Grain, and Babies. Further afield, Italian alliances with Yugoslavia, Albania, Romania, Hungary, Greece, Austria, and Turkey envisaged a Roman presence in the Danube Basin and the Mediterranean, supported by a new, modern navy.

Additionally, Mussolini postured as a world statesman at Locarno in 1925, Stresa in 1935, and Munich in 1938. Force was used at Corfu (1923) and a new Roman Empire saw a victorious war waged against Ethiopia to unite Italian Eritrea with Somaliland between 1935 and 1936.

Aid to Franco's Nationalists in the Spanish Civil War and the 1939 annexation of Albania rounded out some fascist ambitions. This Roman Republican nightmare then collapsed following a series of disastrous defeats during the Second World War and Mussolini's subsequent assassination.

PART 1

ORIGINS

THEORETICAL ORIGINS CONCERNING HUMAN origins abound, the most commonly held theory being that *Homo sapiens* developed in Africa. Penetrating the sub-Saharan barrier, hunter-gatherer man populated Europe, Asia, Australasia, and crossed the land bridge to the Americas. Cave societies developed with Neolithic humankind creating the first major civilizations along river valleys: the Nile, Tigris, Euphrates, Indus and the Huang Ho. In Europe, peoples spread along the Danube and eventually to the Atlantic. Each major civilization was based upon the development of irrigation techniques with which to cultivate cereals, and eventually the domestication of animals, such as pigs, sheep, goats, cattle, donkeys, and horses to provide meat, dairy products, and motive power. Mesopotamia produced a series of societies, renowned for their cuneiform script, while Chinese Shang sites show pictogram writing. The Harappan civilization of the Indus Valley was destroyed by an Indo-European invasion that introduced a Vedic faith whose sacred texts were written in Sanskrit using the Devanagari script. All societies developed social stratification with elite priests and kings dominating their people. Prominent among early states were the Mitanni, the Hittites, Pharaonic Egypt, and Solomonic Israel. Societies benefited from the growth of urban civilization, differentiated labor, and metallurgy based on copper and bronze.

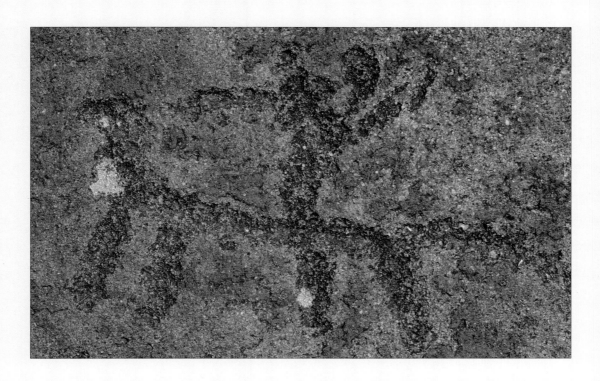

EARLIEST SETTLEMENTS

C. 8000 – 2004 BC

EARLIEST SETTLEMENTS
c. 8000–2004 BC

The discovery of food production methods, such as growing crops, grinding grain with stones, taming wild animals for meat or milk, and making pottery, brought an end to early man's nomadic hunter-gatherer existence. Living in one place led to people building more permanent mud-brick structures. Populations increased and moved to open lands, rich with alluvial soil. Similar societies grew up, all of which were completely unconnected, but all developed politico-religious hierarchies of some kind. Parallel developments in different parts of the world led to early civilizations being born in the river valleys of the Tigris–Euphrates, the Nile, the Yellow River, and the Indus.

CATAL-HÜYÜK
c. 6000 BC

Catal-Hüyük has been described as the oldest city in the world. It was first discovered in 1958 and preliminary excavations began three years later. The site then lay idle for nearly 30 years until excavations resumed in 1993. It is situated in southern Anatolia, southeast of the present-day city of Konya in Turkey and was a complex settlement, apparently consisting entirely of domestic housing with open courtyard areas for dumping rubbish. The average population during the history of this settlement is estimated to have been between 5,000 and 8,000. A number of carefully carved figurines have been discovered in areas thought to have been shrines.

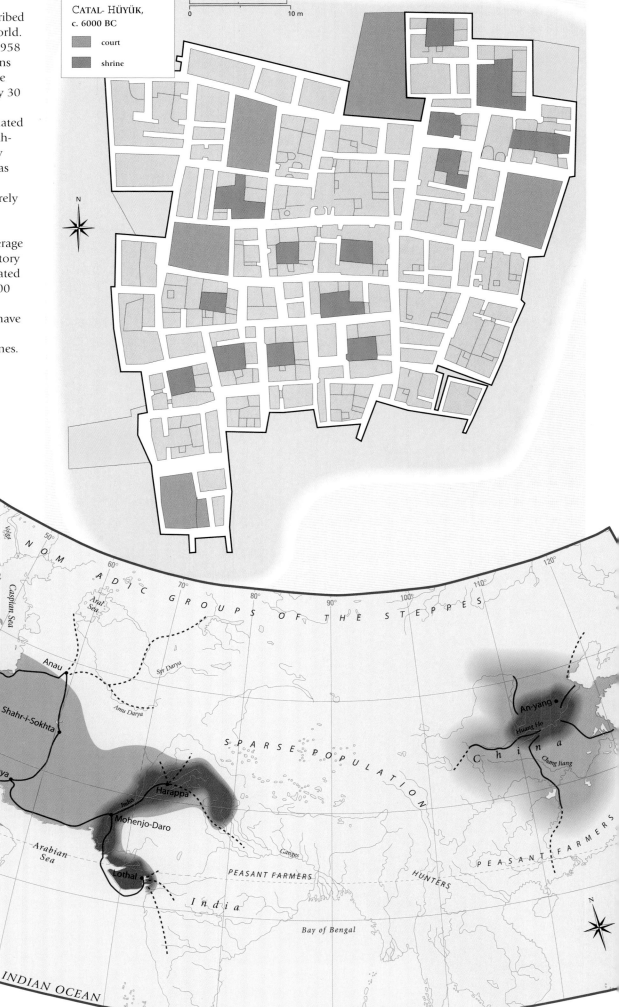

CATAL- HÜYÜK,
c. 6000 BC

court

shrine

EARLIEST
SETTLEMENTS,
c. 8000–3500 BC

- Area of cities/towns
- Area of villages
- Early urban center
- Main trade route of the settled zone
- ---- Route to pastoral/nomadic zones

EMPIRE OF SARGON THE GREAT

EMPIRE OF SARGON THE GREAT

Sargon the Great was an Akkadian king famous for his conquest of the Sumerian city-states in the 24th and 23rd centuries BC. He ruled for 56 years and built up a vast empire that extended from Elam to the Mediterranean Sea and included Mesopotamia, parts of modern-day Iran and

Syria and possibly parts of Anatolia and the Arabian Peninsula. He was regarded as a model ruler by the Mesopotamian kings for some 2000 years after his death and is regarded as one of the first individuals in history to create a multiethnic centrally ruled empire.

EMPIRE OF SARGON
THE GREAT

━━━ Empire of Sargon, 2334–2279 BC

━━━ III Ur Empire, c. 2112–2004 BC

━━━ Earliest Sumerian settlement

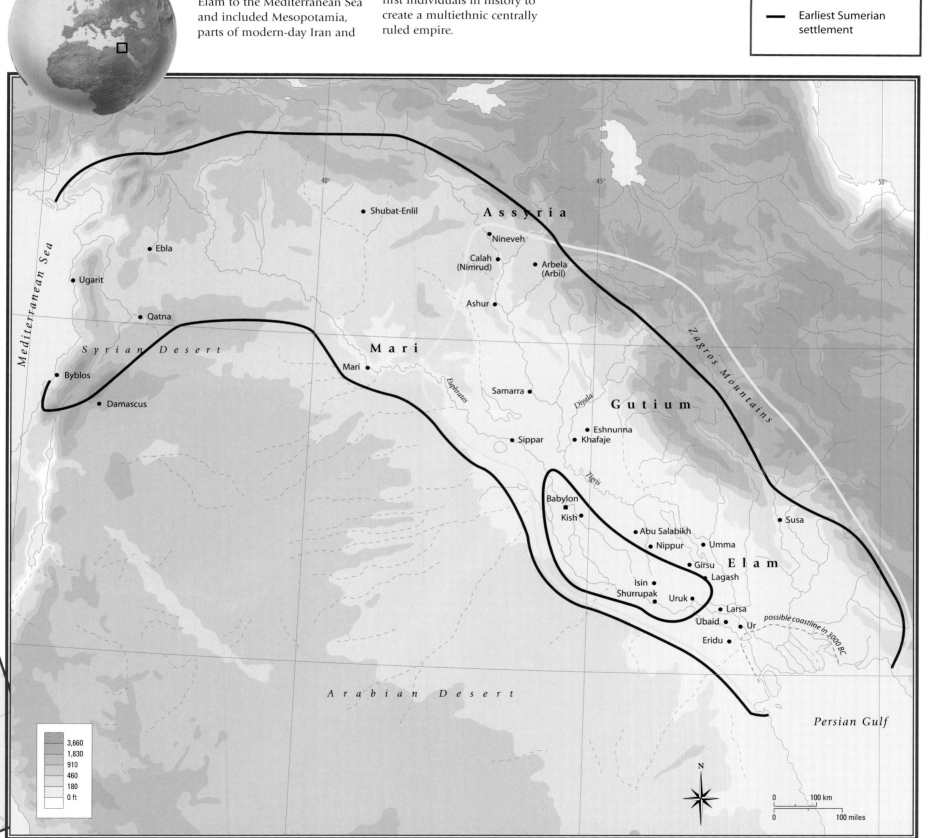

C. 3000 BC – AD 300 # ORIGINS OF WRITING; FIRST SCRIPTS

ORIGINS OF WRITING
As civilizations developed, the need arose to write things down. Records needed to be kept, especially as trade and commerce began to develop. In addition, civilization brought culture, and culture brought the need for the written word. Since early civilizations developed in isolation from each other, it is only to be expected that each developed its own way of doing things. Early writing was often pictographic, but other civilizations like the Sumarians chose a system of cuneiform writing. In Northern Europe the Germanic tribes used runic symbols. Eventually the most favored systems predominated; with the English-speaking world using a Roman alphabet and Arabic numbers.

ORIGINS OF WRITING
- Sumerian cuneiform
- Spread of cuneiform
- Egyptian hieroglyphic
- Spread of hieroglyphic
- Phoenician alphabet
- Spread of alphabet
- Chinese script
- Spread of Chinese script
- Mesoamerican script
- Runic script
- Indus script

North America

ATLANTIC OCEAN

Central America:
Earliest known script,
Zapotec pictographic, c. 600 BC
Maya script (Pictographic/syllabic)
evolves c. 300 BC
Tikal

PACIFIC OCEAN

South America

	OX	HOUSE	WATER	EYE	HEAD	PAPYRUS	
EGYPTIAN HIEROGLYPHICS C. 3000 BC							Egyptian writing did not develop far from the use of pictorial symbols.
CANAANITE C. 2000 BC							Canaanite writing shows its pictorial origins, but in fact symbolizes basic sounds.
PHOENICIAN C. 1000 BC							The 22 basic symbols of the Canaanite system became the standard for the region.
HEBREW C. 700 BC							The Hebrews adopted the Canaanite alphabet in a modified form.
OLD GREEK C. 650 BC							The Canaanite origins can still be seen in archaic Greek script.
ARAMAIC C. 350 BC							Aramaic was the main language of the Persian Empire, and displaced Hebrew in Palestine.
FORMAL HEBREW C. 150 BC							Classical Hebrew was written in a 'square' form of the common script of the region.
FORMAL GREEK C. 450 BC	A	B	M	O	P	Σ	The Greek alphabet allocated vowel sounds to some of the letters, and added more symbols.
ROMAN C. 550 BC	A	B	M	O	R	S	The Romans gained their alphabet from the Etruscans and Greek colonists.

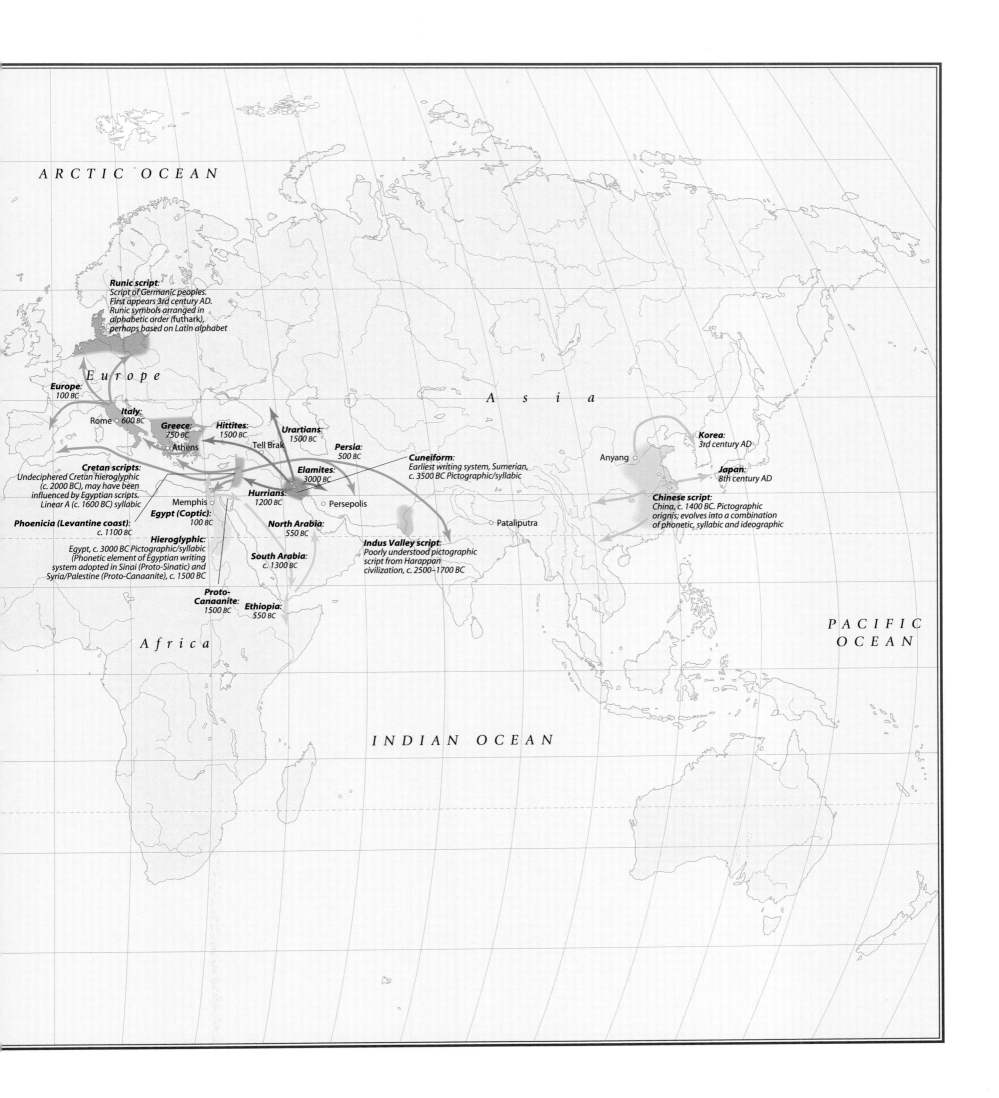

ARCTIC OCEAN

Runic script:
Script of Germanic peoples.
First appears 3rd century AD.
Runic symbols arranged in
alphabetic order (futhark),
perhaps based on Latin alphabet

E u r o p e

Europe:
100 BC

Italy:
Rome ○ *600 BC*

Greece:
750 BC
○ Athens

Hittites:
1500 BC

Tell Brak

Urartians:
1500 BC

A s i a

Persia:
500 BC

Cuneiform:
Earliest writing system, Sumerian,
c. 3500 BC Pictographic/syllabic

Anyang

Korea:
3rd century AD

Japan:
8th century AD

Cretan scripts:
Undeciphered Cretan hieroglyphic
(c. 2000 BC), may have been
influenced by Egyptian scripts.
Linear A (c. 1600 BC) syllabic

Elamites:
3000 BC

Hurrians:
1200 BC
○ Persepolis

Chinese script:
China, c. 1400 BC. Pictographic
orignis; evolves into a combination
of phonetic, syllabic and ideographic

Memphis ○

Phoenicia (Levantine coast):
c. 1100 BC

Egypt (Coptic):
100 BC

North Arabia:
550 BC

○ Pataliputra

Hieroglyphic:
Egypt, c. 3000 BC Pictographic/syllabic
(Phonetic element of Egyptian writing
system adopted in Sinai (Proto-Sinatic) and
Syria/Palestine (Proto-Canaanite), c. 1500 BC

South Arabia:
c. 1300 BC

Indus Valley script:
Poorly understood pictographic
script from Harappan
civilization, c. 2500–1700 BC

**Proto-
Canaanite:**
1500 BC

Ethiopia:
550 BC

A f r i c a

PACIFIC
OCEAN

INDIAN OCEAN

EMERGENCE OF ORGANIZED RELIGIONS

1500 – 500 BC

EMERGENCE OF ORGANIZED RELIGIONS

**Cultural regions
c. 1500–500 BC**

- Adena
- Chavin
- China
- Egypt
- Etruscans
- Greece
- Hopewell
- India
- Maya
- Mesopotamia
- Oaxaca
- Olmec
- Persia
- Phoenicia

EMERGENCE OF ORGANISED RELIGIONS

Religion can be described as a set of common beliefs and practices generally held by a group of people and often codified as prayer, ritual, and religious law. It also encompasses ancestral and cultural traditions, writings, history, and mythology as well as personal faith and mystic experience. It can refer to personal practices related to communal faith, to group rituals, and to communication stemming from shared conviction. Religious development has taken many forms in various cultures, but there are generally a number of common features, such as an all-powerful god or spirit and some form of afterlife.

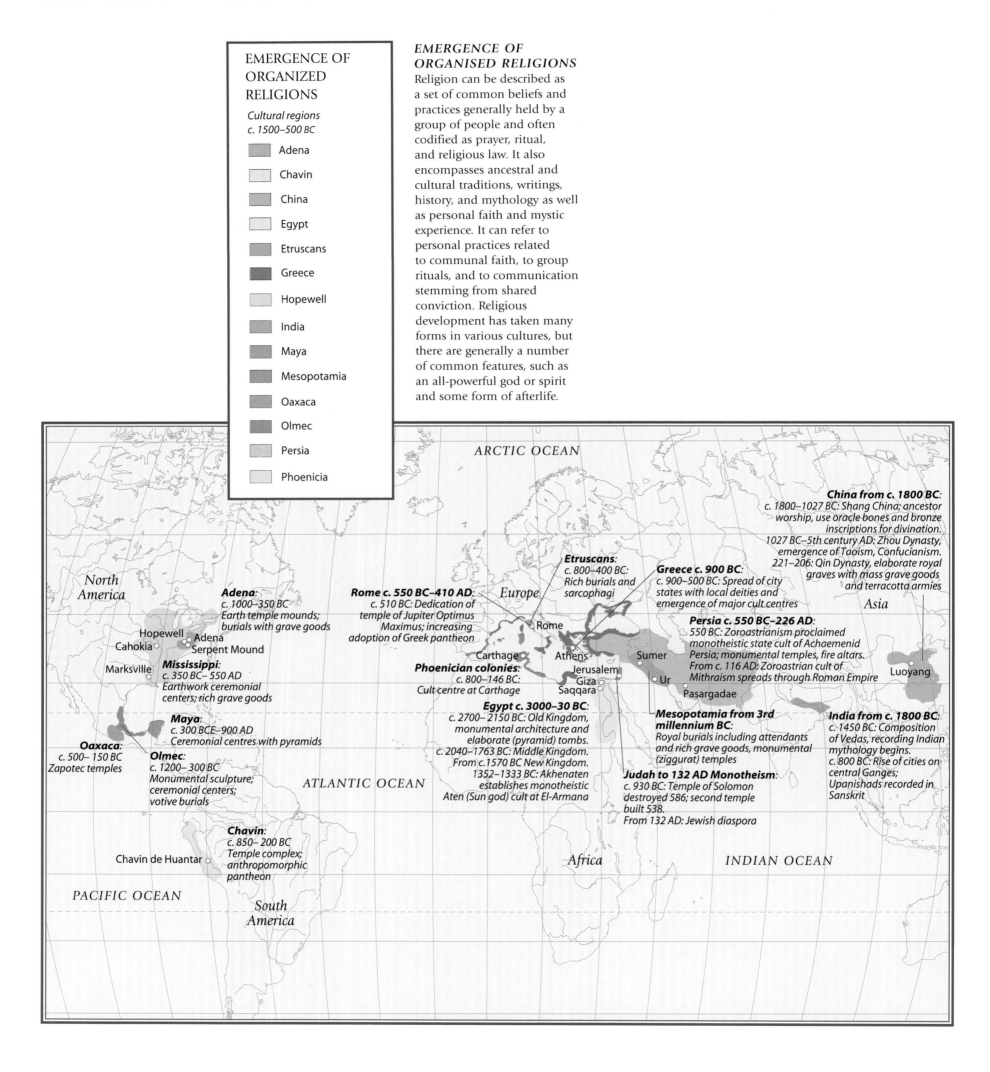

ARCTIC OCEAN

North America

China from c. 1800 BC:
*c. 1800–1027 BC: Shang China; ancestor worship, use oracle bones and bronze inscriptions for divination.
1027 BC–5th century AD: Zhou Dynasty, emergence of Taoism, Confucianism.
221–206: Qin Dynasty, elaborate royal graves with mass grave goods and terracotta armies*

Etruscans:
c. 800–400 BC: Rich burials and sarcophagi

Greece c. 900 BC:
c. 900–500 BC: Spread of city states with local deities and emergence of major cult centres

Rome c. 550 BC–410 AD:
c. 510 BC: Dedication of temple of Jupiter Optimus Maximus; increasing adoption of Greek pantheon

Adena:
*c. 1000–350 BC
Earth temple mounds; burials with grave goods*

Hopewell
Cahokia
Adena
Serpent Mound

Persia c. 550 BC–226 AD:
*550 BC: Zoroastrianism proclaimed monotheistic state cult of Achaemenid Persia; monumental temples, fire altars.
From c. 116 AD: Zoroastrian cult of Mithraism spreads through Roman Empire*

Luoyang

Asia

Marksville

Mississippi:
*c. 350 BC– 550 AD
Earthwork ceremonial centers; rich grave goods*

Carthage
Athens
Jerusalem
Giza
Saqqara
Sumer
Ur
Pasargadae

Phoenician colonies:
*c. 800–146 BC:
Cult centre at Carthage*

Maya:
*c. 300 BCE–900 AD
Ceremonial centres with pyramids*

Mesopotamia from 3rd millennium BC:
Royal burials including attendants and rich grave goods, monumental (ziggurat) temples

India from c. 1800 BC:
*c.1450 BC: Composition of Vedas, recording Indian mythology begins.
c. 800 BC: Rise of cities on central Ganges; Upanishads recorded in Sanskrit*

Oaxaca:
*c. 500– 150 BC
Zapotec temples*

Olmec:
*c. 1200– 300 BC
Monumental sculpture; ceremonial centers; votive burials*

Egypt c. 3000–30 BC:
*c. 2700– 2150 BC: Old Kingdom, monumental architecture and elaborate (pyramid) tombs.
c. 2040–1763 BC: Middle Kingdom.
From c.1570 BC New Kingdom.
1352–1333 BC: Akhenaten establishes monotheistic Aten (Sun god) cult at El-Armana*

Judah to 132 AD Monotheism:
*c. 930 BC: Temple of Solomon destroyed 586; second temple built 538.
From 132 AD: Jewish diaspora*

ATLANTIC OCEAN

Chavin:
*c. 850– 200 BC
Temple complex; anthropomorphic pantheon*

Chavin de Huantar

Africa

INDIAN OCEAN

PACIFIC OCEAN

South America

EVOLUTION OF NUMERICAL SYSTEMS

EVOLUTION OF NUMERICAL SYSTEMS

Regions with earliest dates

- Chinese
- Egyptian
- Greek
- Gupta India
- Hebraic
- Hittite
- Roman

Bases

- ◯ Base 10
- ◯ Base 20
- ◯ Base 60

Symbols

- + Additive
- X Multiplicative
- ● Positional

EVOLUTION OF NUMERICAL SYSTEMS
As civilisations developed, written and numerical systems became necessary. Since early civilisations had no contact with each, other individual systems developed. The Babylonians were great mathematicians and their numbering system is one of the world's oldest. They used base 60 and we still use this for time and geometry: 24 hours in a day, 60 minutes in an hour, 60 seconds in a minute and 360 degrees in a circle. Most other systems used base 10. Measurements were often based on average sizes of hands and feet: 4 finger widths = 1 palm, 4 palms = 1 foot, etc.

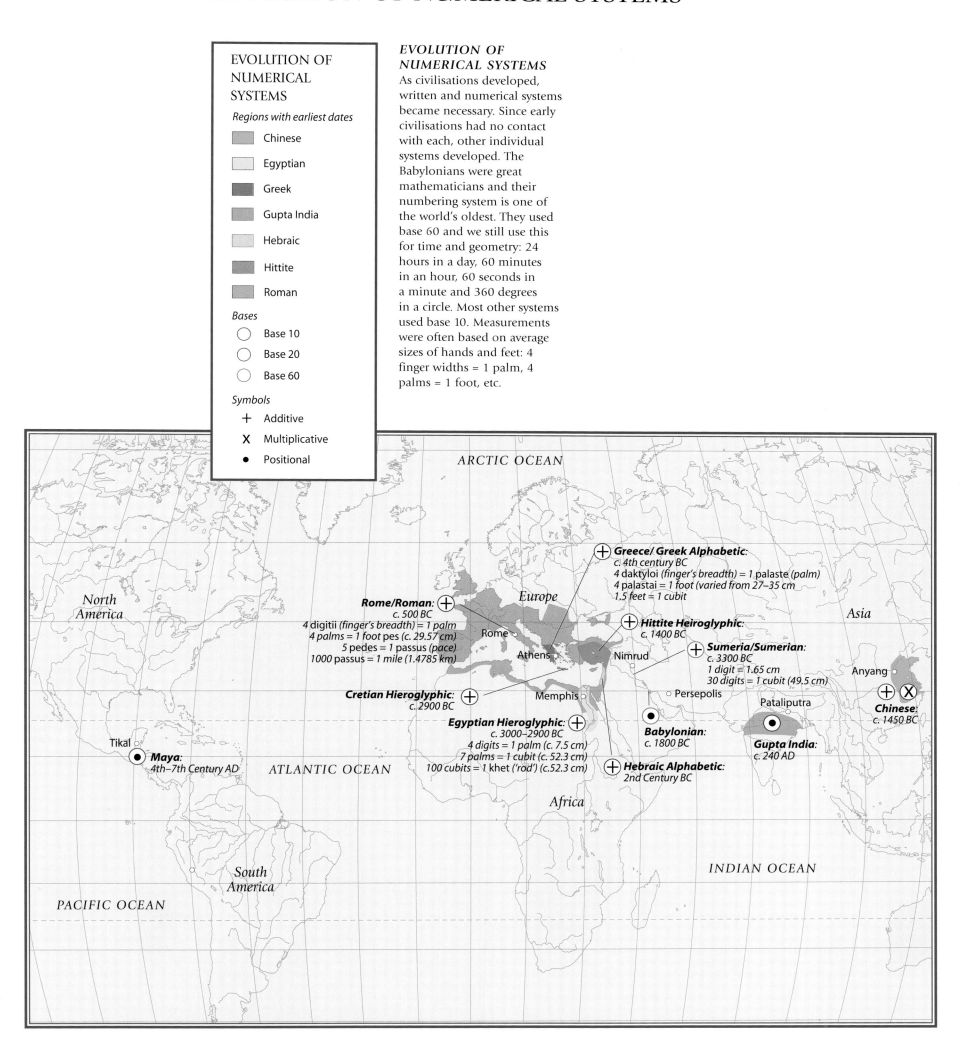

Greece/ Greek Alphabetic:
c. 4th century BC
4 daktyloi (finger's breadth) = 1 palaste (palm)
4 palastai = 1 foot (varied from 27–35 cm
1.5 feet = 1 cubit

Rome/Roman:
c. 500 BC
4 digitii (finger's breadth) = 1 palm
4 palms = 1 foot pes (c. 29.57 cm)
5 pedes = 1 passus (pace)
1000 passus = 1 mile (1.4785 km)

Hittite Heiroglyphic:
c. 1400 BC

Sumeria/Sumerian:
c. 3300 BC
1 digit = 1.65 cm
30 digits = 1 cubit (49.5 cm)

Cretian Hieroglyphic:
c. 2900 BC

Egyptian Hieroglyphic:
c. 3000–2900 BC
4 digits = 1 palm (c. 7.5 cm)
7 palms = 1 cubit (c. 52.3 cm)
100 cubits = 1 khet ('rod') (c.52.3 cm)

Babylonian:
c. 1800 BC

Gupta India:
c. 240 AD

Chinese:
c. 1450 BC

Hebraic Alphabetic:
2nd Century BC

Maya:
4th–7th Century AD

ARCTIC OCEAN
North America
Europe
Asia
Rome
Athens
Nimrud
Anyang
Memphis
Persepolis
Pataliputra
Tikal
ATLANTIC OCEAN
Africa
South America
INDIAN OCEAN
PACIFIC OCEAN

THE WORLD IN 1250 BC

THE WORLD IN 1250 BC
With the introduction of iron technology and better cultivation techniques, civilisations that had adopted these techniques began to spread out into larger areas that would ultimately become empires. The biggest concentrations of people were in Europe and Asia, although there were substantial populations in Africa, South-east Asia and parts of the Americas.

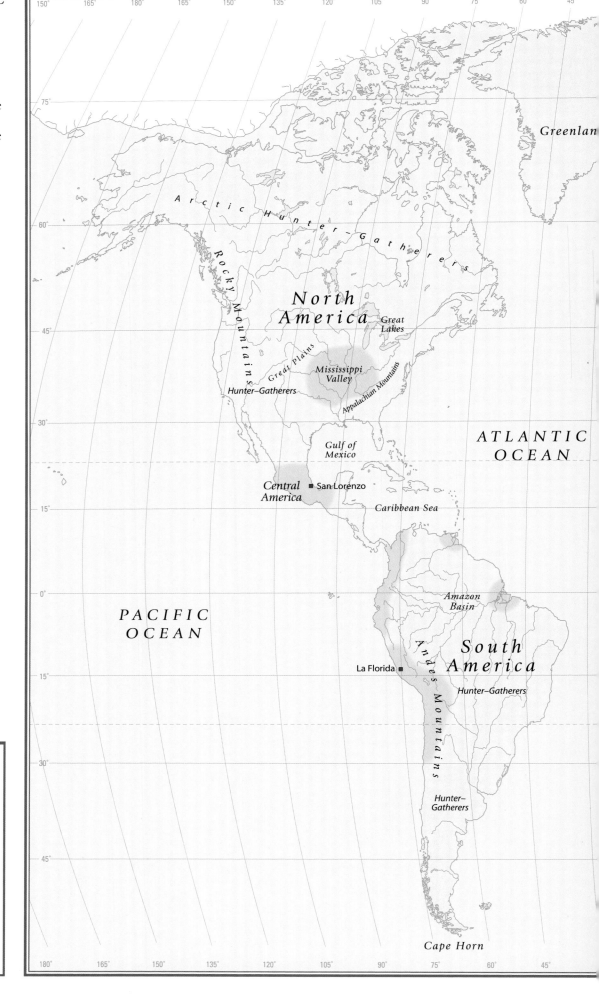

THE WORLD IN 1250 BC

- ■ Important sites
- New Kingdom of Egypt
- Hittites
- Mitanni
- Elam
- Shang China
- Mycenaean civilization

- Transition from hunting and gathering to agriculture
- Other urbanized regions

Major Bronze-using Regions

- Andronova steppe cultures
- Bronze Age Europe
- Mainland Southeast Asia

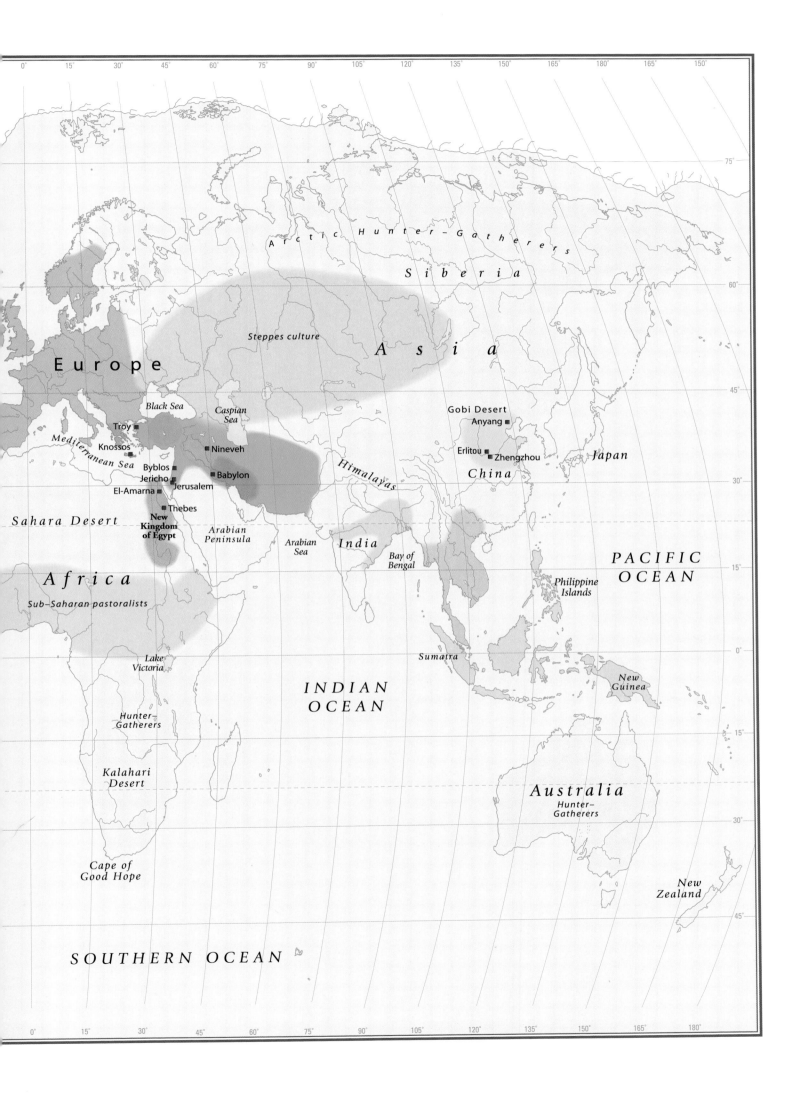

Arctic Hunter–Gatherers

Siberia

Steppes culture

Europe

Asia

Black Sea

Caspian Sea

Troy

Knossos

Mediterranean Sea

Byblos

Jericho

Jerusalem

El-Amarna

Thebes

New Kingdom of Egypt

Nineveh

Babylon

Arabian Peninsula

Sahara Desert

Africa

Sub–Saharan pastoralists

Lake Victoria

Hunter–Gatherers

Kalahari Desert

Cape of Good Hope

Arabian Sea

India

Himalayas

Bay of Bengal

Sumatra

INDIAN OCEAN

Gobi Desert

Anyang

Erlitou

Zhengzhou

China

Japan

Philippine Islands

PACIFIC OCEAN

New Guinea

Australia

Hunter–Gatherers

New Zealand

SOUTHERN OCEAN

INDO-EUROPEAN MIGRATION

5000 – 900 BC

INDO-EUROPEAN MIGRATION 5000–900 BC

Migration denotes any population movement from one locality to another, often over long distances or in large groups. Humans are known to have migrated extensively throughout history and prehistory. Since there are obviously no records of early migrations it is necessary to rely on comparative linguistics and archaeology. Using such indicators it can be speculated that somewhere between 3000 and 2000 BC there were movements from Central Asia into the Black Sea region. These were followed some thousand years later by more extensive movements covering much of Europe, the Middle East, and Northern India.

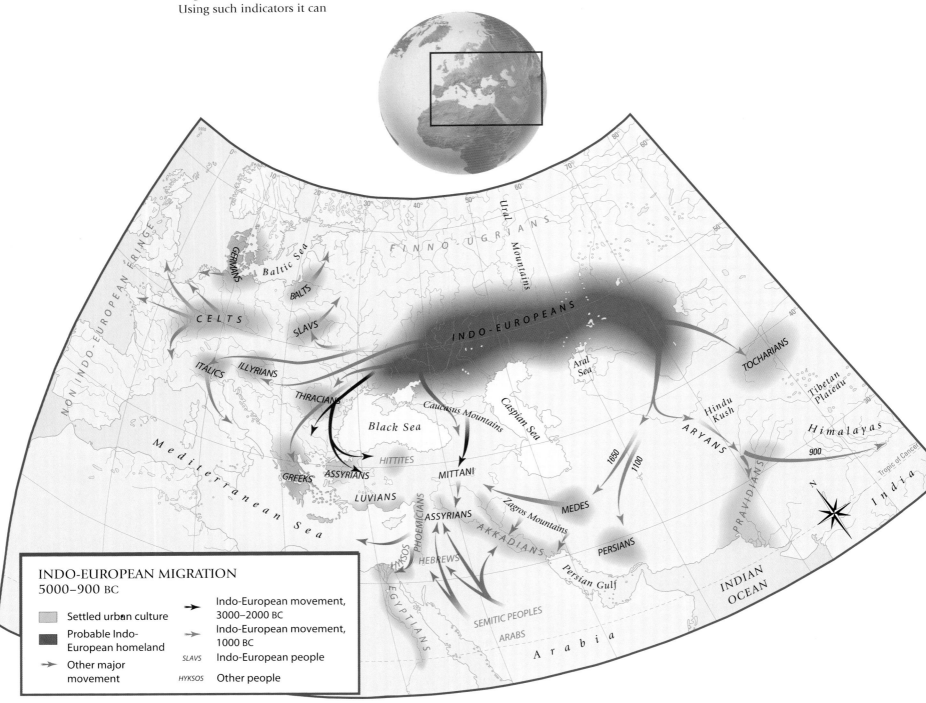

INDO-EUROPEAN MIGRATION
5000–900 BC

▢ Settled urban culture	⟶ Indo-European movement, 3000–2000 BC
▮ Probable Indo-European homeland	⟶ Indo-European movement, 1000 BC
⟶ Other major movement	*SLAVS* Indo-European people
	HYKSOS Other people

PART 2

EGYPT AND THE NEAR EAST

EARLY EGYPTIANS WERE FARMERS settling near the Nile. Communities learned to cooperate in building irrigation channels that would diffuse flood water and its silt onto fields. Common methods of agricultural exploitation were generated by administrative and commercial centers capable of controlling large stretches of the Nile. Prior to pharaonic Egypt, integrated trading systems developed, with carefully planned fortified towns being built at Nagada, Hierakonpolis, and Elephantine. Kingship developed under the pharaoahs leading to dynasties lasting from c. 2900 BC to Alexander the Great's conquest in 332 BC when Persian tutelage was eradicated. Alexander's successors and Rome ended Egyptian independence. The Near East and Mesopotamia were the home of several civilizations fed by the granary of the Tigris–Euphrates river systems. Ancient Sumerians were followed by Akkadians, Gutians, Babylonians, and Assyrians who conflicted with other cultures and empires such as the Mitanni and Hittites. The latter, an Indo-European people, eventually fought Pharaoh Ramesses II at Kadesh in 1275 BC as powers at different ends of the Fertile Crescent sought to expand through Palestine, a cockpit of war in which the Hebrew states of Israel and Judah were created and then destroyed.

3250 – 552 BC EGYPT: OLD KINGDOM

EGYPT: OLD KINGDOM
The Old Kingdom covers the period between 2650 and 2134 BC. It was the richest and most creative period in Egyptian history. All the enormous pyramids were built at this time in the lifetimes of only four kings, Snofru, Cheops, Chephren, and Mycerinus and the growth in population and wealth allowed the kings to apportion vast amounts of labor and materials to these monuments to themselves. The Nile was the lifeline of Egypt and at the end of the 6th Dynasty the annual floods suddenly fell off precipitously; people began to starve and the kingdom fell into disarray.

EGYPT: OLD KINGDOM

- ● Town or city, c. 3250–2000 BC
- ▬ Cemetery
- ▮ Royal tomb, c. 3250–2650 BC
- ▫ Noble's tomb, c. 2500–2000 BC
- ▲ Pyramid, c. 2500–2000 BC
- ⛏ Mines/raw materials
- ▨ Gold
- — Desert routes

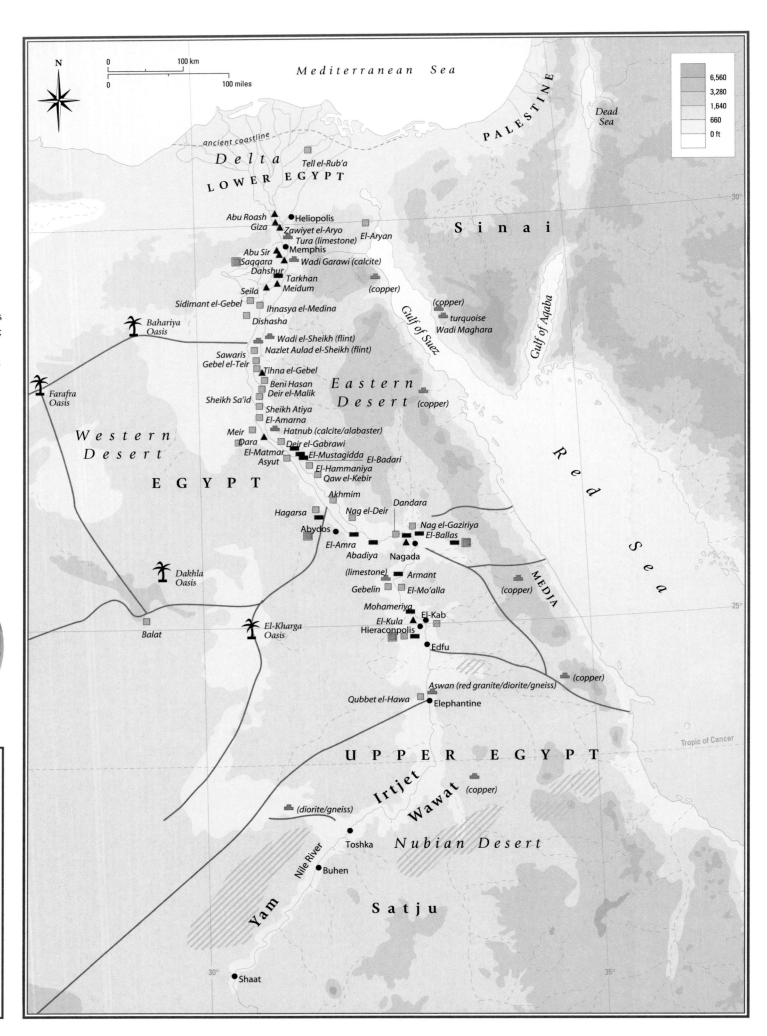

THE BABYLONIAN EMPIRE

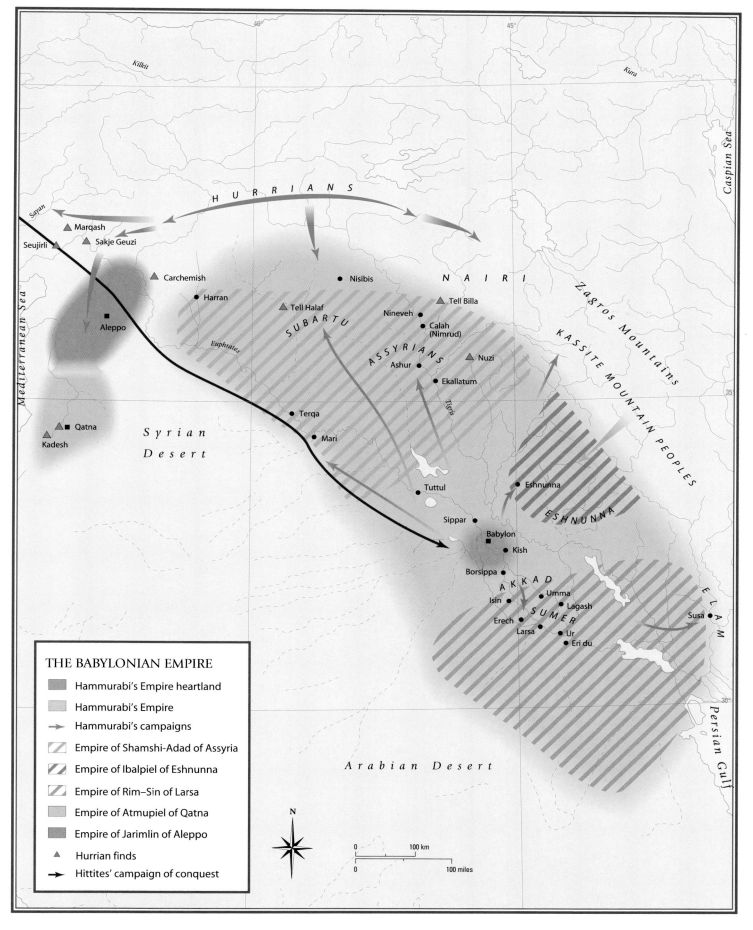

THE BABYLONIAN EMPIRE 2000–552 BC

Babylonia was a state south of Mesopotamia in modern Iraq, combining the territories of two ethnic groups, the Sumerians and the Akkadians. It was an intensively irrigated area, strategically located for trade routes and commerce and throughout its history was often under threat from outsiders. In the 18th century BC Hammurabi became ruler of Mesopotamia. He was a highly efficient ruler who drew up a very influential code of law. This gave the region stability and transformed it into the central power of Mesopotamia. The empire continued for another 440 years.

THE BABYLONIAN EMPIRE

- Hammurabi's Empire heartland
- Hammurabi's Empire
- → Hammurabi's campaigns
- Empire of Shamshi-Adad of Assyria
- Empire of Ibalpiel of Eshnunna
- Empire of Rim–Sin of Larsa
- Empire of Atmupiel of Qatna
- Empire of Jarimlin of Aleppo
- ▲ Hurrian finds
- → Hittites' campaign of conquest

EGYPT: MIDDLE KINGDOM

2030 – 1100 BC

EGYPT: THE MIDDLE KINGDOM

The Middle Kingdom covers the period between 2030 and 1640 BC. The country had been in chaos for about 100 years, but order was restored, trade with other countries began again, and irrigation projects were repaired. Local villages and cities had grown accustomed to operating independently but as the king began to regain authority the country grew in wealth and population. Many of the population were foreigners, and as their numbers increased their communities became larger and their leaders became kings in their own right. This led to a decline in the power of the Egyptian king and once again the country fell into disorder.

THE HITTITE EMPIRE AND NEIGHBORING STATES (FACING PAGE)

The Hittites originated in north-central Anatolia during the 14th century BC. They expanded their empire to include central Anatolia, northwestern Syria, and Upper Mesopotamia. Hittite prosperity was mostly dependent on control of trade routes and sources of metal. Control of the routes linking northern Syria with Mesopotamia was vital, but Egypt was making threatening moves. Things came to a head at the Battle of Kadesh in 1274. This was the biggest chariot battle the world had ever seen. The result was a draw, although both sides claimed a great victory. However, by 1200 BC the Hittite Empire had virtually disappeared.

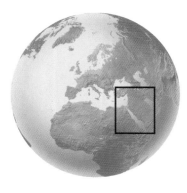

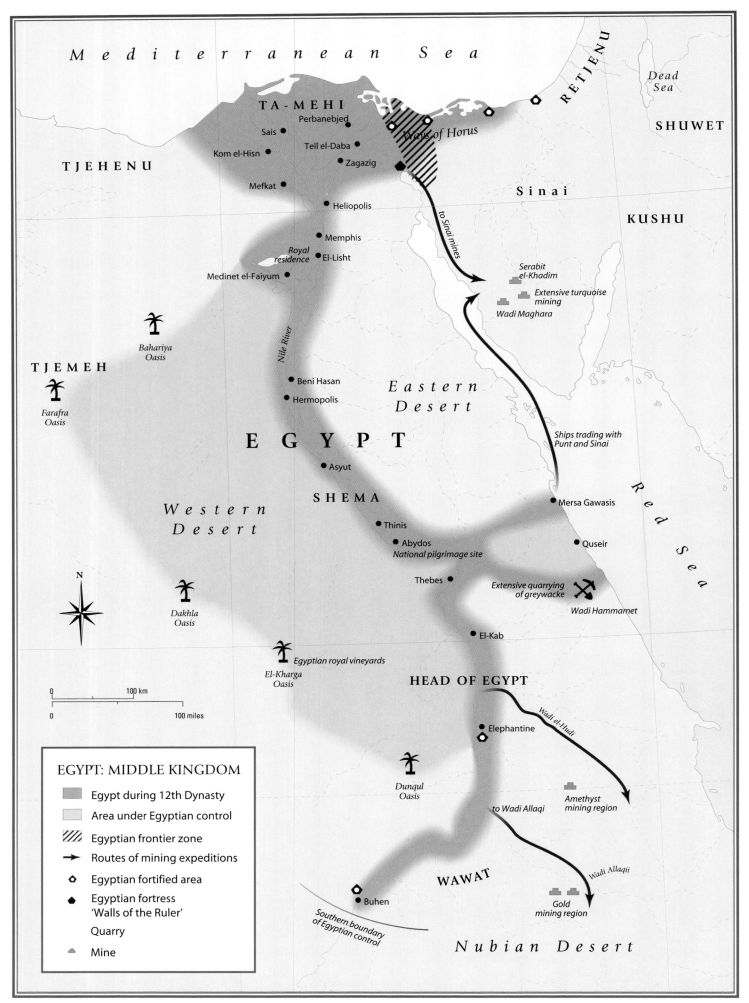

Mediterranean Sea

RETJENU

Dead Sea

TA-MEHI

SHUWET

Perbanebjed

Sais

Tell el-Daba

Ways of Horus

Kom el-Hisn

Zagazig

Sinai

TJEHENU

Mefkat

KUSHU

Heliopolis

to Sinai mines

Memphis

Serabit el-Khadim

Royal residence

El-Lisht

Extensive turquoise mining

Medinet el-Faiyum

Wadi Maghara

Nile River

Bahariya Oasis

Beni Hasan

Eastern Desert

Hermopolis

TJEMEH

E G Y P T

Farafra Oasis

Ships trading with Punt and Sinai

Asyut

SHEMA

Mersa Gawasis

Western Desert

Thinis

Abydos
National pilgrimage site

Red Sea

Quseir

N

Thebes

Extensive quarrying of greywacke

Dakhla Oasis

Wadi Hammamet

El-Kab

0   100 km

Egyptian royal vineyards

0   100 miles

El-Kharga Oasis

HEAD OF EGYPT

Wadi el-Hudi

Elephantine

Dunqul Oasis

Amethyst mining region

to Wadi Allaqi

EGYPT: MIDDLE KINGDOM

Wadi Allaqi

Egypt during 12th Dynasty

Gold mining region

Area under Egyptian control

Egyptian frontier zone

WAWAT

Routes of mining expeditions

Egyptian fortified area

Southern boundary of Egyptian control

Egyptian fortress 'Walls of the Ruler'

Buhen

Quarry

Nubian Desert

Mine

THE HITTITE EMPIRE AND NEIGHBORING STATES, MIDDLE EAST

THE HITTITE EMPIRE AND NEIGHBORING STATES

- Hittite Kingdom, c. 1400
- ○ Hittite Empire at its maximum extent, c. 1322
- Hurrian Kingdom of Mittani, c. 1400
- Kassile Kingdom of Babylon, c. 1400
- Assyrian heartland
- ○ Assyrian Empire
- New Egyptian Kingdom, c. 1490
- → Migrations, 1200–1100

PHRYGIANS

Black Sea

Troy

MYSIANS

AHHIYAMA   ARZAWA

AHHIYAWA EMPIRE

Beycesultan
Mendares

LUVIANS

Crete

Alaca Hüyük
Hattusas   Masal Hüyük
Yazilikaya   Palace
Alisar Hüyük
HATTI
Kültepe

Kara Hüyük
Eflatun Pinar
Spring sanctuary

Malatya

URARTIANS

Karatepe

Tarsus
Mersin

Mediterranean
Sea

Cyprus

Carchemish
Ugarit   Aleppo
Emar

HURRIANS   1115

MITTANI

Nineveh
Kalhu   Arbela
(Arbil)
Ashur   ASSYRIA
Nuzi

Euphrates

Tigris

Byblos
Kadesh
1285

Tadmor
(Palmyra)

ARAMEANS

Zagros Mountains

Tyre

Sippar   Der
BABYLONIA
Babylon

ELAM

Susa

Canopus
Ramases   Jerusalem
(Tanis)   1180   Gaza

HEBREWS

Nippur
Isin

Ur

Memphis

Elath

NEW EGYPTIAN EMPIRE

R. Nile

Red Sea

Persian Gulf

CHALDEANS

Thebes

Tropic of Cancer

N

0   200 km

0   200 miles

EGYPT: NEW KINGDOM

1550 – 728 BC

EGYPT: THE NEW KINGDOM

The New Kingdom covers the period from 1550 to 1070 BC. After the fall of the Middle Kingdom, Egypt was ruled by foreign invaders, the Hyksos. In 1550 Amosis drove them out, founded the 18th Dynasty and ushered in the New Kingdom. Egypt dedicated itself to ensuring that no such invasion happened again. The kings were warriors who built up border defenses and actively seized territory outside Egypt. Foreigners were not tolerated and were often treated badly. This was the time of Moses and the Hebrew slaves. Eventually more foreigners began to encroach and following a series of weaker kings, Egypt once again collapsed into chaos.

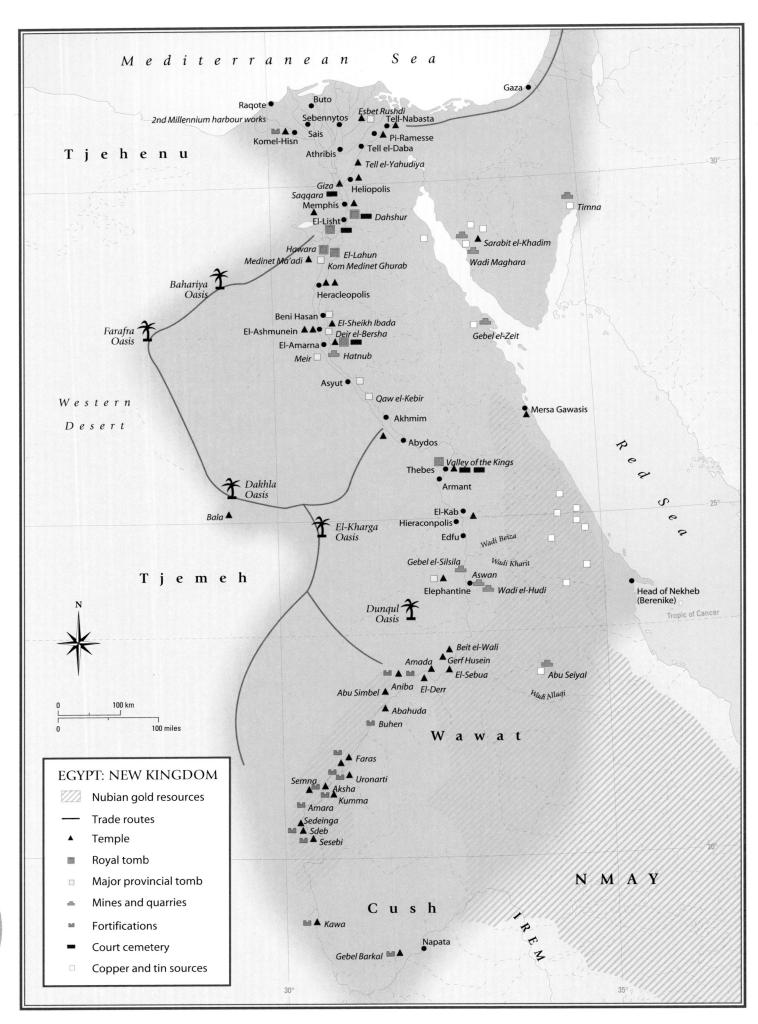

EGYPT: NEW KINGDOM

- ▨ Nubian gold resources
- — Trade routes
- ▲ Temple
- ▪ Royal tomb
- ☐ Major provincial tomb
- ⛏ Mines and quarries
- ▬ Fortifications
- ▬ Court cemetery
- ☐ Copper and tin sources

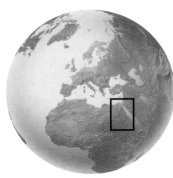

NUBIA ASCENDANT

NUBIA ASCENDANT

In 728 BC, after 300 years of political chaos, Egypt was invaded by its sister civilization to the south, Nubia. The Nubians had modelled their civilization on the Egyptians and had maintained Egyptian values and culture with a high degree of conservatism. Under the command of Piy the Nubians rushed northward and, defeating all opposition, conquered the whole of Egypt. The aim of the Nubians was to return Egypt to its old ways and to restore the Egyptian traditions and religious practices that had died out. They were successful, but not long after everything changed once more when the Assyrians invaded.

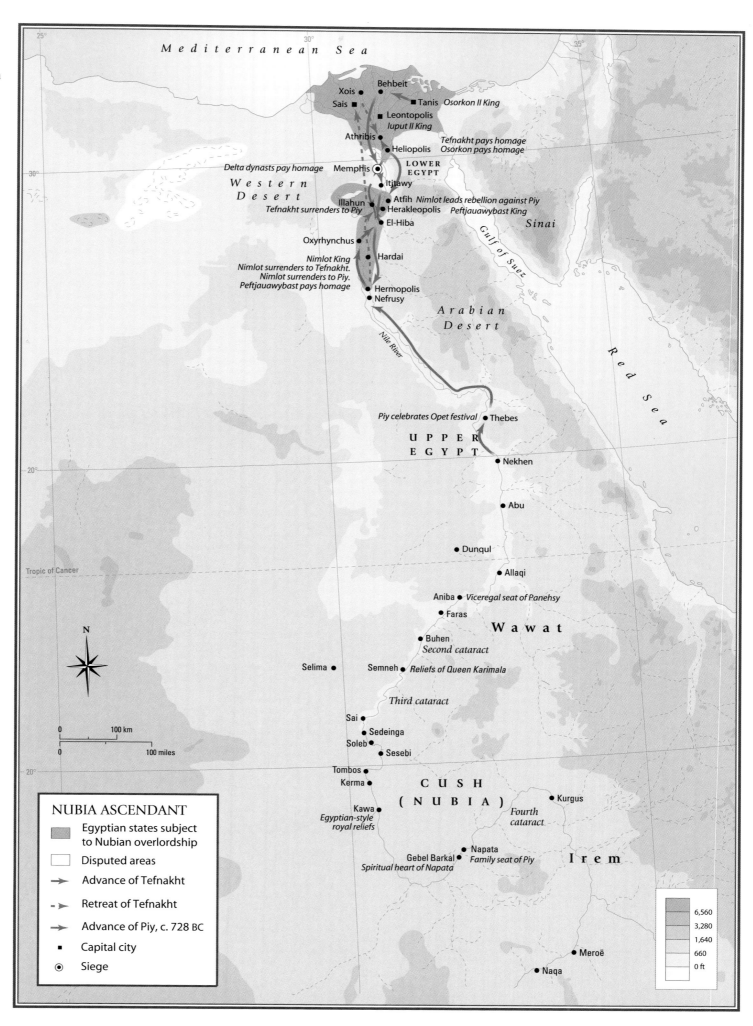

Mediterranean Sea

Xois • Behbeit •
Sais ■ ■ Tanis   *Osorkon II King*
■ Leontopolis
Iuput II King
Athribis •
Tefnakht pays homage
• Heliopolis   *Osorkon pays homage*

Delta dynasts pay homage   Memphis ⊙   **LOWER EGYPT**

• Ititawy

Western Desert

Illahun • • Atfih   *Nimlot leads rebellion against Piy*
• Herakleopolis   *Peftjauawybast King*
Tefnakht surrenders to Piy   • El-Hiba

Oxyrhynchus •

• Hardai

Nimlot King
Nimlot surrenders to Tefnakht.
Nimlot surrenders to Piy.
Peftjauawybast pays homage   • Hermopolis
• Nefrusy

Arabian Desert

Gulf of Suez   *Sinai*

Nile River

Red Sea

Piy celebrates Opet festival • Thebes

UPPER EGYPT

• Nekhen

• Abu

• Dunqul

• Allaqi

Aniba • *Viceregal seat of Panehsy*
• Faras

Wawat

• Buhen
Second cataract

Selima •   Semneh • • *Reliefs of Queen Karimala*

Third cataract

Sai •
• Sedeinga
Soleb •
• Sesebi

Tombos •
Kerma •   **CUSH (NUBIA)**   *Fourth cataract*   • Kurgus

Kawa •
Egyptian-style royal reliefs

Gebel Barkal • • Napata   **Irem**
Spiritual heart of Napata   *Family seat of Piy*

• Meroë

• Naqa

Tropic of Cancer

N

0   100 km
0   100 miles

NUBIA ASCENDANT

◼ Egyptian states subject to Nubian overlordship

▢ Disputed areas

→ Advance of Tefnakht

⇢ Retreat of Tefnakht

→ Advance of Piy, c. 728 BC

■ Capital city

⊙ Siege

6,560
3,280
1,640
660
0 ft

733 – 663 BC

ASSYRIAN CAMPAIGNS OF TIGLATH-PILESER; THE STRUGGLE FOR EGYPT

ASSYRIAN CAMPAIGNS OF TIGLATH-PILESER III

The Assyrians under Tiglath-Pileser III launched a series of seasonal campaigns against the Medes, the Syrians and the Babylonians. His major policy change was to incorporate newly conquered territories into his empire rather than creating a series of dependent ministates.

In the years following Tiglath-pileser's death in 725 BC, a number of battles were fought, where the Assyrians gradually won control of Egypt from the Nubians. In 663 BC a decisive battle drove the Nubians out of Egypt for good.

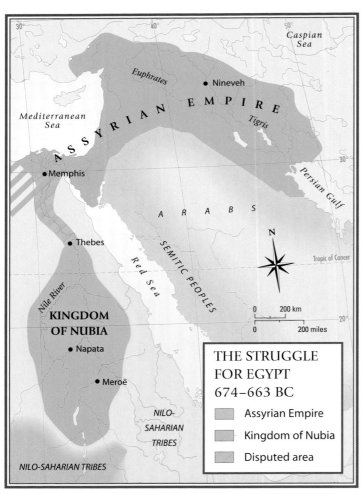

THE STRUGGLE
FOR EGYPT
674–663 BC

- Assyrian Empire
- Kingdom of Nubia
- Disputed area

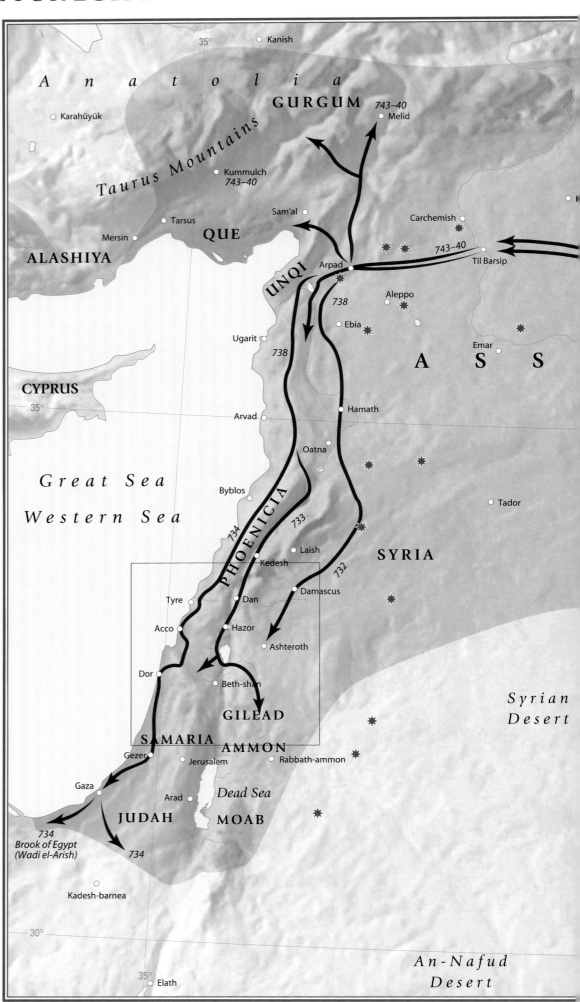

CAMPAIGN IN PALESTINE

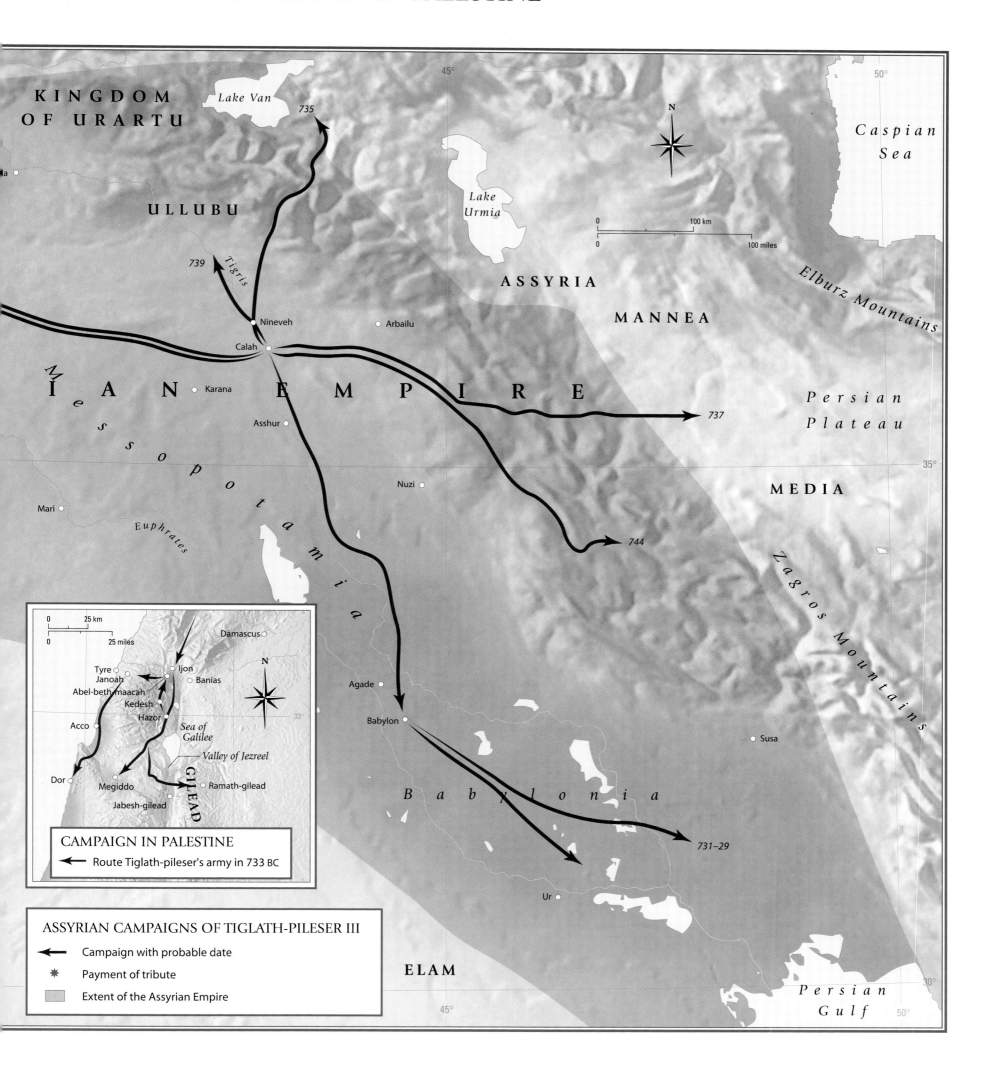

CAMPAIGN IN PALESTINE

→ Route Tiglath-pileser's army in 733 BC

ASSYRIAN CAMPAIGNS OF TIGLATH-PILESER III

→ Campaign with probable date

✳ Payment of tribute

▨ Extent of the Assyrian Empire

THE BABYLONIAN EMPIRE

THE BABYLONIAN EMPIRE 625–539 BC
For centuries the Assyrians had dominated Babylonia, but this all changed following the death of the last strong Assyrian ruler, Ashurbanipal in 627. Nabopolassar the Chaldean became ruler and he was followed by his son Nebuchadnezzar.

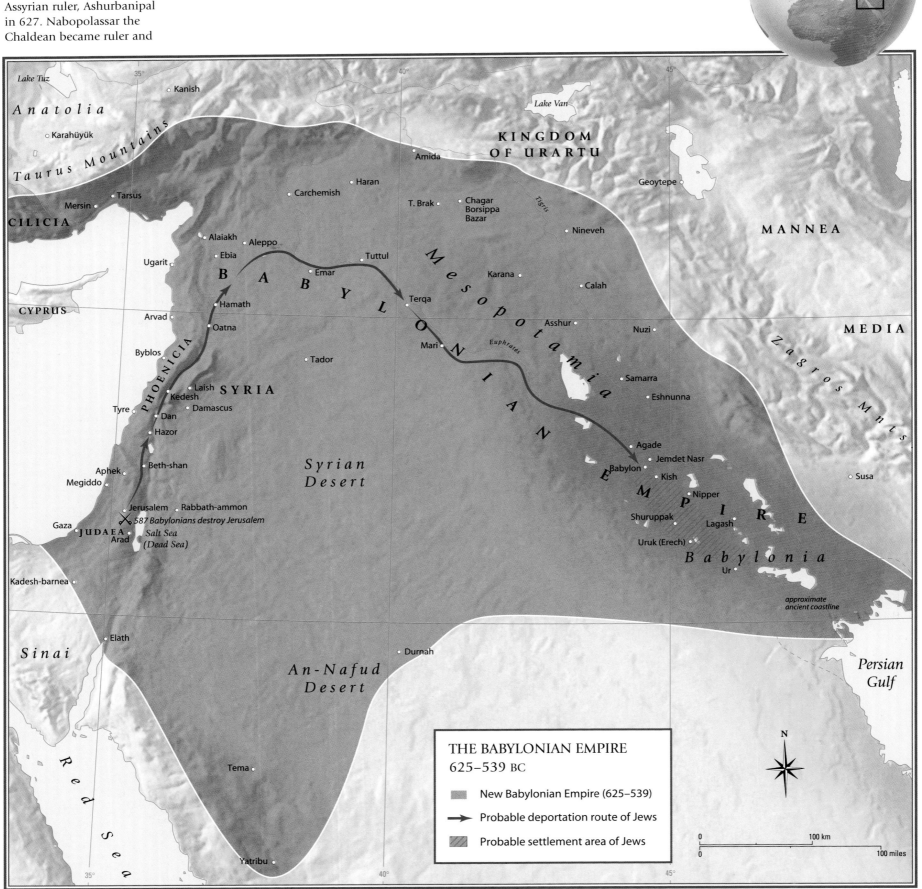

THE BABYLONIAN EMPIRE
625–539 BC

New Babylonian Empire (625–539)

Probable deportation route of Jews

Probable settlement area of Jews

0   100 km

0   100 miles

PART 3

GREECE

GREEK CIVILIZATION PROGRESSED THROUGH several phases. Initially, Greeks speaking a variety of dialects settled Greece, the Aegean islands, the Cyclades, and coastal Anatolia. Trade routes connected these regions with sizable settlements emerging in Crete and the Cyclades (c. 5000 BC). Cretan Minoan society competed with Mycenae for access to the Near East until 1200 BC when the former collapsed. The Mycenaean world was destroyed at about the same time, which many historians believe was a result of internecine strife between rival city-states.

The ending of Mycenaean cities ushered in three centuries known as the 'dark ages', a period shrouded in obscurity. Yet Greek Cyprus, partially peopled by refugees from the mainland, traded with the Near East and mainland Greece. An explosion in trade saw products exported to Egypt and artistic motifs were borrowed from Assyria and Armenia. Dynamic trade was partnered with political developments as city states toyed with constitutions, the most renowned being Sparta, Athens, and Corinth. Innovations commenced with an Athenian version of democracy while the various Greek cultural areas colonized the Mediterranean, with important settlements at Marseille (Massilia), Kyrene, and Sicily. Eventually, internal bickering led to the Peloponnesian War with weakness allowing subjection by Alexander the Great and eventually, Rome

750 – 400 BC

ANCIENT GREECE

EARLY ATTICA 4TH & 5TH CENTURIES BC
Attica is a peninsula jutting out into the Aegean Sea. The Persians had occupied it in 480 and 479 BC and after their departure work began on rebuilding the Athenian walls that had been destroyed. This project drew opposition from the Spartans and their Peloponnesian allies but the Athenians ignored the protests and carried on building. Despite fighting between Athens and Sparta's various Peloponnesian allies in the 460s BC, work on the walls continued. New long walls connected Athens with the ports and ensured that as long as Athens controlled the sea she would never be cut off from supplies..

EURASIA 750 BC (RIGHT)
By 750 BC, although the world was fairly well settled, most ethnic groups remained isolated. Agrarian-based economies were the first to show significant development and early settled civilizations were all based on the banks of large rivers with extensive floodplains. The Yellow River, the Indus, the Tigris-Euphrates, and the Nile were all important examples. This agrarian development led to the growth of trade and the growth of manufacturing industries. Other trappings

of civilization followed, such as a hierarchy of government, a legal system, and the development of writing as a means of record keeping.

EARLY ATTICA
4th and 5th centuries

- ○ Settlement
- ● Sacred site
- ▄ Fortress and sacred site
- ▄ Fortresses of the 4th century BC
- —— National border
- —— District boundary
- ---- Frontiers of the Trittyen
- —— Main highways (assumed)
- —— the "Long Walls"

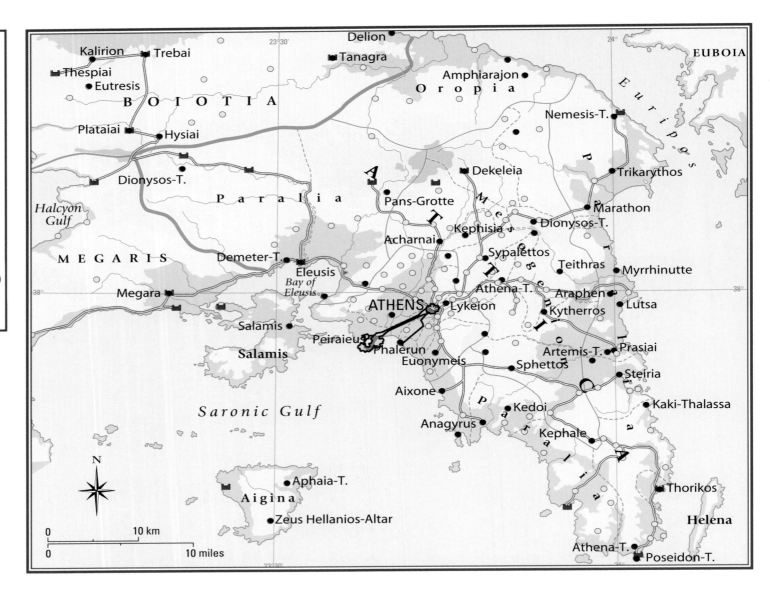

EURASIA

ARCTIC OCEAN

Iceland

FINNO-UGRIAN PEOPLES

SAMOYEDS

Siberia

PALAEOSIBERIANS

GERMANIC PEOPLES

BALTIC PEOPLES

SLAVS

Europe

Asia

ALTAIC PEOPLES

AINU

CELTS

THRACIANS

CAUCASIAN PEOPLES

Black Sea

Caspian Sea

Gobi Desert

KOREANS

JAPANESE

Japan

ILLYRIANS

IBERIAN PEOPLES

LIGUARIANS

ETRUSCANS

Rome
Cumae

GREEK STATES

Gordium

PHRYGIA

URARTU
Tushpa

IRANIANS

TIBETANS

Himalayas

Zhengzhou

CHINESE STATES

Wu

Carthage

Olympia

Mediterranean Sea

Nineveh
ASSYRIA
Byblos
Tyre

Nimrud

BABYLONIA
Babylon
ELAM

SINITIC PEOPLES

YUE

BERBERS

ISRAEL
Jerusalem
Memphis

AMMON
MOAB
JUDEA

Sahara Desert

EGYPT
Thebes

SEMITES

Arabian Peninsula

Arabian Sea

INDIAN STATES

NON-KHMER PEOPLES

Bay of Bengal

PACIFIC OCEAN

CUSH
Napata

NILO-SAHARAN PEOPLES

CUSHITES

DRAVIDIANS

CHADIANS

Sahel

NIGER-CONGO PEOPLES

Africa

Congo Basin

MALAYS

Borneo

Sumatra

MALAYS

PAPUANS
New Guinea

ATLANTIC OCEAN

INDIAN OCEAN

KHAISAN PEOPLES

Kalahari Desert

Australia

ABORIGINES

Cape of Good Hope

SOUTHERN OCEAN

EURASIA 750 BC

■ Important site or city

15° 0° 15° 30° 45° 60° 75° 90° 105° 120° 135° 150° 165°

75
60
45
30
15
0
15
30

PALACE OF KNOSSOS; MINOAN CRETE

2000 – 1200 BC

THE PALACE OF KNOSSOS

Excavations show that the area around Knossos had been inhabited since Neolithic times, possibly earlier than 6000 BC. The first palace was built around 2000 BC and stood for 300 years before it was destroyed. It was rebuilt a number of times following a series of earthquakes. Each time the palace was rebuilt it got larger and more splendid. Knossos was by now a major city with an estimated 100,000 inhabitants. The king used the palace as a royal residence until at least 1380 BC.

MINOAN CRETE

This is the period in Minoan history when smaller residences that we call villas began to appear on the rural landscape. These were probably the homes of affluent landlords and were modelled after the large palaces, with storage facilities, workshops, and places of worship. Small towns also began to develop near the palaces. There is also evidence at this time of administrative and economic unity throughout the island. Women played a powerful role in Minoan society and the gold artifacts, seals, and spears that have been found speak of a very affluent upper class.

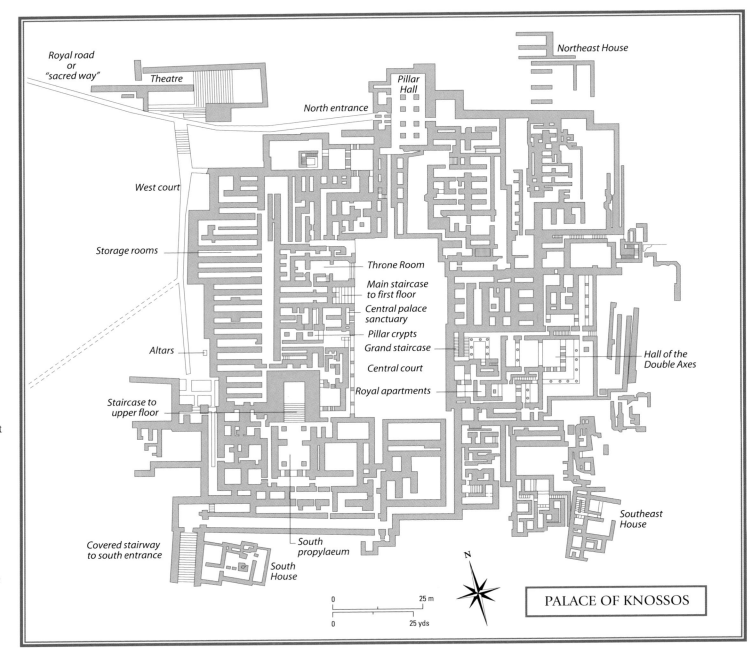

PALACE OF KNOSSOS

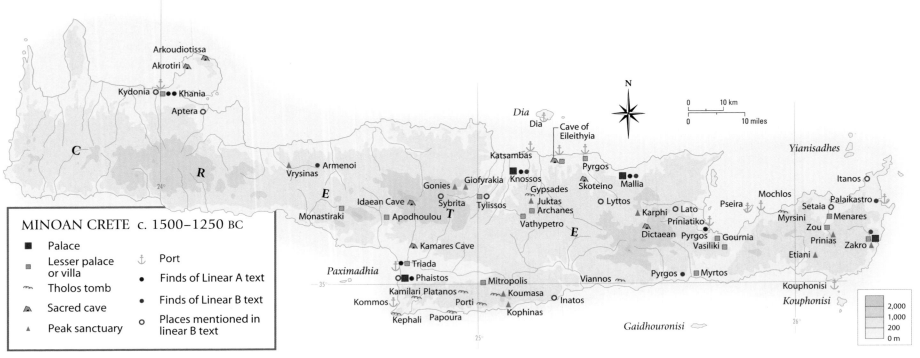

MINOAN CRETE c. 1500–1250 BC

- ■ Palace
- ▪ Lesser palace or villa
- ⌒ Tholos tomb
- ▲ Sacred cave
- ▴ Peak sanctuary
- ⚓ Port
- • Finds of Linear A text
- ● Finds of Linear B text
- ○ Places mentioned in linear B text

THE COLLAPSE OF MYCENAE

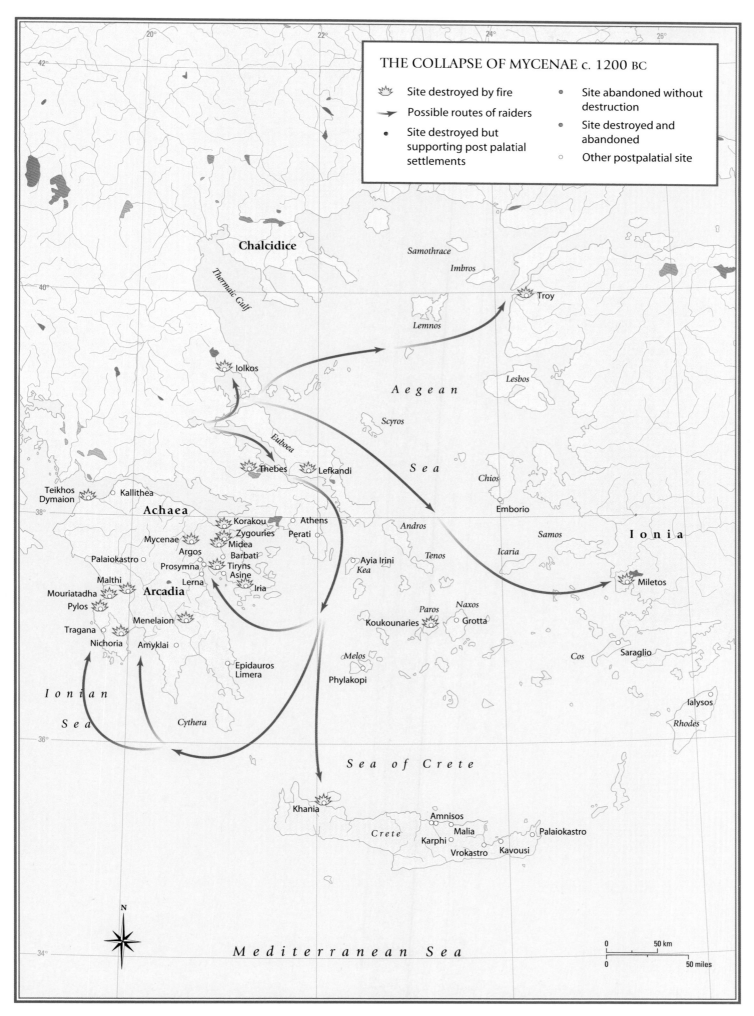

THE COLLAPSE OF MYCENAE c. 1200 BC

�fire Site destroyed by fire

→ Possible routes of raiders

• Site destroyed but supporting post palatial settlements

• Site abandoned without destruction

• Site destroyed and abandoned

○ Other postpalatial site

THE COLLAPSE OF MYCENAE

For 500 years from about 1600 BC, Mycenae was one of the major centres of Greek civilization. It was a military stronghold that dominated much of southern Greece, but by 1200 BC the power of Mycenae was declining and its dominance soon collapsed. There seems to have been a universal catastrophe. Within a short time around 1250 BC all the palaces of southern Greece were burned, including that at Mycenae, which was abandoned at the end of the 12th century. Though there are many theories as to why this happened, there is no conclusive evidence to support any one hypothesis. Historians disagree on why this should have occurred: it may have been famine or raiders from the sea, but it may also have been due to substantial invasions by Dorian Greeks armed with iron weapons that overwhelmed their bronze-equipped Mycenean opponents. Another theory favors intense rivalry between individual city-states that ignited into all-out war.

CLASSICAL GREECE: THE DELIAN LEAGUE

500 – 369 BC

THE DELIAN LEAGUE
The Delian League was an association of Ionian Greek city-states in 5th century BC. Athens set the level of payment that each of these states had to make and they all became subject to Athenian dictates. Athens also began to control the internal affairs of the other states, occasionally garrisoning soldiers there. At its height the Athenian Empire was composed of 172 tribute-paying states and it controlled the Aegean Sea. Many states that were outside the empire, notably Sparta, felt very threatened by the growth of Athenian power and this created a very volatile situation in the mid-5th century BC.

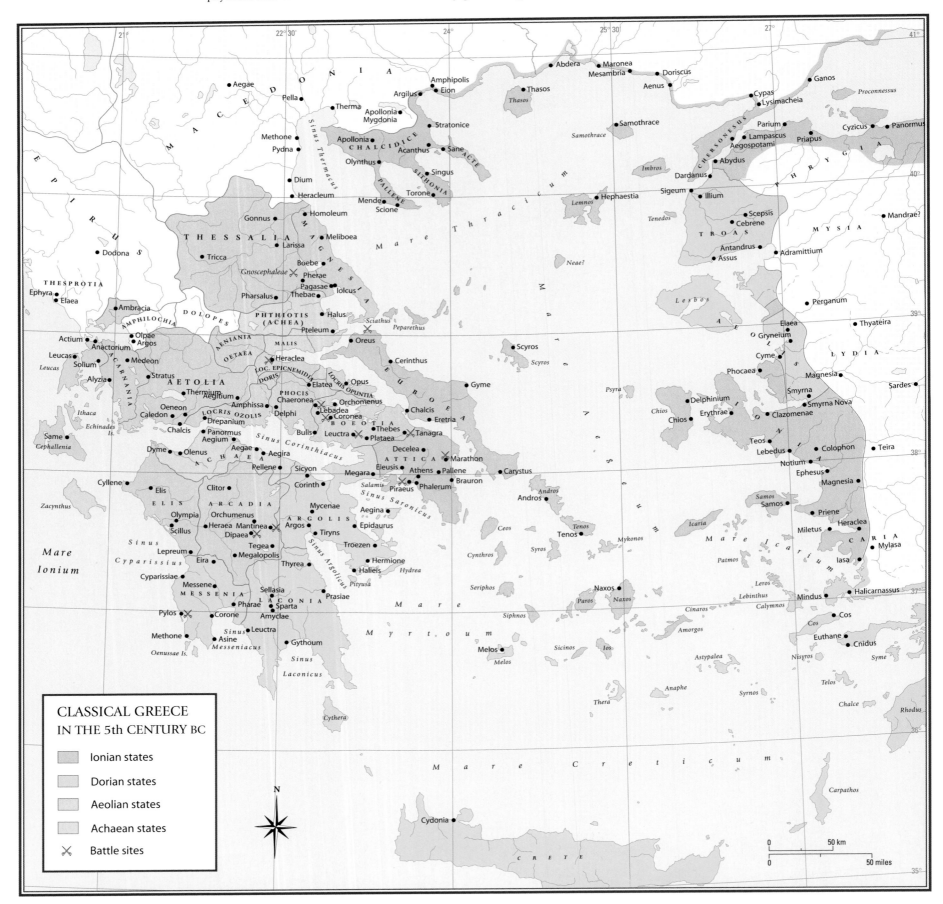

CLASSICAL GREECE
IN THE 5th CENTURY BC

- Ionian states
- Dorian states
- Aeolian states
- Achaean states
- ✕ Battle sites

MAJOR CULT CENTRES OF CLASSICAL GREECE;
THE FORTIFIED CITY OF MESSENE

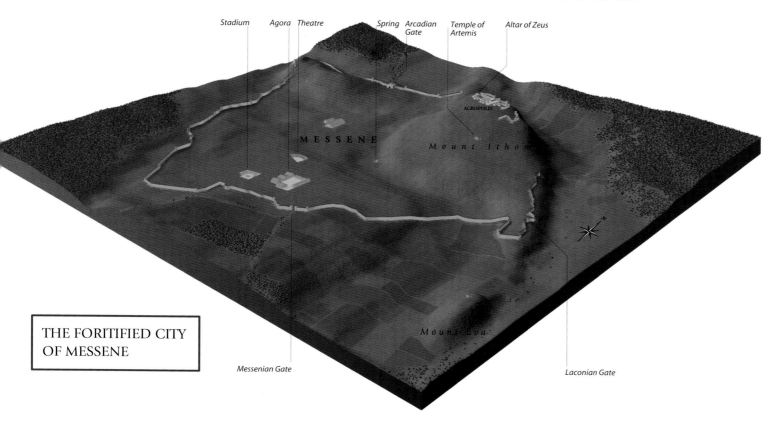

Stadium Agora Theatre   Spring Arcadian Gate   Temple of Artemis   Altar of Zeus

ACROPOLIS

MESSENE

Mount Ithome

Mount Eva

THE FORITIFIED CITY OF MESSENE

Messenian Gate

Laconian Gate

THE FORTIFIED CITY OF MESSENE

Messene is situated on the southwest Peloponnese in Greece and was founded in 369 BC after the liberation of Messenia from Spartan rule. It was constructed by the Thebans on the slopes of Mount Ithome. Its great stone walls were a monument to Greek military engineering and were effectively the seal of Sparta's doom. Messene became an independent city-state that was intransigently hostile to its former master, and cut its supply of slaves and conscripts to the Spartan army. Having lost its ready supply of forced labor, Sparta could no longer maintain its military traditions. It was still capable of winning the occasional border skirmish, but it was no longer a major player in the area.

CULTS IN CLASSICAL GREECE

The Greeks did not have any form of organized religion or belief, but they did recognize a group of twelve major gods who they worshipped under a variety of names and identities depending on the location. Although several of these main deities would have temples in each major city, some gods were strongly associated with one particular place, such as Apollo at Delphi or Zeus at Olympia. Rituals varied from site to site and within individual households. Smaller cults also developed based on the deeds of local heroes, who ranged from Olympic athletes to warriors, healers, and temple leaders.

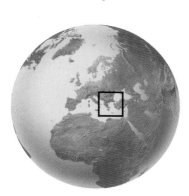

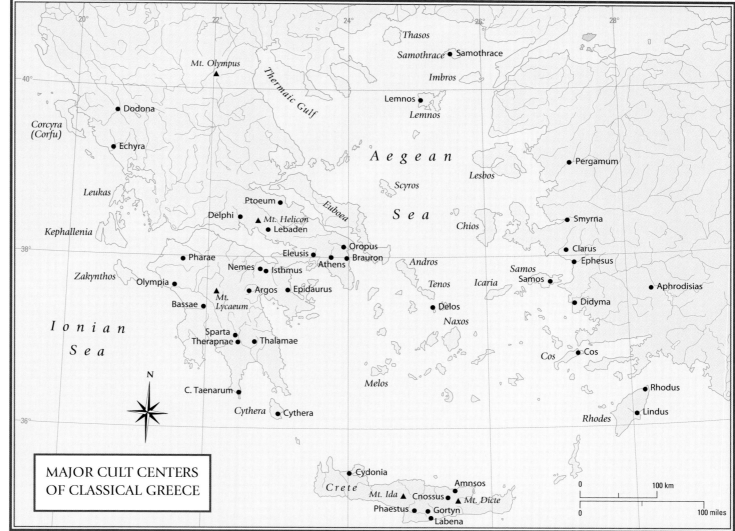

MAJOR CULT CENTERS OF CLASSICAL GREECE

ATHENIAN EMPIRE; PHOENICIANS AND GREEKS COLONISE THE MEDITERRANEAN

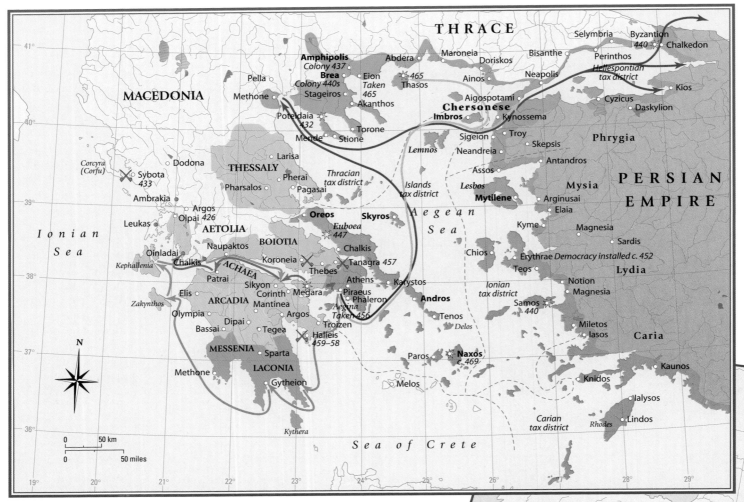

ATHENIAN EMPIRE

- Persian Empire
- Sparta 446 BC
- Spartan allies 446 BC
- Delian League 470s BC
- New Athenian allies 460–446 BC

Brea
Lesbos — Athenian cleruchy

- ☀ Region/State revolting against Athens
- --- Tax district boundary

Campaigns
- → Kimon 465 BC
- → Tolmides 455 BC
- → Perikles 450 BC
- → Perikles 435 BC
- ✗ Major battle site

COLLAPSE OF THE ATHENIAN EMPIRE

The Persians invaded Greece in 492 BC. They were finally defeated two years later, but made another attempt in 481. As a result the Delian League was formed under the leadership of Athens. At this time Greece was made up of a number of small city-states and they effectively began to pay tribute to Athens. Athens began to grow in power, which concerned Sparta and led to the first Peloponnesian war of 431. Following a brief respite a second war then broke out which resulted in a victory for Sparta and the complete defeat of Athens in 404. Athens never regained its preeminence in the region, and Sparta dominated Greece for many years. The wars marked the end of the golden age of classical Greece

THE PHOENICIANS & GREEKS COLONISE THE MEDITERRANEAN: 9TH–6TH CENTURY BC (RIGHT)

The Phoenicians came from the region of Tyre and were the major trading power in the Mediterranean in the early part of the first millennium BC. They had trading contacts in Egypt and Greece and had established colonies as far west as Spain and even traded as far north as Britain. Their most successful colony would eventually be known as Carthage. Many of the Greek city-states had colonies throughout the Mediterranean world. Melitus in Asia Minor, for example, had 90 colonies scattered along the shores of the Black Sea and around the Mediterranean. In most colonies the motivation was to foster trade and further the wealth of the mother city.

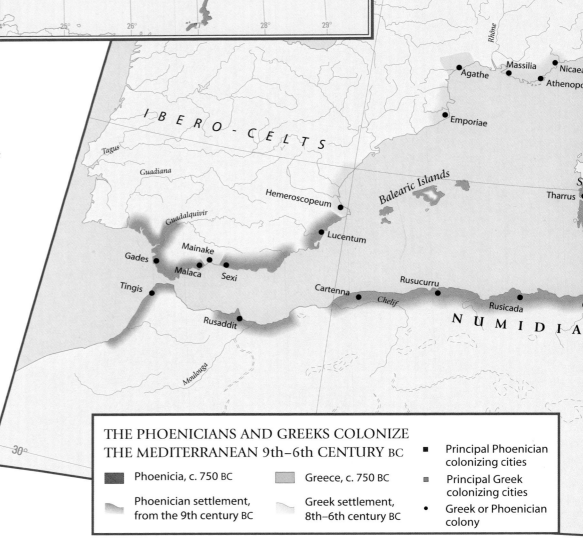

THE PHOENICIANS AND GREEKS COLONIZE THE MEDITERRANEAN 9th–6th CENTURY BC

- Phoenicia, c. 750 BC
- Phoenician settlement, from the 9th century BC
- Greece, c. 750 BC
- Greek settlement, 8th–6th century BC
- ■ Principal Phoenician colonizing cities
- ■ Principal Greek colonizing cities
- • Greek or Phoenician colony

GREEK TYRANNIES

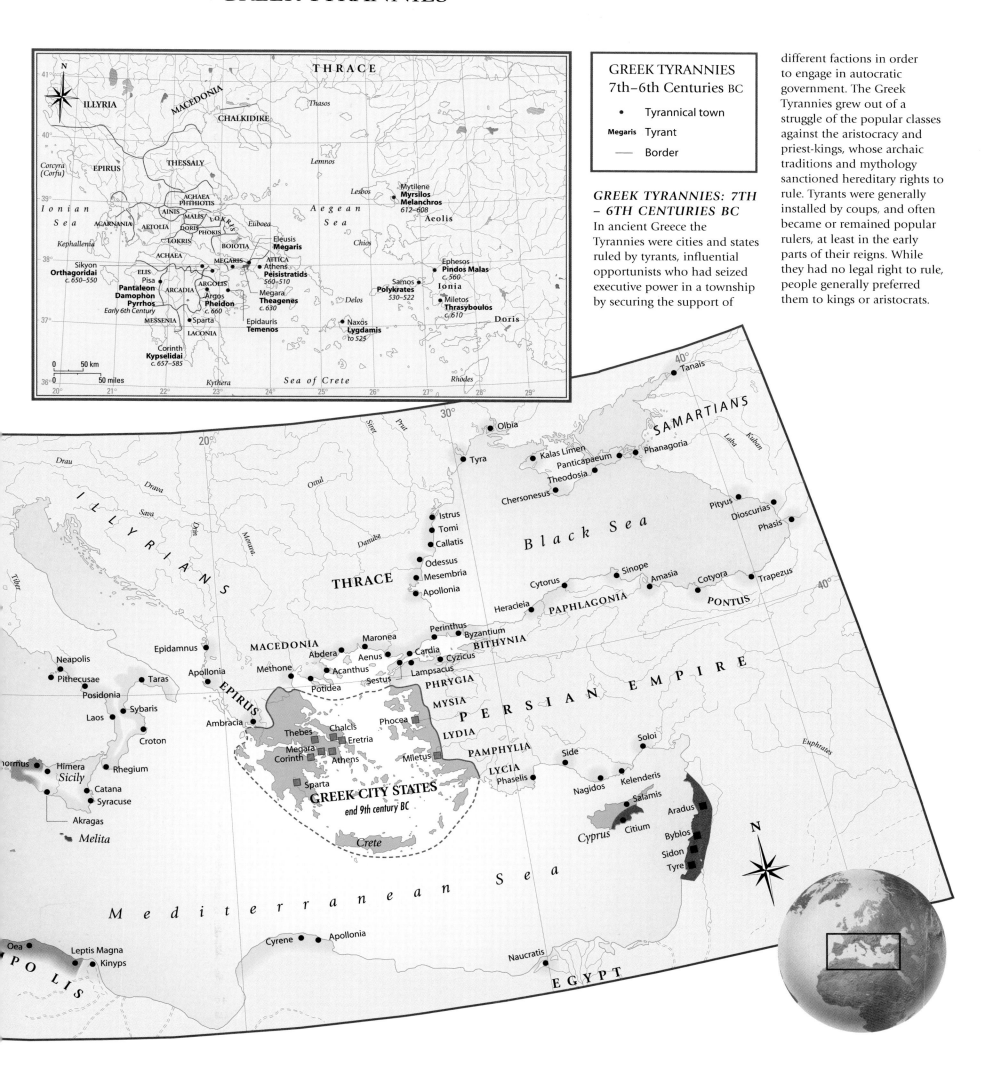

**GREEK TYRANNIES
7th–6th Centuries** BC

- • Tyrannical town
- **Megaris** Tyrant
- — Border

***GREEK TYRANNIES: 7TH
– 6TH CENTURIES BC***
In ancient Greece the
Tyrannies were cities and states
ruled by tyrants, influential
opportunists who had seized
executive power in a township
by securing the support of

different factions in order
to engage in autocratic
government. The Greek
Tyrannies grew out of a
struggle of the popular classes
against the aristocracy and
priest-kings, whose archaic
traditions and mythology
sanctioned hereditary rights to
rule. Tyrants were generally
installed by coups, and often
became or remained popular
rulers, at least in the early
parts of their reigns. While
they had no legal right to rule,
people generally preferred
them to kings or aristocrats.

INVASION ROUTES INTO GREECE; XERXES' INVASION

INVASION ROUTES INTO GREECE

Invading Greece by land from the north involved facing various natural difficulties. The invaders would have to pass through Thessaly to reach southern Laconia. Doing so would entail crossing a series of large plains separated by mountain ranges. Thus Greece's natural terrain provided choke points. At these places Greek phalanxes could be successfully deployed, thus denying large parts of Greece to an invader. The Spartan stand at the Pass of Thermopylae in 480 BC against Xerxes' invading Persian army exemplifies this tactic of denial.

INVASION ROUTES IN GREECE

→ major routes of invasion and campaigns

① Route of invasion from the north

② Choke point, the pass of Thermopylae

③ Route of invasion from the south

④ Choke point, the isthmus of Corinth

⑤ Great plain of Boeotia

XERXES INVASION, 480 BC

→ Route of Persian land forces

→ Route of Persian fleet

XERXES' INVASION 480 BC

In 480 BC, after massive preparation, the Persian king Xerxes led a very large force to conquer Greece. At the Battle of Thermopylae a vastly outnumbered Greek force, led by the Spartan king, Leonidas, held back the Persians for three days. The Persians eventually took the pass, but the delay gave the Athenians time to prepare for a decisive naval battle at Salamis that destroyed the Persian navy. Xerxes left his army in Greece to fight one last battle at Platea where it suffered a comprehensive defeat by the Greeks. Thus ended the threat of Persian expansion into Europe.

PELOPONNESIAN WAR; CAMPAIGN IN SICILY

PELOPONNESIAN WAR 431–404 BC

- ▧ Athens and members of the Delian League, c. 431 BC
- Athens's allies
- → Athenian campaign
- ✗ Athenian victory
- Sparta and Spartan allies, c. 431 BC
- → Spartan campaign
- ✗ Spartan victory
- ✺ Revolt against Athens
- Persian Empire
- Neutral states

PELOPONNESIAN WAR

The Peloponnesian war was a defining point in the history of Greece. Fought between Athens and Sparta the first phase of the war saw repeated incursions by the Spartans into Attica, while Athens used its superior naval power to attack towns along the Peloponnesian coast. In 415 BC the second phase began when Athens launched an attack on Syracuse in Sicily, which was populated by settlers from Corinth, an ally of Sparta. The Athenians were comprehensively defeated. The final phase saw an alliance between Sparta and Persia that led to the collapse and fall of the Athenian empire.

CAMPAIGN IN SICILY

- ▧ Athens and allied to Athens
- • Athenian ally in Sicily or Italy
- Sparta or allied to Sparta
- • Spartan ally in Sicily or Italy
- Greek settlement in Sicily and Southern Italy
- Neutral Greek states
- → Route of Athenian force under Alcibiades, 415
- ✗ Spartan victory

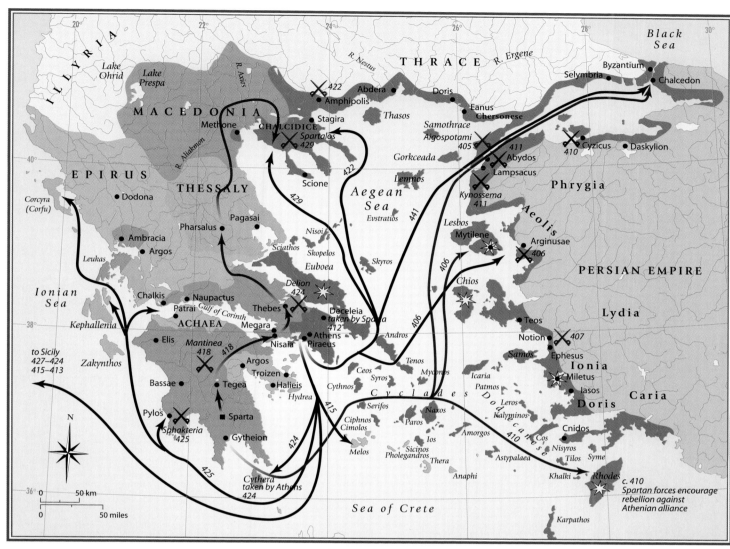

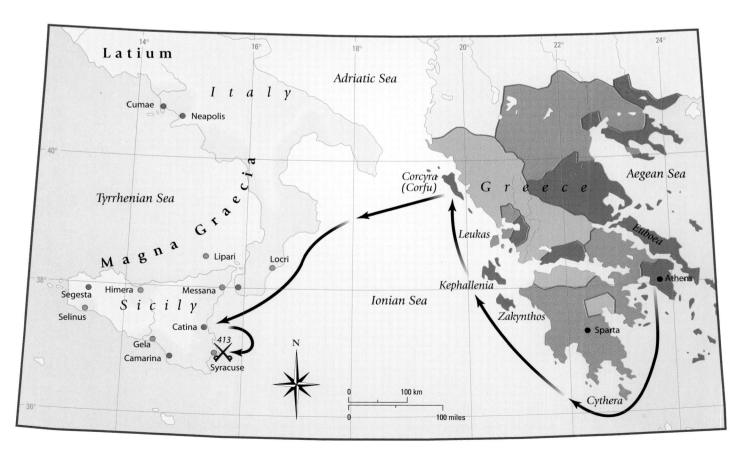

THEBAN AND SPARTAN CAMPAIGNS

382 – 336 BC

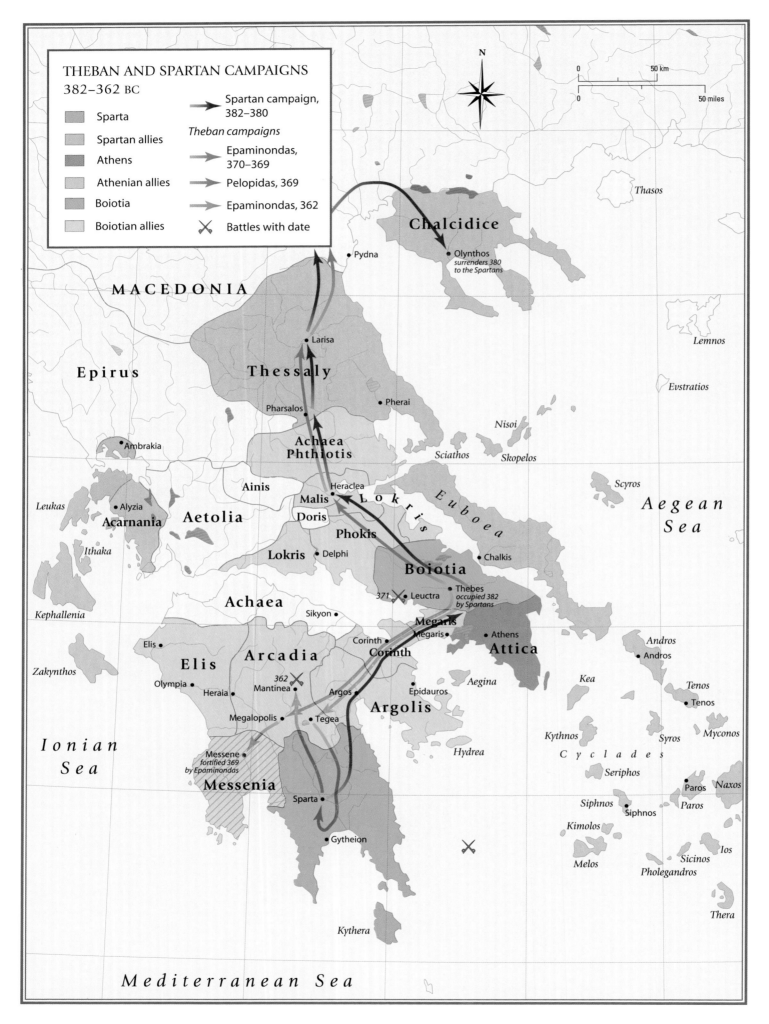

THEBAN AND SPARTAN CAMPAIGNS
382–362 BC

- Sparta
- Spartan allies
- Athens
- Athenian allies
- Boiotia
- Boiotian allies

→ Spartan campaign, 382–380

Theban campaigns

→ Epaminondas, 370–369
→ Pelopidas, 369
→ Epaminondas, 362
✗ Battles with date

THEBAN AND SPARTAN CAMPAIGNS 382–362 BC
After the defeat of Athens by Sparta in 404 BC, Sparta proved that its skills in civilian administration did not match up to its skills on the battlefield. Any people who opposed them were simply executed, imprisoned, or exiled. Sparta was hated and feared in more or less equal measure. For some 30 years Sparta had been a leading state in Greece, but now it was facing a different world: Thebes was growing in strength and had turned back a series of Spartan invasions. Eventually the two sides met on the battlefield at Leuctra in 371. The result was indecisive, but Thebes was able to carve out an independent state for itself within Spartan territory.

THE RISE OF MACEDONIA

THE RISE OF MACEDONIA

For a brief period Macedonia became the most powerful state in the ancient Near East after Alexander the Great had conquered most of the known world, but it only really started to expand after Philip II came to power in 359 BC. By 348 BC Philip had conquered Thrace and Chalcidice. Two years later, Philip intervened in a war between Thebes and Phocis. His victory allowed him to replace Phocis in the Amphictyonic League. This membership gave Macedonia the right to participate in Greek political issues and Philip was made the senior military commander of all league forces. However, Athens grew concerned at the growth of Macedonia's power. A subsequent alliance between Athens and Thebes was destroyed by Philip's army at Chaeronea in 338 BC, leaving Philip the master of Greece.

While preparing an invasion of Persia, Philip was murdered. He was immediately succeeded by his son Alexander, who ruthlessly executed all those accused of his father's murder and any possible rivals or factions that could threaten his position. Macedonia was once again poised for further conquests.

THE EMPIRE OF ALEXANDER THE GREAT

336 – 323 BC

***THE EMPIRE OF
ALEXANDER THE GREAT
336–323 BC
336–323 BC***

Following the unification of
the city-states of ancient
Greece by this father, Philip II
of Macedon, Alexander
conquered the Persian Empire
including Anatolia, Syria,
Phoenicia, Judaea, Gaza, Egypt,
Bactria, and Mesopotamia. He
extended the boundaries of his
own empire as far as the
borders of the Punjab. He
encouraged marriage between
his army and foreigners and
as a result his conquests
ushered in centuries of Greek
settlement and cultural
influence. Alexander died in
323 BC possibly from malaria,
West Nile virus, typhoid,
viral encephalitis, or the
consequences of heavy
drinking. At the time of his
death he was making plans
to conquer Europe.

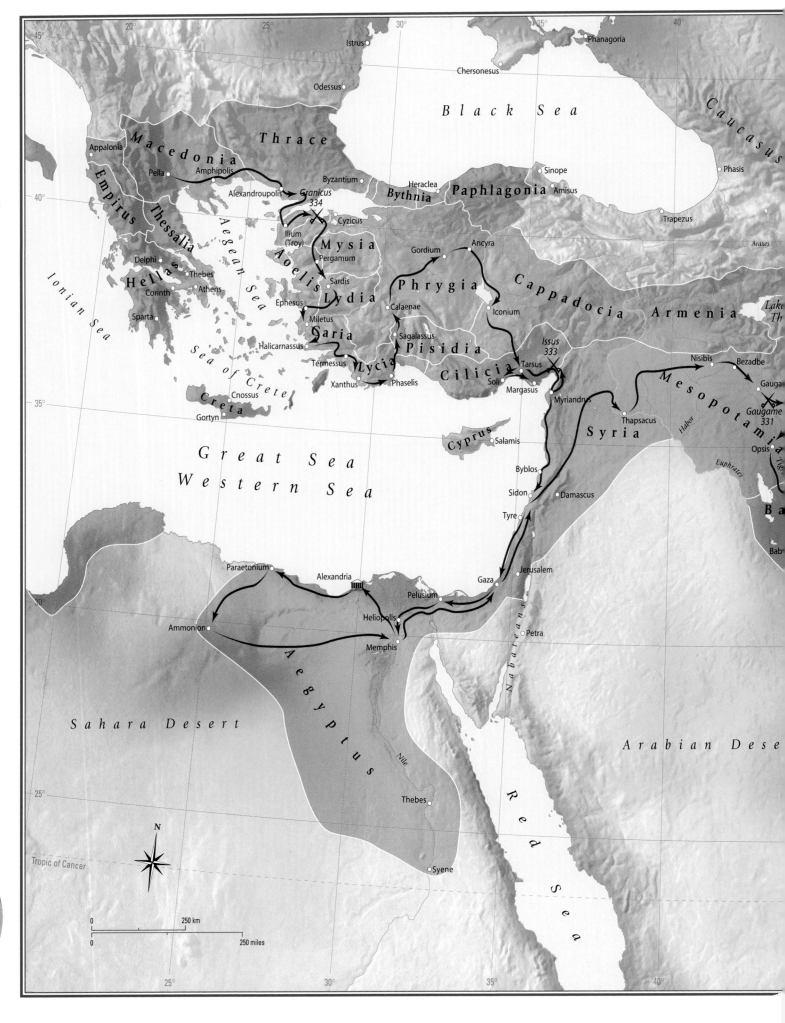

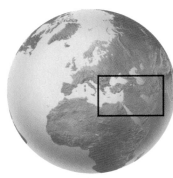

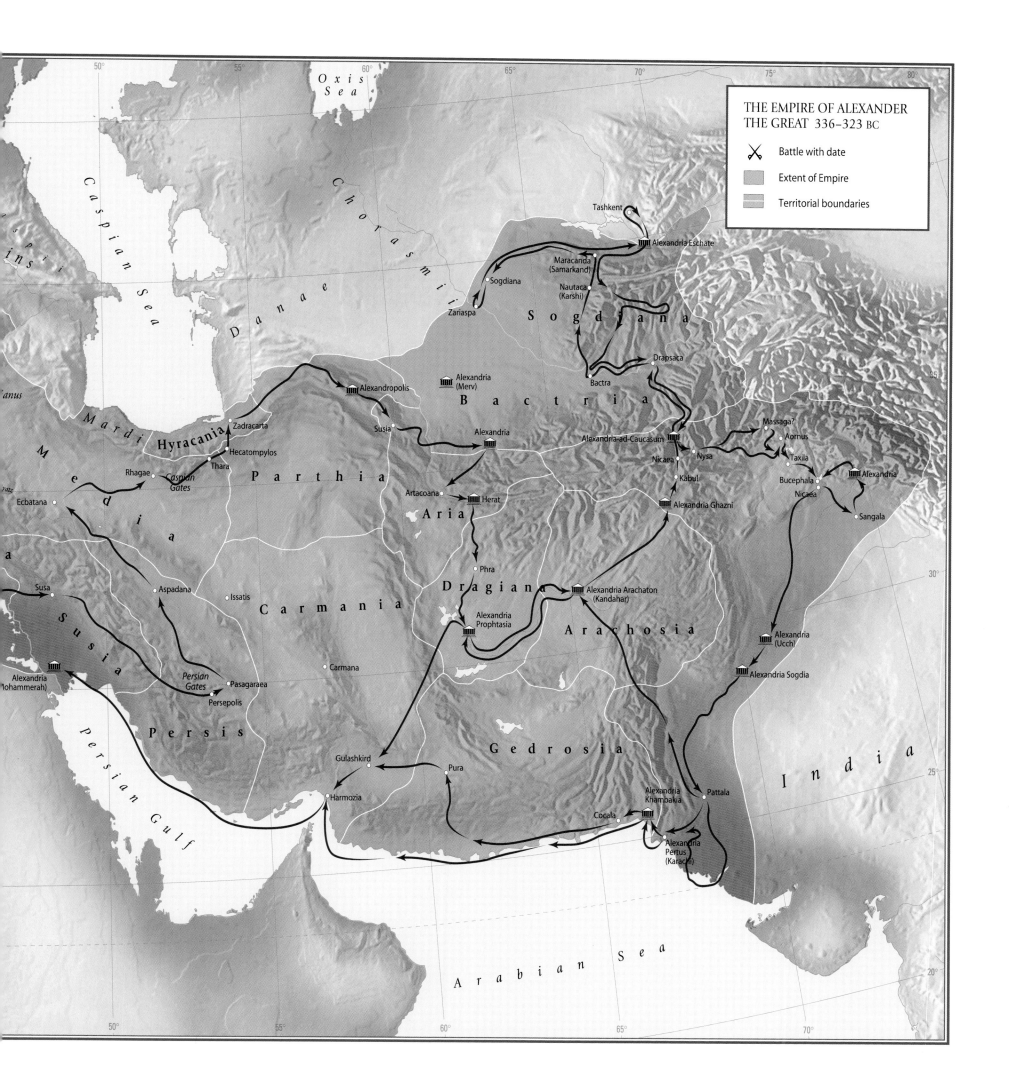

THE EMPIRE OF ALEXANDER
THE GREAT 336–323 BC

✕ Battle with date

Extent of Empire

Territorial boundaries

*Oxis
Sea*

*Caspian
Sea*

C h o r a s m i i

Tashkent

Alexandria Eschate

D a n a e

Maracanda
(Samarkand)

Sogdiana

Nautaca
(Karshi)

Zariaspa

S o g d i a n a

Drapsaca

Bactra

Alexandropolis

Alexandria
(Merv)

B a c t r i a

Susia

Alexandria

Alexandria-ad-Caucasum

Massaga?

Aornus

Mardi

Zadracarta

Nysa

Taxila

Hyracania

Hecatompylos

Nicaea

Kabul

Bucephala

Alexandria

M e d i a

Thara

P a r t h i a

Nicaea

Rhagae

Caspian
Gates

Artacoana

Herat

Sangala

Ecbatana

A r i a

Alexandria Ghazni

Phra

D r a g i a n a

Alexandria Arachaton
(Kandahar)

Susa

Aspadana

Issatis

C a r m a n i a

Alexandria
Prophtasia

A r a c h o s i a

Alexandria
(Ucch)

Carmana

Alexandria
(Mohammerah)

S u s i a

Persian
Gates

Pasagaraea

Alexandria Sogdia

Persepolis

P e r s i s

I n d i a

*Persian
Gulf*

Gulashkird

G e d r o s i a

Pura

Harmozia

Pattala

Alexandria
Khambakia

Cocala

Alexandria
Pertus
(Karachi)

A r a b i a n   S e a

C. 275 BC

THE DIVISION OF ALEXANDER'S EMPIRE C. 275 BC

THE DIVISION OF ALEXANDER'S EMPIRE; C. 275 BC

Alexander's empire grew quickly, but its collapse was even quicker. When he died suddenly in 323 BC he had made no provision for his succession. His half-brother was mentally ill and his son had not yet been born. The result was a power struggle. Egypt was secured by Ptolomy, Macedonia and Greece were taken by Antigonus, and Seleucus took Anatolia, Syria, Parthia, and the rest of Alexander's kingdom in Asia. Later, Lysimachus, another general who had sided with Seleucus and Ptolomy against Antigonus at the Battle of Issus in 301, took control of Thrace. Roman support ensured his security.

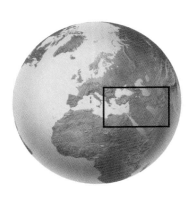

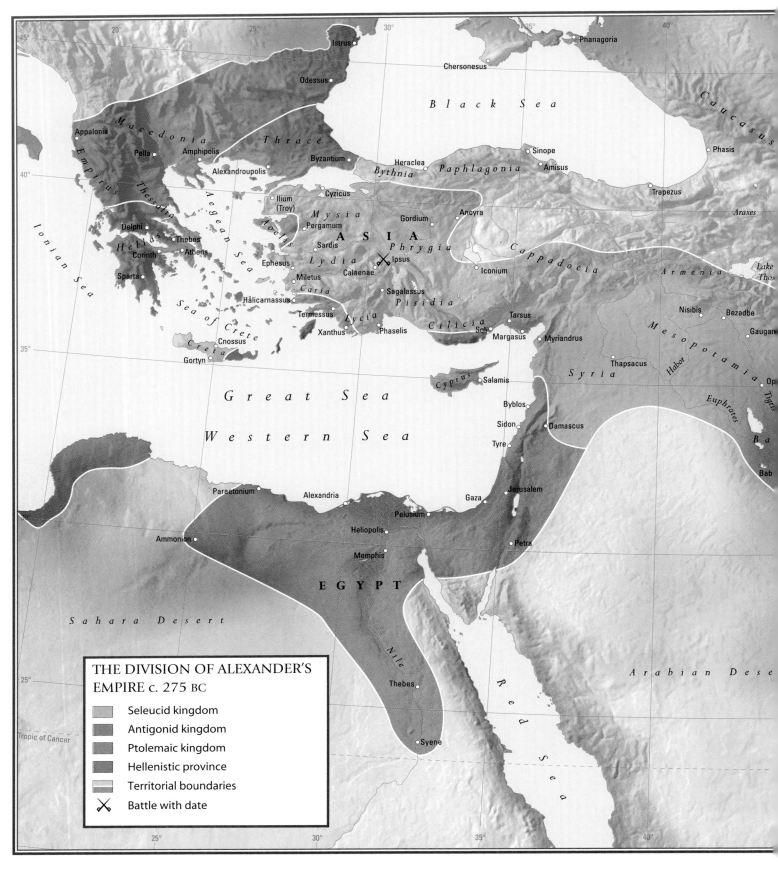

THE DIVISION OF ALEXANDER'S
EMPIRE c. 275 BC

Seleucid kingdom

Antigonid kingdom

Ptolemaic kingdom

Hellenistic province

Territorial boundaries

✕ Battle with date

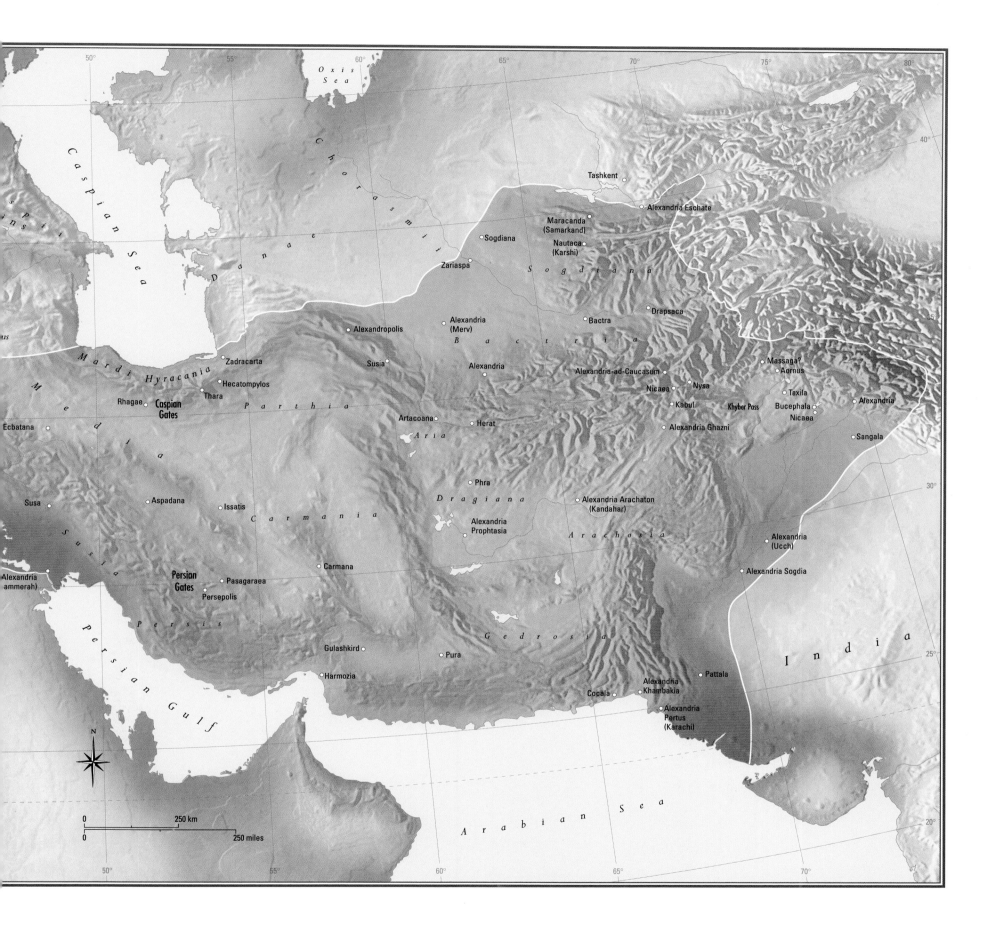

Oxis
Sea

Caspian Sea

Chorasmii

Danae

Tashkent

Alexandria Eschate

Maracanda
(Samarkand)

Sogdiana

Nautaca
(Karshi)

Sogdiana

Zariaspa

Mardi

Hyracania

Zadracarta

Alexandropolis

Alexandria
(Merv)

Bactra

Drapsaca

Bactria

Susia

Alexandria

Massaga?

Aornus

Medi

Hecatompylos

Thara

Alexandria-ad-Caucasum

Nicaea

Nysa

Taxila

Rhagae

Caspian
Gates

Parthia

Kabul

Khyber Pass

Bucephala

Alexandria

Ecbatana

a

Artacoana

Herat

Aria

Alexandria Ghazni

Nicaea

Sangala

Susa

Aspadana

Issatis

Phra

Dragiana

Alexandria Arachaton
(Kandahar)

Alexandria
(Ucch)

Alexandria
(ammerah)

Susia

Carmania

Alexandria
Prophtasia

Arachosia

Persian
Gates

Pasagaraea

Carmana

Alexandria Sogdia

Persepolis

Persis

Gedrosia

India

Gulashkird

Pura

Alexandria

Harmozia

Pattala

Persian Gulf

Alexandria
Khambakia

Cocala

N

Alexandria
Pertus
(Karachi)

250 km

250 miles

Arabian   Sea

57

700 – 168 BC

GREEK BATTLES

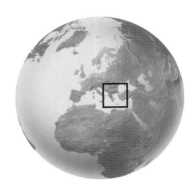

GREEK BATTLES, 700 – 168 BC

Greek States

① Lelantine, 700 BC	⑩ Coronea, 447 BC	⑲ Corinth, 390 BC
② Hysiae, 669 BC	⑪ Pylos, 425 BC	⑳ Tegyra, 375 BC
③ Marathon, 490 BC	⑫ Delium, 424 BC	㉑ Leuctra, 371 BC
④ Thermopylae, 480 BC	⑬ Mantinea, 418 BC	㉒ Cynoscephalae, 364 BC
⑤ Salamis, 480 BC	⑭ Decelea, 413 BC	㉓ Chaeronea, 338 BC
⑥ Plataea, 479 BC	⑮ Arginusae, 406 BC	㉔ Granicus, 334 BC
⑦ Mycale, 479 BC	⑯ Aegospotami, 404 BC	㉕ Sellasia , 221 BC
⑧ Oenophyta, 457 BC	⑰ Haliartus, 395 BC	㉖ Pydna, 168 BC
⑨ Tanagra, 457 BC	⑱ Nemea, 394 BC	

PART 4

ROME

$\mathscr{F}$OUNDED IN 753 BC, ROME was the central city of the Latin peoples of Italy. To the north lay the lands of the Indo-European Etruscans and to the south, Greek colonies and other Italian tribes. Rome became a republic in 510 BC. By 266 BC, Rome controlled the Italian peninsula, then moved into Sicily to oppose Carthaginian power. Victory in the Punic Wars (264–241, 218–201, 149–146 BC) gave Rome an empire that included Spain, Sardinia, Corsica, Sicily, and Tunisia, with annexations in north Italy and areas of southern France. Military leaders such as Julius Caesar, Pompey, and Crassus acquired Gaul, Illyria, Greece, parts of Anatolia, and Syria with allies and client states in Anatolia, Egypt, and Palestine. Octavian, Caesar's adoptive son and heir, became Caesar Augustus in 27 BC and pushed Roman borders over the Alps and to the rivers Rhine and Danube. The empire reached its widest extent under Marcus Aurelius with the Pax Romana (a period of relative peace and stability), and stretched from the Atlantic to the Persian Gulf and from Hadrian's Wall in Britain to the deserts of North Africa. Under Diocletian (AD 285–305), the empire was reorganized and strengthened but ultimately fell to barbarian tribes, including the Huns, Ostrogoths, Visigoths, Vandals, Franks, Angles, and Saxons.

ETRUSCAN EXPANSION

600 – 200 BC

ETRUSCAN EXPANSION
The Etruscans were an early people of ancient Italy and Corsica. They had their own language and their civilization lasted from some unknown prehistoric time to the foundation of Rome and its subsequent assimilation into the Roman Republic. At its maximum extent, during the foundation of Rome and the Roman kingdom, Etruscan civilization flourished in three confederacies. Rome was situated in Etruscan territory and there is evidence to suggest that the Etruscans dominated Rome until the sacking of the city of Veii in 396 BC. Etruscan influence gradually declined as Roman influence in the area grew.

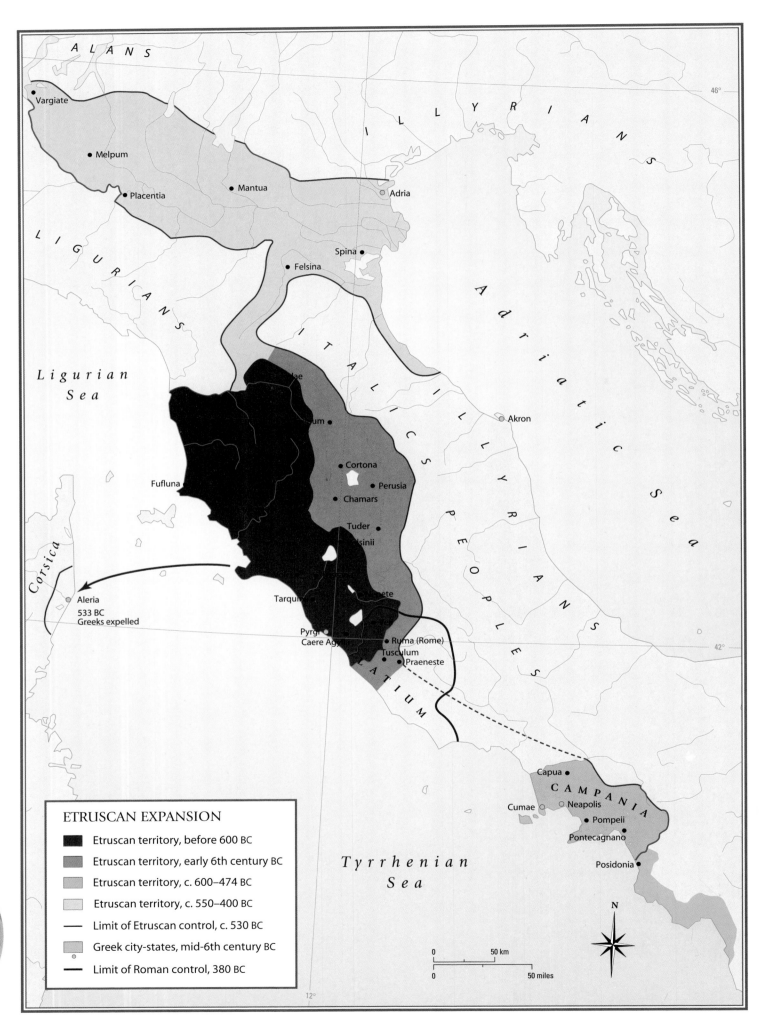

ETRUSCAN EXPANSION

- ■ Etruscan territory, before 600 BC
- ■ Etruscan territory, early 6th century BC
- ■ Etruscan territory, c. 600–474 BC
- ■ Etruscan territory, c. 550–400 BC
- — Limit of Etruscan control, c. 530 BC
- ■ Greek city-states, mid-6th century BC
- — Limit of Roman control, 380 BC

THE CELTS

THE CELTS

Genealogists have traditionally placed Celtic origins along a broad band either side of Germany's river Rhine and down into Austria. Somewhere between the 5th and 8th centuries BC it is believed that there was a slow movement outward into modern France, Britain, and Iberia. By the 4th century Celts were moving into Northern Italy and by the 3rd century into the Balkan region and as far as Galatia in present-day Turkey. The Celts had a distinctive art form, producing beautifully intricate metalwork, many examples of which have been preserved in their burial sites. They were also great warriors.

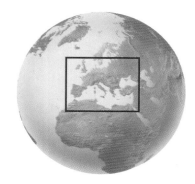

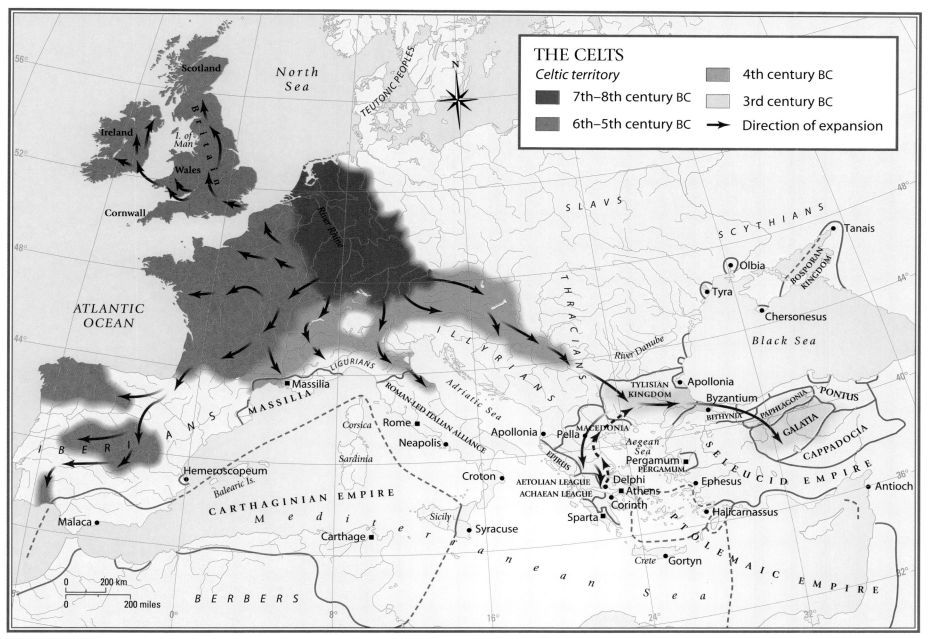

THE CELTS
Celtic territory

■ 7th–8th century BC

■ 6th–5th century BC

■ 4th century BC

□ 3rd century BC

→ Direction of expansion

THE LANGUAGES IN ITALY

LANGUAGES IN 5TH CENTURY ITALY

In the 5th century BC there was no unified language in Italy. Many of the population, especially in the central and southern areas spoke Osco-Umbrian. This would eventually die out as Latin-speaking Roman influence increased. The Venetians had their own language and many people along the Adriatic coast spoke Massapic, another language that disappeared once Latin gained prominence. The same happened to the Etruscan language. In many southern coastal areas where there were Greek colonies, Greek was the major language. Again Latin took over as the Greeks were eventually expelled.

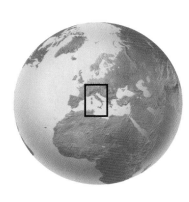

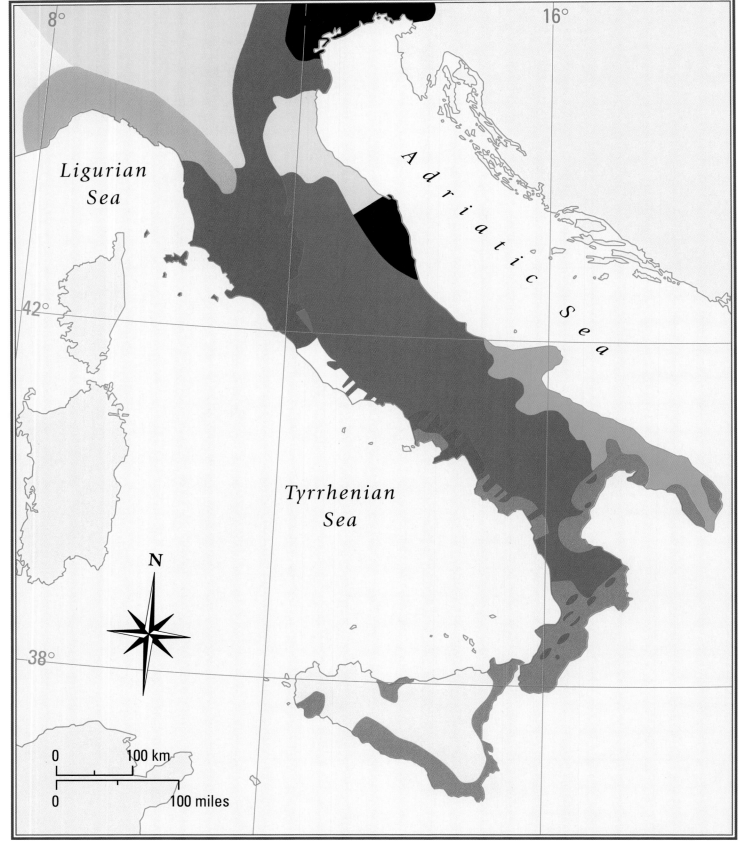

LANGUAGES IN ITALY 5th CENTURY BC

Italic Group

- ■ East Italic
- ■ Faliscan
- □ Latin
- ■ Osco-Umbrian
- ■ Venetic

Other Indo-European

- ■ Celtic
- ■ Greek
- ■ Massapic

Unclassified

- ■ Etruscan
- ■ Ligurian

THE RISE OF ROME

THE RISE OF ROME

After its foundation in 753 BC, Rome remained in the Etruscan sphere of influence for almost 250 years. Rome commanded a strategic crossing point of the river Tiber; to the north lay the powerful Etruscan cities, to the south the numerous Greek settlements. For 200 years the Romans slowly extended their power over one tribe after another. Eventually the last Etruscan king was overthrown in 510 BC, and Rome became a republic. However Rome's position remained insecure; an Etruscan bid to retake Rome was beaten off. Other Latin cities joined Rome and finally won total independence from the Etruscans at the Battle of Aricia in 506 BC.

Rapidly growing in importance, Rome was now able to expand its power southward. The Romans took on their one-time allies, the Samnites, defeating them completely by 290 BC. By 266 BC Roman control extended north to the river Rubicon conferring Roman citizenship throughout this region.

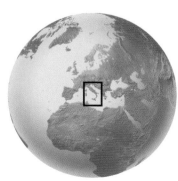

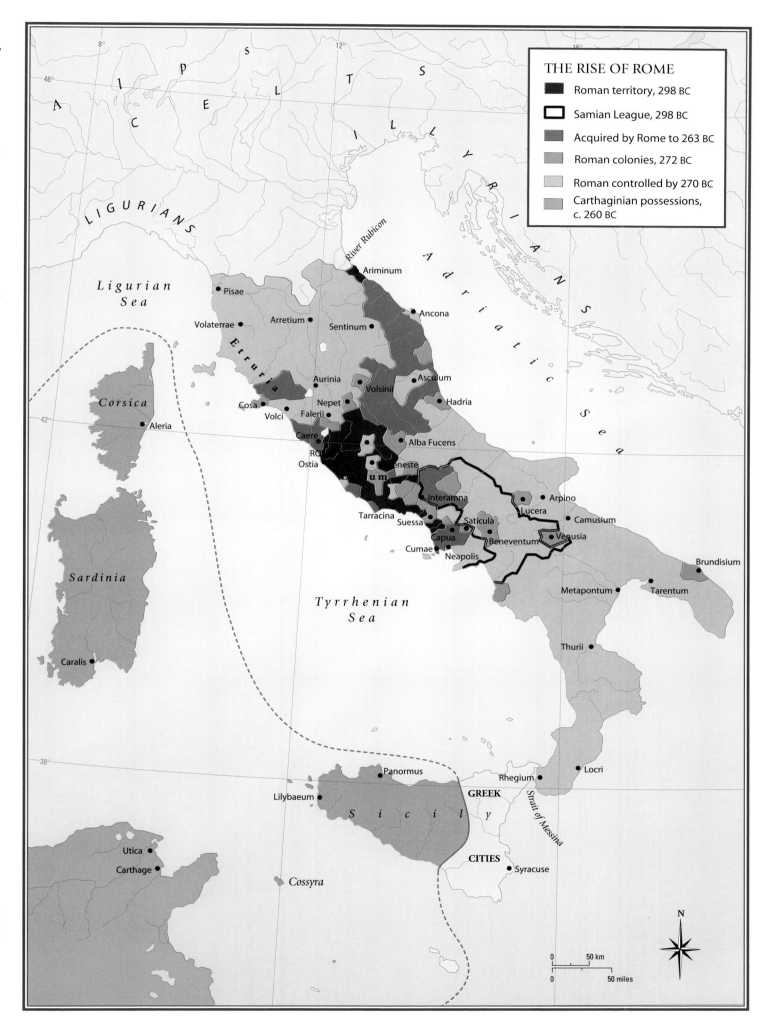

THE RISE OF ROME
- Roman territory, 298 BC
- Samian League, 298 BC
- Acquired by Rome to 263 BC
- Roman colonies, 272 BC
- Roman controlled by 270 BC
- Carthaginian possessions, c. 260 BC

PUNIC WARS

264 – 146 BC

PUNIC WARS 264–146 BC
Carthage was a powerful city-state with a large commercial empire and, with the exception of Rome, was the strongest power in the western Mediterranean. Although the might of its navy was uncontested, it did not maintain a strong standing army. Rome's policies of expanding influence around the Mediterranean led to a total of three Punic Wars against Carthage. The first began as a local conflict in Sicily and was largely a naval war, although partly fought on land. It resulted in a nearly unbroken string of Roman victories, leading to Rome's acquisition of Sicily, Sardinia, and Corsica and Rome's undisputed control of the Mediterranean.

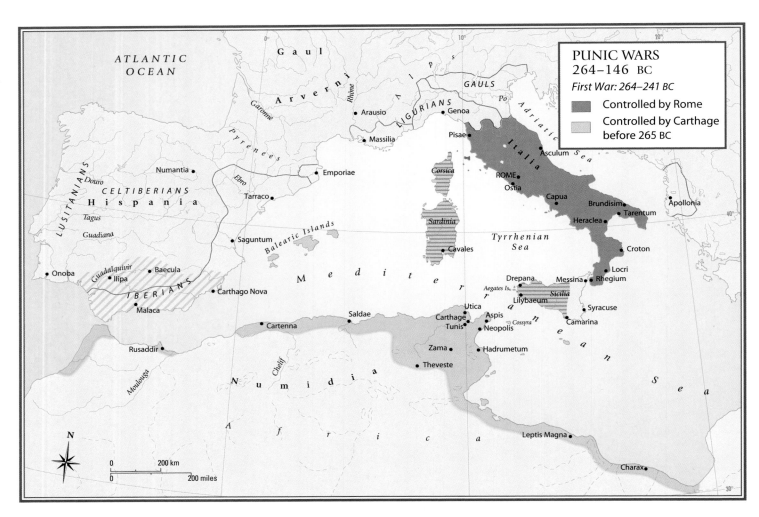

PUNIC WARS
264–146 BC
First War: 264–241 BC

■ Controlled by Rome
□ Controlled by Carthage before 265 BC

THE PUNIC WARS
264–146 BC

Second War: 218–201 BC

■ Carthaginian gains by 218 BC
■ Roman gains by 201 BC
→ Scipio's campaign 218–210 BC
→ Roman campaign against Macedonia 216–211 BC
→ Movements of Carthaginian fleet 215–209 BC
→ Hannibal's campaign 216–203 BC
→ Hasdrupal's campaign 208–207 BC
→ Mago's campaign 205–203 BC
✕ Site of battle with date

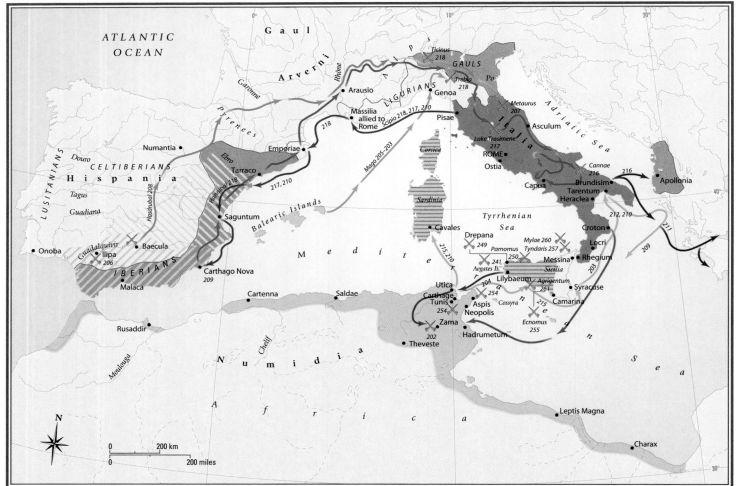

BATTLE OF ZAMA 202 BC

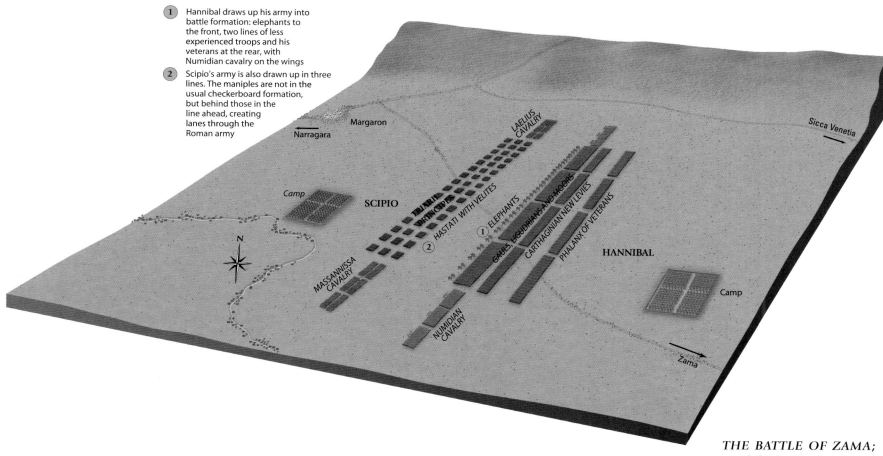

① Hannibal draws up his army into battle formation: elephants to the front, two lines of less experienced troops and his veterans at the rear, with Numidian cavalry on the wings

② Scipio's army is also drawn up in three lines. The maniples are not in the usual checkerboard formation, but behind those in the line ahead, creating lanes through the Roman army

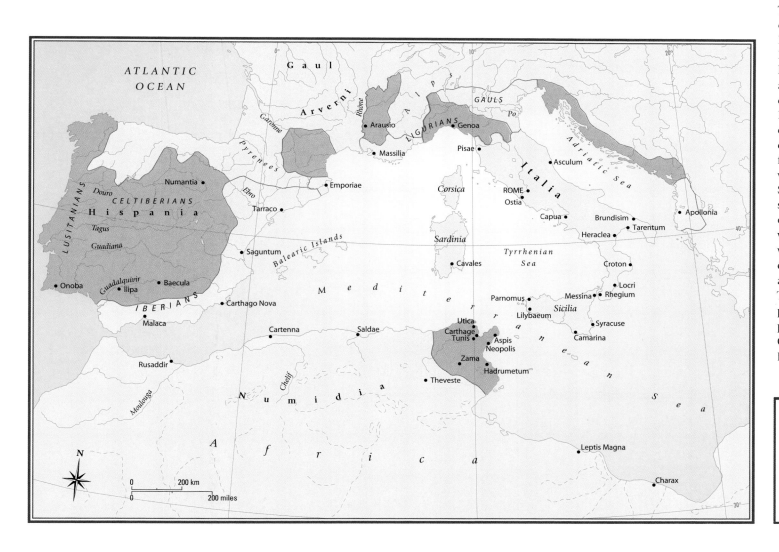

THE BATTLE OF ZAMA; 19 OCTOBER 202 BC
This battle marked the decisive end of the Second Punic War. It was fought between the Roman army under the leadership of Scipio Africanus and the Carthaginian commander, Hannibal. Hannibal hoped that a combination of his war elephants and the depth of his first two lines of infantry would be enough to stop Scipio. The Roman cavalry was superior to its Carthaginian opponents. Hannibal's army was hastily assembled and was no match against the experienced, well-trained, and confident Roman soldiers. The Carthaginians sued for peace and suffered terms so punishing that never again was Carthage able to challenge Rome in the Mediterranean.

THE PUNIC WARS 264–146 BC

Third War, 149–146 BC

■ Annexed by Rome by 121 BC

EASTERN MEDITERRANEAN 100 BC

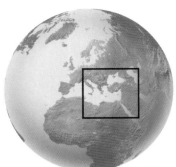

EASTERN MEDITERRANEAN 100 BC In 100 BC the Roman Empire was expanding in the east but there was still plenty of evidence of earlier empires, although many were pale shadows of what they once were. The mighty Seleucid Empire that had stretched from the Mediterranean to the Punjab was now reduced to little more than Antioch and a few Syrian cities. The Seleucids only existed because no other nation wished to absorb them. The Ptolemies still ruled Egypt, but since they had adopted the Egyptian custom of brothers marrying sisters, their leaders were becoming increasingly inbred and feeble. The whole region was ready for a complete Roman takeover.

EASTERN MEDITERRANEAN 100 BC

■ Roman provinces with date of acquisition

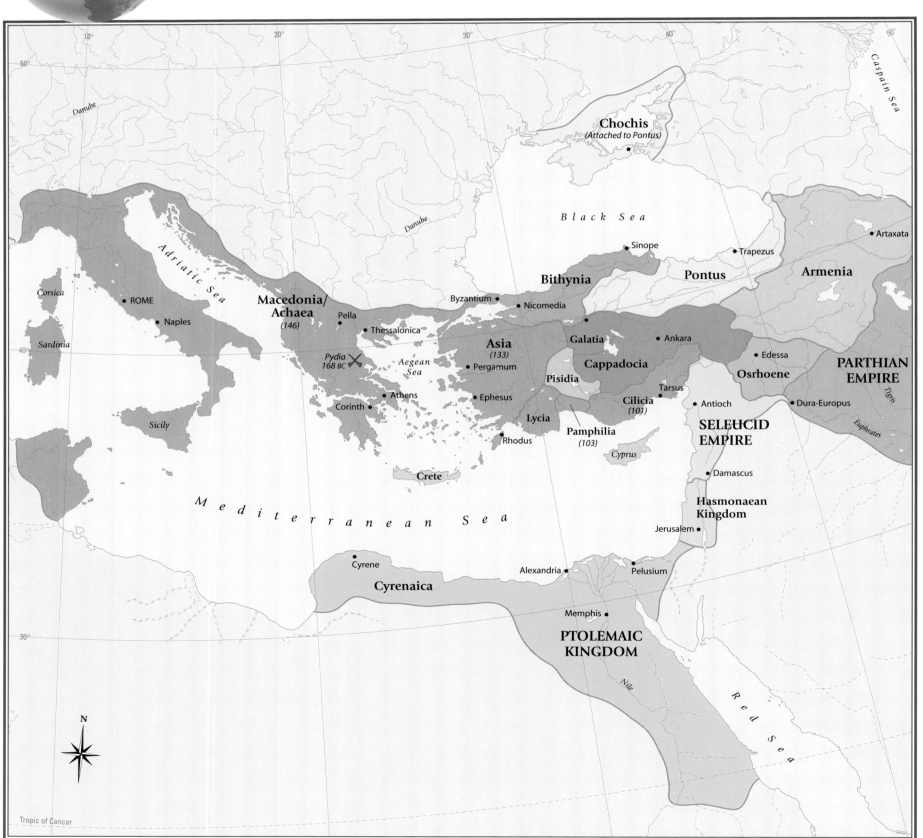

THE ROMAN EMPIRE 55 BC; IMPERIAL ROME

THE ROMAN EMPIRE 55 BC

In 55 BC the Roman Empire was still expanding. Most areas to the north of the Mediterranean, including the Balkans, Gaul, and Spain were now part of the empire. This was the time of the First Triumvirate, formed in 60 BC between Caesar, Pompey, and Crassus. Caesar was given control of Gaul, Pompey got Hispania, and Crassus was given Syria. The alliance lasted until the death of Crassus in 53 BC, and allowed the three members of the Triumvirate to maneuver themselves into a position where they completely dominated Roman politics.

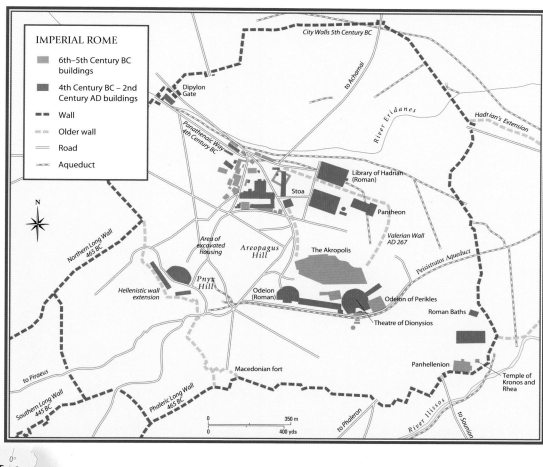

IMPERIAL ROME

- 6th–5th Century BC buildings
- 4th Century BC – 2nd Century AD buildings
- Wall
- Older wall
- Road
- Aqueduct

IMPERIAL ROME

The Imperial City of Rome was the largest urban center of its time, with a population of about one million, roughly the size of London in the early 19th century. The constant noise of horses and iron chariot wheels led to proposals to ban traffic at night. The city was located on seven hills and had vast monumental structures, including the Colosseum, the Forum, and the Pantheon. It had fountains of fresh water fed by aqueducts, theatres, gymnasiums, bath complexes, libraries, shops, market places, and functional sewers. The rich lived in elegant residences but the low and middle classes were packed into city center apartments.

THE ROMAN EMPIRE 55 BC

The First Triumvirate

- Caesar
- Pompey
- Crassus
- Other Roman possessions
- Allied to Rome

CAESAR'S CAMPAIGNS IN GAUL

53 – 48 BC

CAESAR'S CAMPAIGN IN GAUL 58–50 BC
To many historians Caesar's prime reason for fighting the Gallic wars was to boost his political career and pay off his massive debts, but one must not underestimate the importance of Gaul to the Romans. Conquering Gaul allowed Rome to secure a natural border of the river Rhine. Caesar also mounted two expeditions to Britain. The first, in 56 BC nearly ended in disaster when most of his ships were sunk. He returned the following year and successfully defeated the powerful Catuvellauni. These expeditions had little lasting effect but were great propaganda victories for Caesar, keeping him in the public eye back home.

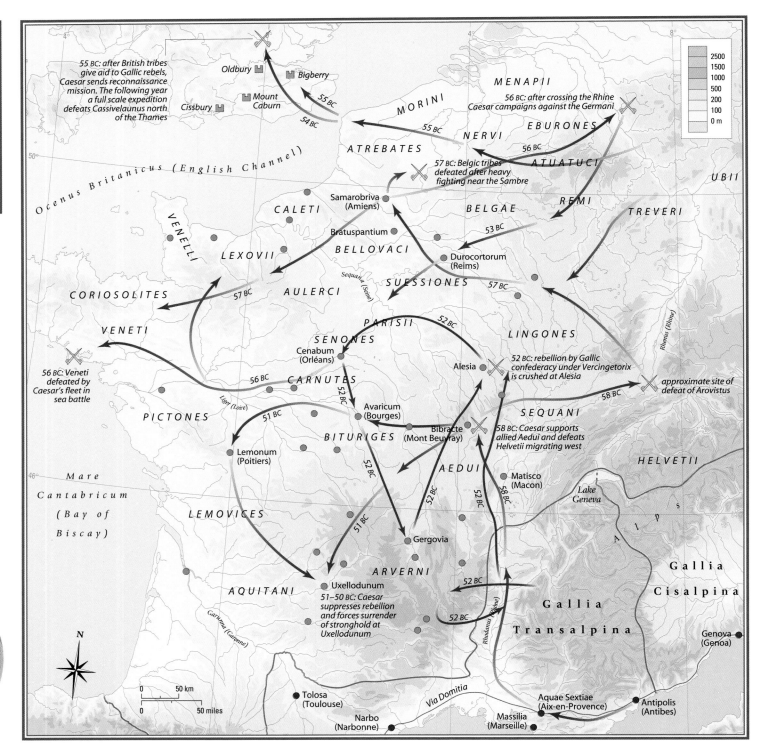

CAESAR'S CAMPAIGN IN GAUL 58–50 BC

➤ Caesar's route (with date)
✕ Site of battle
● Major Gallic settlement
🏯 Major British hill fort
⬤ Major Roman city
— Roman road

55 BC: after British tribes give aid to Gallic rebels, Caesar sends reconnaissance mission. The following year a full scale expedition defeats Cassivelaunus north of the Thames

56 BC: after crossing the Rhine Caesar campaigns against the Germani

57 BC: Belgic tribes defeated after heavy fighting near the Sambre

56 BC: Veneti defeated by Caesar's fleet in sea battle

52 BC: rebellion by Gallic confederacy under Vercingetorix is crushed at Alesia

approximate site of defeat of Arovistus

58 BC: Caesar supports allied Aedui and defeats Helvetii migrating west

51–50 BC: Caesar suppresses rebellion and forces surrender of stronghold at Uxellodunum

Oldbury
Bigberry
Cissbury
Mount Caburn

MENAPII
MORINI
NERVI
EBURONES
ATREBATES
ATUATUCI
UBII
Samarobriva (Amiens)
BELGAE
REMI
TREVERI
CALETI
Bratuspantium
BELLOVACI
Durocortorum (Reims)
LEXOVII
SUESSIONES
VENELLI
CORIOSOLITES
AULERCI
LINGONES
VENETI
PARISII
SENONES
Cenabum (Orléans)
Alesia
SEQUANI
CARNUTES
Avaricum (Bourges)
Bibracte (Mont Beuvray)
PICTONES
BITURIGES
AEDUI
Matisco (Macon)
HELVETII
Lemonum (Poitiers)
Lake Geneva
LEMOVICES
Gergovia
Gallia Cisalpina
AQUITANI
Uxellodunum
ARVERNI
Gallia Transalpina
Genova (Genoa)
Tolosa (Toulouse)
Via Domitia
Aquae Sextiae (Aix-en-Provence)
Antipolis (Antibes)
Narbo (Narbonne)
Massilia (Marseille)

Ocenus Britanicus (English Channel)

Mare Cantabricum (Bay of Biscay)

Sequana (Seine)
Liger (Loire)
Garumna (Garonne)
Rhenus (Rhine)
Rhodanus (Rhône)

N

0   50 km
0   50 miles

BATTLE OF PHARSALUS

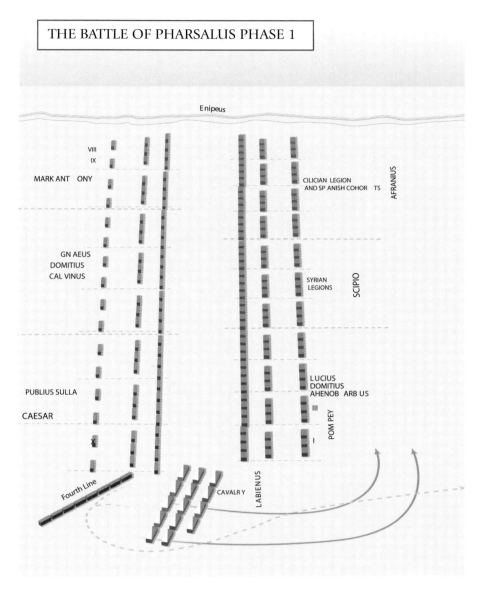

Phase 2 – the battle

Once the two generals had deployed their troops the infantry began to close. Pompey ordered his troops not to charge, hoping to tire his enemy. Caesar's experienced troops realized the trap and stopped, but Pompey's multilingual troops did not understand their orders and got confused. Labenus then led a cavalry charge, but Caesar's Fourth Line of heavy infantry pushed this back. With the cavalry out of the way, the Fourth Line wheeled around to Pompey's rear. Pompey saw that defeat was at hand.

Phase 3 – the rout

Pompey realized that he had no hope of winning the battle and, while his troops were being defeated under extreme pressure, he fled from the battlefield. Caesar ransacked Pompey's camp and took control of the remainder of his army. Pompey fled to Egypt where he was assassinated. Caesar spent the next few years "mopping up" before returning to Rome, where he too was assassinated.

THE BATTLE OF PHARSALUS PHASE 2

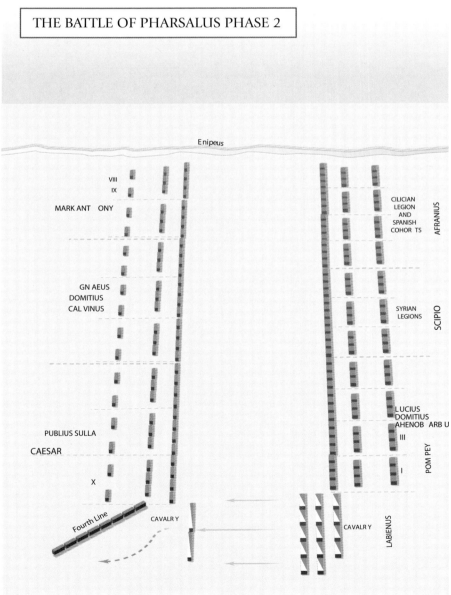

BATTLE OF PHARSALUS

This was a battle that took place in Greece in 48 BC between the Populares faction of the Roman Republic, led by Julius Caesar and the Optimates faction led by Pompey. Pompey and the Roman Senate had fled to Greece in 49 BC to prepare an army. When they finally met on 9 August, Caesar had fewer men, but his were more experienced.

Phase 1 – the preparation

Pompey hoped to win by using his superior cavalry to mount a two-front attack on Caesar's forces. He placed a large contingent of cavalry on Caesar's right. Caesar placed his cavalry on his right, with a fourth battle line in reserve and at right angles to the main body.

49 – 31 BC

CIVIL WARS

CIVIL WARS 49–31 BC
When Caesar returned to Rome in January 49 BC he ignited a civil war. Pompey and the Roman Senate fled to Greece and, after solidifying his control over Spain, North Africa, and the western Mediterranean, Caesar followed him. Pompey was defeated at the Battle of Pharsalus in 48 BC and fled to Egypt where he was murdered. After re-establishing his control in the region Caesar returned to Rome in 45 BC. The following year he was assassinated by a group of senators. The power struggle continued until in 31 BC Caesar's adopted heir Octavian defeated Mark Antony at the Battle of Actium, and took the name Augustus. This marked the end of the civil war, the end of the Roman Republic, and the beginning of the Roman Empire.

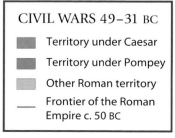

CIVIL WARS 49–31 BC
- Territory under Caesar
- Territory under Pompey
- Other Roman territory
- Frontier of the Roman Empire c. 50 BC

THE BATTLE OF ACTIUM

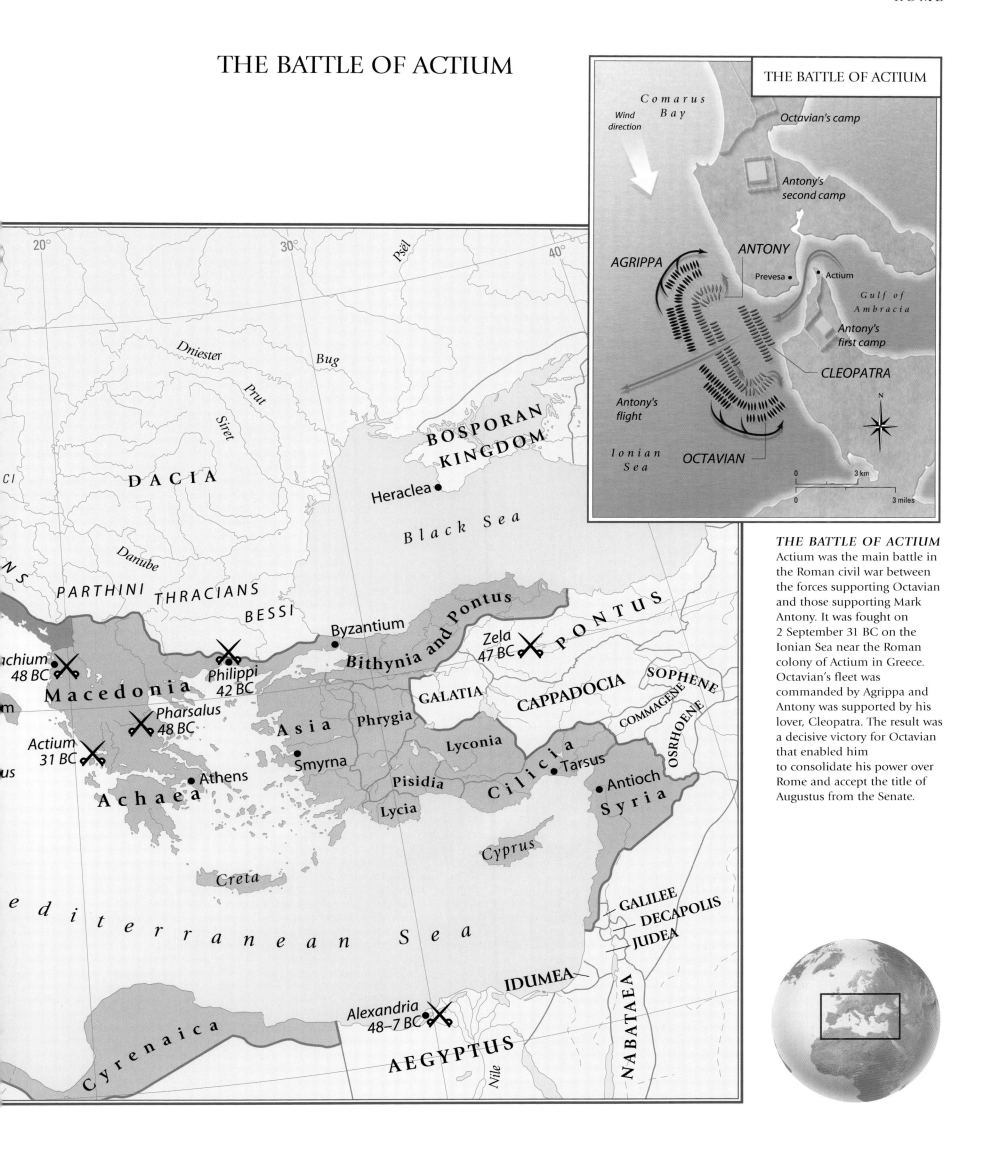

THE BATTLE OF ACTIUM

Comarus Bay

Wind direction

Octavian's camp

Antony's second camp

AGRIPPA

ANTONY

Prevesa •

• Actium

Gulf of Ambracia

Antony's first camp

CLEOPATRA

Antony's flight

Ionian Sea

OCTAVIAN

N

0   3 km

0   3 miles

THE BATTLE OF ACTIUM
Actium was the main battle in
the Roman civil war between
the forces supporting Octavian
and those supporting Mark
Antony. It was fought on
2 September 31 BC on the
Ionian Sea near the Roman
colony of Actium in Greece.
Octavian's fleet was
commanded by Agrippa and
Antony was supported by his
lover, Cleopatra. The result was
a decisive victory for Octavian
that enabled him
to consolidate his power over
Rome and accept the title of
Augustus from the Senate.

Dniester

Bug

Prut

Siret

Psël

DACIA

BOSPORAN KINGDOM

Danube

Heraclea •

Black Sea

PARTHINI   THRACIANS

BESSI

Byzantium •

Zela
47 BC

PONTUS

chium
48 BC

Philippi
42 BC

Bithynia and Pontus

GALATIA

CAPPADOCIA

SOPHENE

Macedonia

Pharsalus
48 BC

Asia

Phrygia

COMMAGENE

OSRHOENE

Actium
31 BC

Lyconia

Cilicia

• Tarsus

Achaea

• Athens

Smyrna •

Pisidia

• Antioch

Syria

Lycia

Cyprus

Creta

GALILEE

DECAPOLIS

JUDEA

e d i t e r r a n e a n   S e a

IDUMEA

NABATAEA

Alexandria
48–7 BC

Cyrenaica

AEGYPTUS

Nile

12 BC – AD 168   AUGUSTAS'S CAMPAIGN IN GERMANIA; THE WORLD KNOWN TO PTOLEMY

PTOLEMY'S ROMAN EMPIRE

Claudius Ptolomaeus, also known as Ptolemy, was an astronomer, geographer, and mathematician who lived in Alexandria, Egypt, sometime between AD 90 and 168. One of his great works was a geography of the Roman world at this time. Many of his maps were based on sound principles, but were limited by a lack of accurate data and wrong assumptions about the size of the earth. However, the Romans' knowledge of the extent of the world's land mass can clearly be seen in this map, which is based on one described by Ptolemy.

AUGUSTUS'S CAMPAIGN IN GERMANIA 12 BC– AD 9

In 12 BC Emperor Augustus had Gaul firmly under control and turned his sights on Germany. He sent his adopted son Drusus to conquer and pacify the Germans. The campaign was a success and Publius Quintilius Varus was installed as consul. Varus is described as being a barely competent administrator and the result was a rebellion in AD 9. Varus had mistakenly thought that Arminius, the rebel leader was an ally, but Varus was ambushed, together with three legions and three squadrons of auxiliary cavalry, in the Teutoburg forest. The Roman soldiers were completely wiped out.

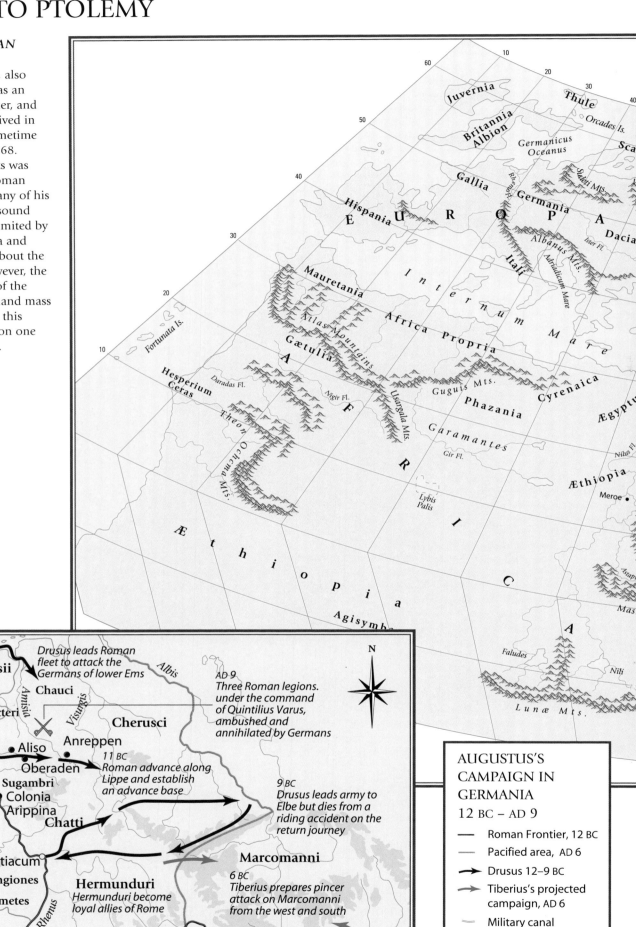

AUGUSTUS'S CAMPAIGN IN GERMANIA
12 BC – AD 9

— Roman Frontier, 12 BC
— Pacified area, AD 6
➤ Drusus 12–9 BC
➤ Tiberius's projected campaign, AD 6
— Military canal

Legionary bases or camps

○ Founded before 12 BC
● Founded 12 BC
✕ Military canal

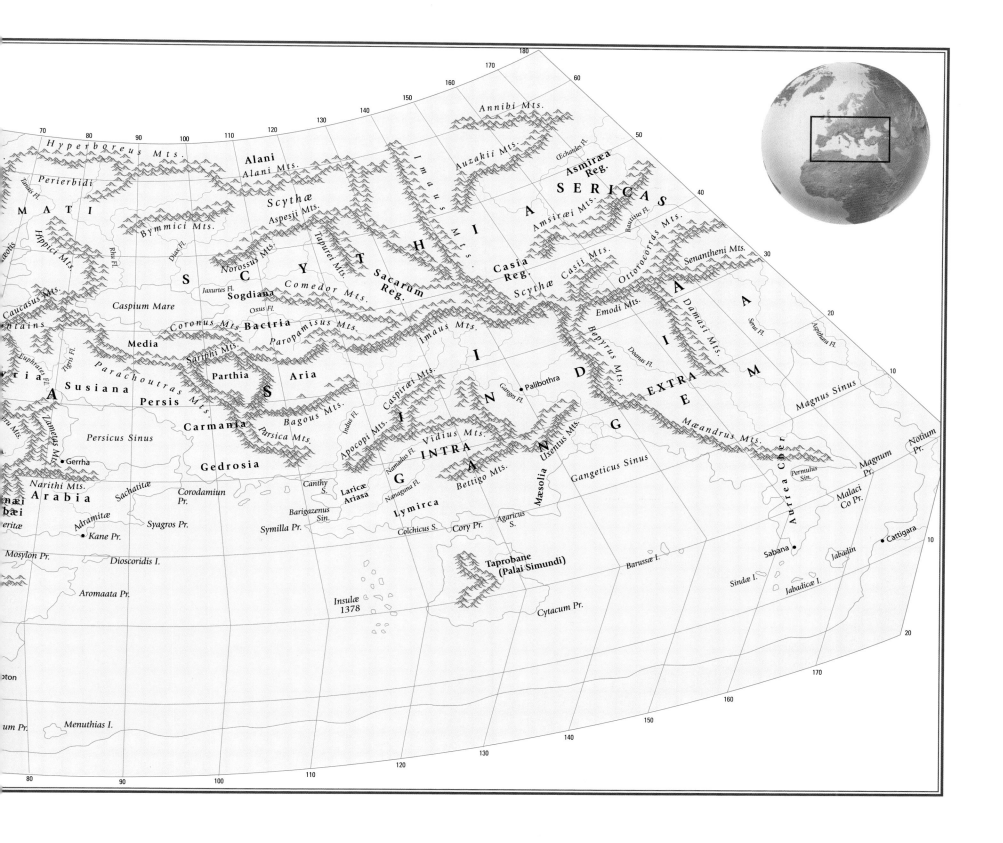

Hyperboreus Mts.
Alani
Alani Mts.
Annibi Mts.
Auzakii Mts.
Œchardes fl.
Asmiræa Reg.
SERICA S
Perierbidi
MATI
Scythæ
Aspesii Mts.
Byrmmici Mts.
Amsiræi Mts.
Imaus Mts.
Batisus fl.
Ottorocorras Mts.
Senantheni Mts.
Hippici Mts.
SCY
Norossus Mts.
Tapurei Mts.
T
Sacarum Reg.
Casia Reg.
Scythæ
Casii Mts.
Rhu fl.
Dix fl.
Jaxurtes fl.
Sogdiana
Comedor Mts.
H
Emodi Mts.
Damasi Mts.
Serus fl.
Caucasus Mts.
Caspium Mare
Oxus fl.
Coronus Mts.
Bactria
Paropamisus Mts.
Imaus Mts.
I
Bepyrus Mts.
Aspithara fl.
htains
Media
Sariphi Mts.
Parachoutras Mts.
Aria
A
Doanas fl.
A
Euphrates fl.
Tigris fl.
Parthia
S
N
Gyndes fl.
Palibothra
D
EXTRA
M
tria
A
Susiana
Persis
Bagous Mts.
Apocopi Mts.
Caspiræi Mts.
Ganges fl.
Magnus Sinus
Zametus fl.
Carmania
Parsica Mts.
Indus fl.
I
Uxentus Mts.
G
Mæandrus Mts.
E
Gerrha
Persicus Sinus
Gedrosia
INTRA
Vidius Mts.
N
Aurrea Cher
Notium Pr.
Narithi Mts.
Sachatitæ
Corodamiun Pr.
Canthy S.
G
Bettigo Mts.
Mæsolia
Gangeticus Sinus
Permulis Sin.
Magnum Pr.
Arabia
Laricæ Ariasa
A
Malaci Co Pr.
bæi
Adramitæ
Syagros Pr.
Barigazenus Sin.
Namaguna fl.
Lymirca
Jabadin
Cattigara
eritæ
Kane Pr.
Symilla Pr.
Colchicus S.
Cory Pr.
Agaricus S.
Sabana
Jabadicæ I.
Mosylon Pr.
Dioscoridis I.
Taprobane
(Palai Simundi)
Barussæ I.
Sindæ I.
Aromaata Pr.
Insulæ 1378
Cytacum Pr.
oton
um Pr.
Menuthias I.

C. AD 14

ROMAN EMPIRE AD 14

ROMAN EMPIRE AD 14
By AD 14 the Roman Empire already covered a significant area, but it was still expanding. Much territory had been added and consolidated during the time of Julius Caesar, but after his assassination in 44 BC and the subsequent rise in power of his adopted heir Augustus, further territory was added. Although the Senate outwardly governed the Roman Republic, in effect Augustus ruled as an autocratic dictator for 41 years. He ended the civil wars and initiated an era of peace that was to last for more than 200 years. He made many reforms and was known as the "father of the country."

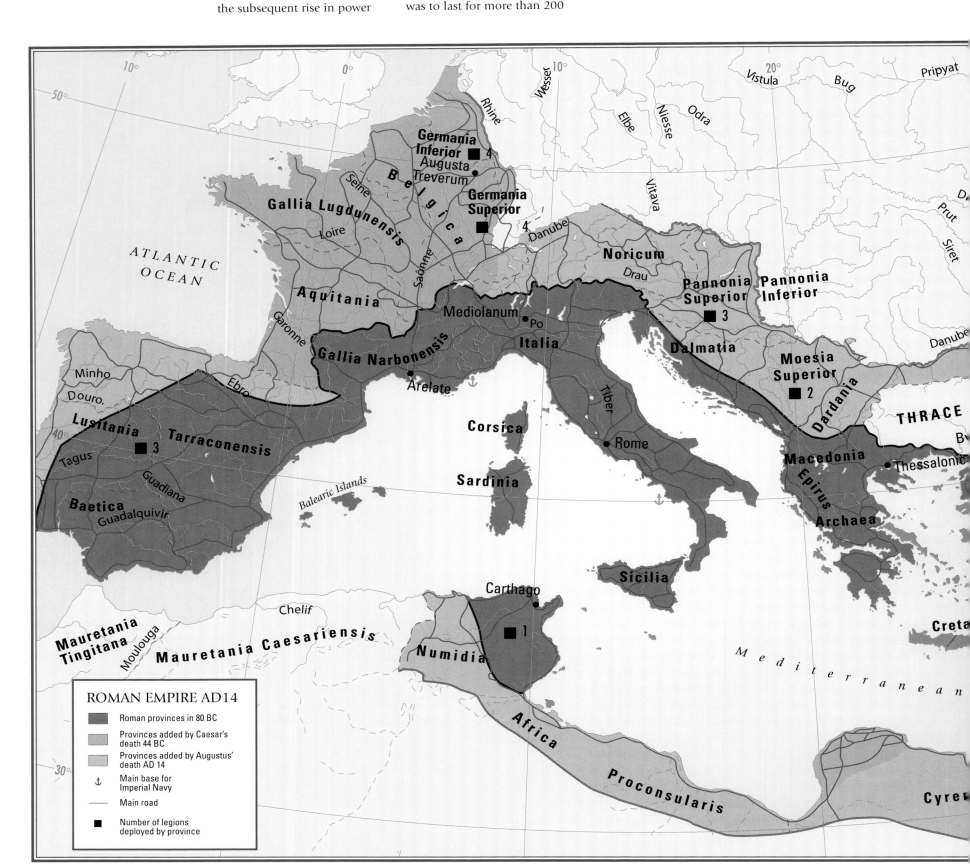

ROMAN EMPIRE AD14

- Roman provinces in 80 BC
- Provinces added by Caesar's death 44 BC
- Provinces added by Augustus' death AD 14
- ⚓ Main base for Imperial Navy
- Main road
- ■ Number of legions deployed by province

THE CITY OF ROME AD 14

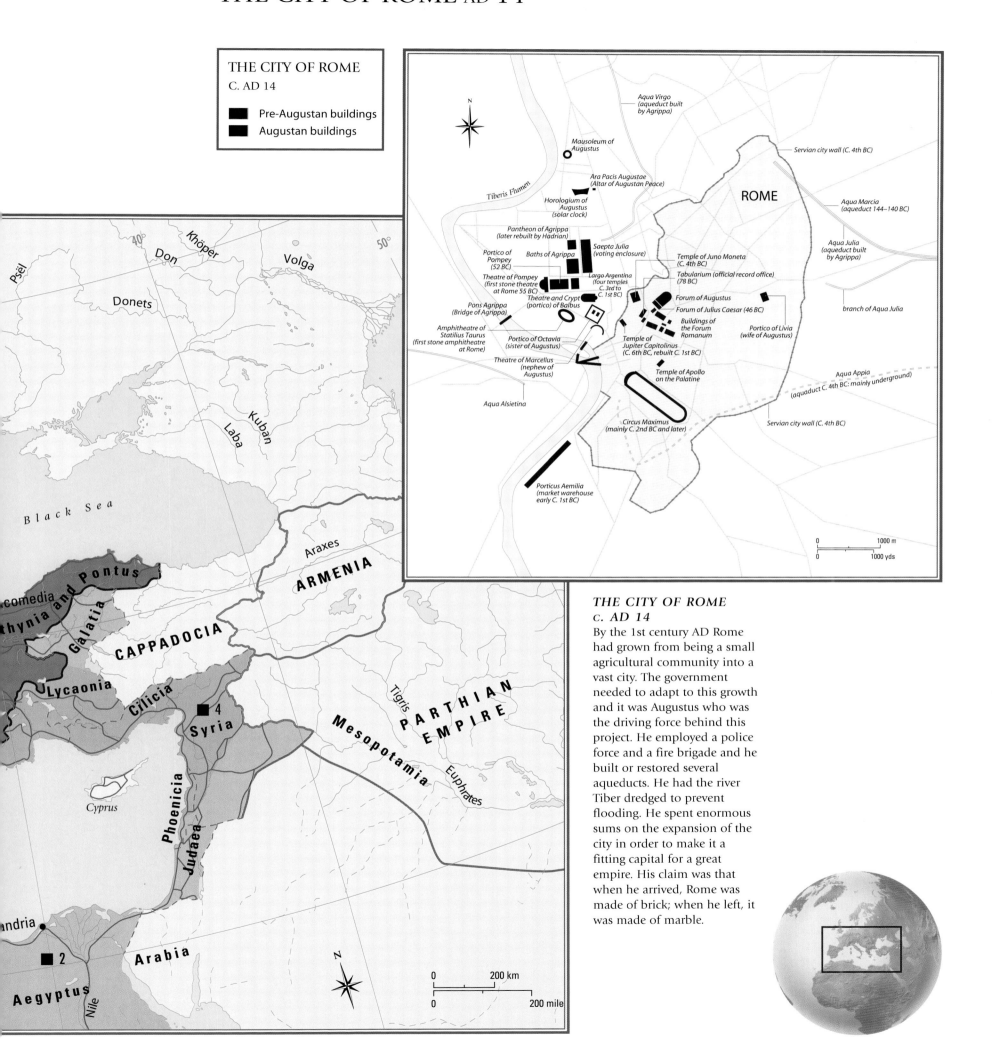

THE CITY OF ROME
C. AD 14

■ Pre-Augustan buildings
■ Augustan buildings

Aqua Virgo
(aqueduct built
by Agrippa)

Mausoleum of
Augustus

Servian city wall (C. 4th BC)

Ara Pacis Augustae
(Altar of Augustan Peace)

Tiberis Flumen

ROME

Horologium of
Augustus
(solar clock)

Aqua Marcia
(aqueduct 144–140 BC)

Pantheon of Agrippa
(later rebuilt by Hadrian)

Aqua Julia
(aqueduct built
by Agrippa)

Portico of
Pompey
(52 BC)

Baths of Agrippa

Saepta Julia
(voting enclosure)

Temple of Juno Moneta
(C. 4th BC)

Theatre of Pompey
(first stone theatre
at Rome 55 BC)

Largo Argentina
(four temples
C. 3rd to
C. 1st BC)

Tabularium (official record office)
(78 BC)

branch of Aqua Julia

Theatre and Crypt
(portico) of Balbus

Forum of Augustus

Pons Agrippa
(Bridge of Agrippa)

Forum of Julius Caesar (46 BC)

Buildings of
the Forum
Romanum

Portico of Livia
(wife of Augustus)

Amphitheatre of
Statilius Taurus
(first stone amphitheatre
at Rome)

Portico of Octavia
(sister of Augustus)

Temple of
Jupiter Capitolinus
(C. 6th BC, rebuilt C. 1st BC)

Theatre of Marcellus
(nephew of
Augustus)

Temple of Apollo
on the Palatine

Aqua Appia

Aqua Alsietina

(aqueduct C. 4th BC: mainly underground)

Circus Maximus
(mainly C. 2nd BC and later)

Servian city wall (C. 4th BC)

Porticus Aemilia
(market warehouse
early C. 1st BC)

0   1000 m
0   1000 yds

Black Sea

Psël

Don

Khöper

Volga

Donets

Kuban

Laba

Araxes

ARMENIA

comedia

thynia and Pontus

Galatia

CAPPADOCIA

Lycaonia

Cilicia

■ 4
Syria

Tigris

PARTHIAN
EMPIRE

Mesopotamia

Euphrates

Cyprus

Phoenicia

Judaea

andria

■ 2

Arabia

Aegyptus

Nile

0   200 km
0   200 mile

THE CITY OF ROME
c. AD 14

By the 1st century AD Rome
had grown from being a small
agricultural community into a
vast city. The government
needed to adapt to this growth
and it was Augustus who was
the driving force behind this
project. He employed a police
force and a fire brigade and he
built or restored several
aqueducts. He had the river
Tiber dredged to prevent
flooding. He spent enormous
sums on the expansion of the
city in order to make it a
fitting capital for a great
empire. His claim was that
when he arrived, Rome was
made of brick; when he left, it
was made of marble.

THE ROMAN EMPIRE AD 68

THE ROMAN EMPIRE AD 68

AD 68 was the year of the death of Emperor Nero. During his 14-year reign he had focused much of his attention on diplomacy, trade, and increasing the cultural capital of the empire. There had also been a successful war with the Parthian empire and improved diplomatic ties with Greece, but after a military coup in AD 68 Nero reportedly committed suicide. There followed a brief civil war and it became known as the Year of the Four Emperors as one followed another until Vespasian, the first ruler of the Flavian Dynasty, assumed power in December AD 69.

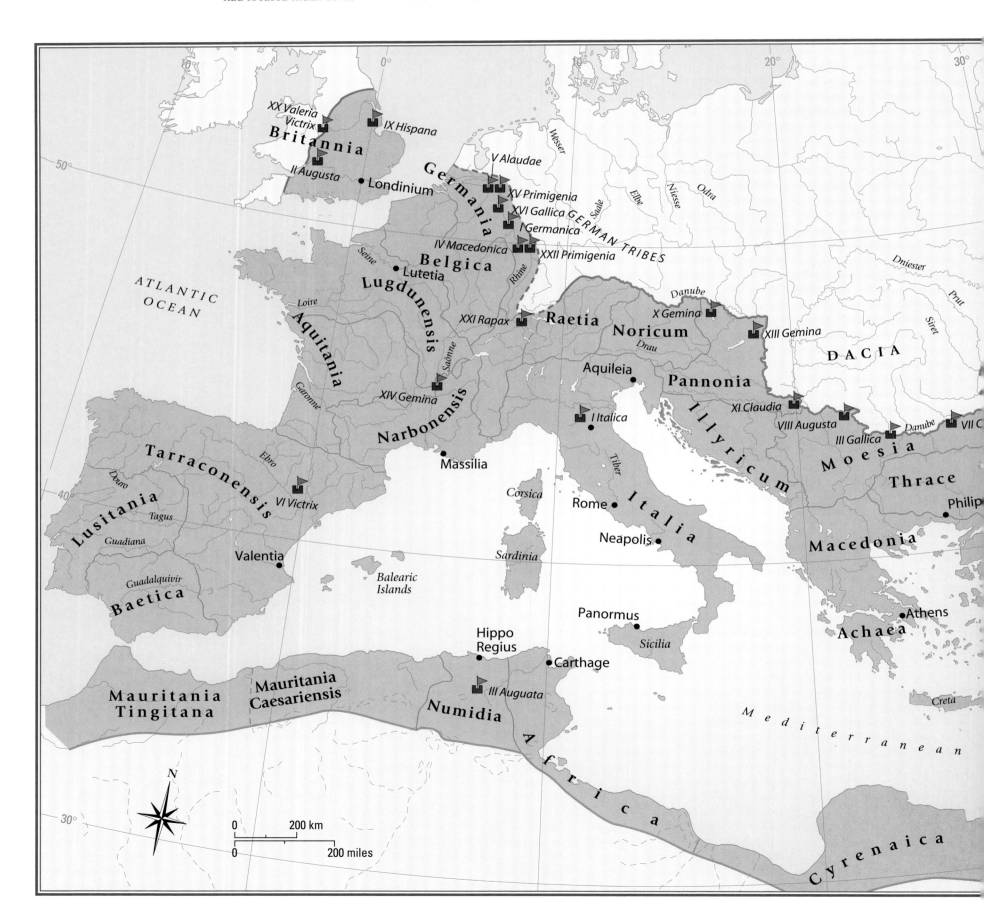

LEPCIS MAGNA: A ROMAN NORTH AFRICAN CITY

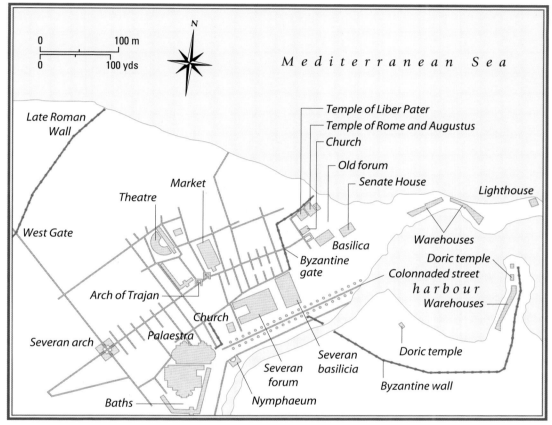

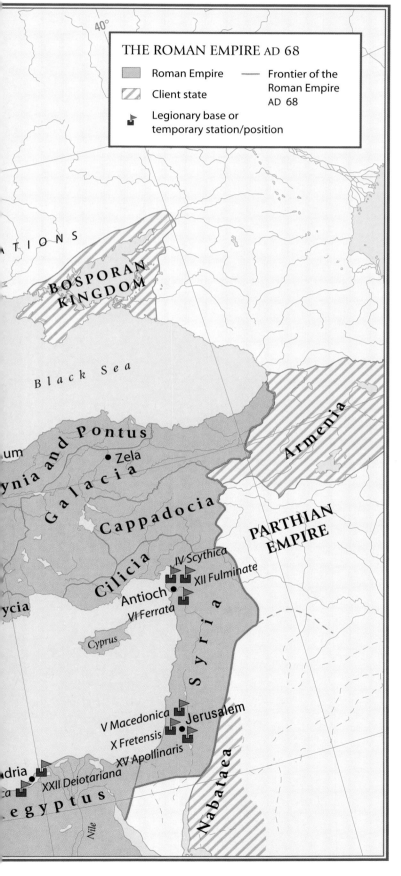

LEPCIS MAGNA, ROMAN NORTH AFRICAN CITY

LEPCIS MAGNA: A ROMAN NORTH AFRICAN CITY

Situated on the Mediterranean coast in the present-day Tripolitania region of Libya, Lepcis Magna was originally founded by the Phoenicians in the 10th century BC. It became prominent in the 4th century after Carthage became a major power in the Mediterranean region. It remained part of Carthage's dominions until the end of the Third Punic War in 146 BC, when it became part of the Roman Republic. From about 200 BC it had operated very much as an independent city, but when Tiberius became emperor it became part of the Roman Province of Africa. It soon became a major trading post of Roman Africa.

ROMAN BRITAIN

AD 43 – 400

FRONTIERS OF NORTHERN BRITAIN

Hadrian's Wall was built after a visit to Britain by the Emperor Hadrian in AD 122. The aim of the wall was to prevent military raids by Pictish tribes and to improve economic stability in the Roman province to the south. For many years it physically marked the frontier of the empire. After Hadrian's death in 138 the new emperor, Antonius Pius abandoned Hadrian's Wall and built another one 100 miles further north, but the northern tribes remained unconquered. Antonius's successor, Marcus Arelius abandoned the Antonine Wall and in 164 reoccupied Hadrian's Wall. It remained occupied until the Roman withdrawal in about 407.

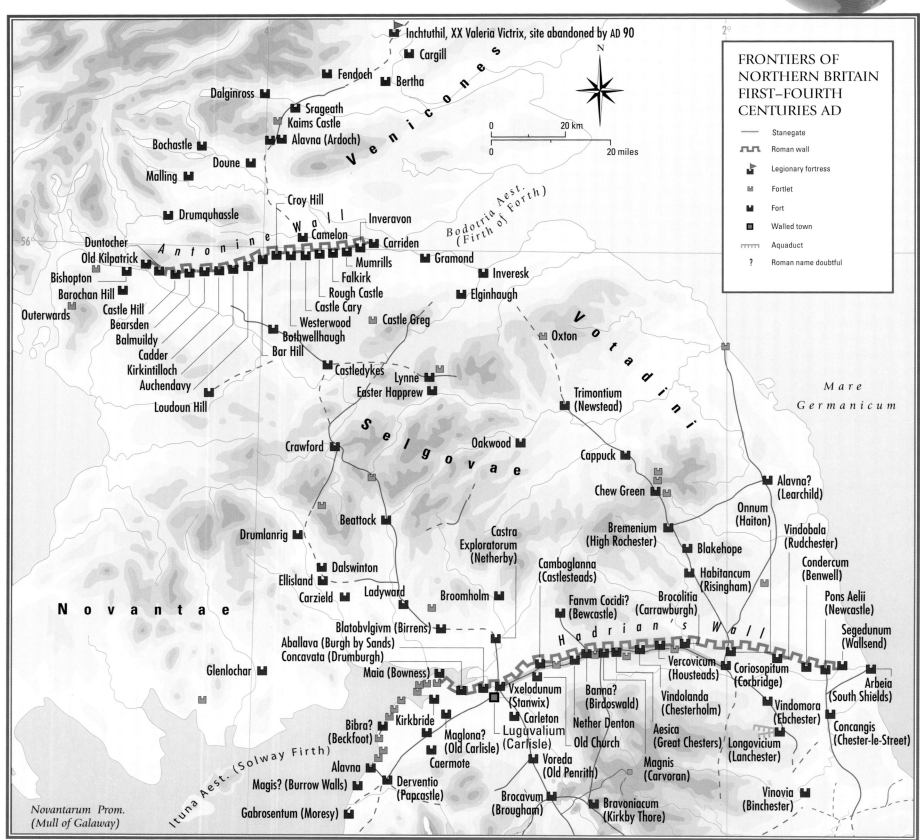

FRONTIERS OF NORTHERN BRITAIN FIRST–FOURTH CENTURIES AD

- Stanegate
- Roman wall
- Legionary fortress
- Fortlet
- Fort
- Walled town
- Aquaduct
- ? Roman name doubtful

Inchtuthil, XX Valeria Victrix, site abandoned by AD 90

N

0   20 km
0   20 miles

Cargill
Fendoch
Bertha
Dalginross
Srageath
Kaims Castle
Bochastle
Alavna (Ardoch)
Doune
Malling
Croy Hill
Drumquhassle
Inveravon
Camelon
Carriden
Duntocher
Old Kilpatrick
Mumrills
Gramond
Bishopton
Falkirk
Inveresk
Barochan Hill
Rough Castle
Elginhaugh
Outerwards
Castle Cary
Castle Hill
Westerwood
Castle Greg
Oxton
Bearsden
Bothwellhaugh
Balmuildy
Bar Hill
Cadder
Castledykes
Trimontium
Kirkintilloch
Lynne
(Newstead)
Auchendavy
Easter Happrew
Loudoun Hill

Venicones
Bodotria Aest.
(Firth of Forth)
Votadini
Mare Germanicum

Crawford
Oakwood
Cappuck
Chew Green
Alavna?
(Learchild)
Beattock
Onnum
(Haiton)
Drumlanrig
Castra
Exploratorum
(Netherby)
Bremenium
(High Rochester)
Vindobala
(Rudchester)
Dalswinton
Camboglanna
(Castlesteads)
Blakehope
Condercum
(Benwell)
Ellisland
Ladyward
Habitancum
(Risingham)
Carzield
Broomholm
Brocolitia
(Carrawburgh)
Pons Aelii
(Newcastle)
Fanvm Cocidi?
(Bewcastle)
Blatobvlgivm (Birrens)
Aballava (Burgh by Sands)
Vercovicum
(Housteads)
Segedunum
(Wallsend)
Concavata (Drumburgh)
Coriosopitum
(Corbridge)
Glenlochar
Maia (Bowness)
Vxelodunum
(Stanwix)
Banna?
(Birdoswald)
Vindolanda
(Chesterholm)
Arbeia
(South Shields)
Vindomora
(Ebchester)
Bibra?
(Beckfoot)
Kirkbride
Carleton
Nether Denton
Aesica
(Great Chesters)
Longovicium
(Lanchester)
Concangis
(Chester-le-Street)
Maglona?
(Old Carlisle)
Luguvalium
(Carlisle)
Old Church
Alavna
Caermote
Voreda
(Old Penrith)
Magnis
(Carvoran)
Magis? (Burrow Walls)
Derventio
(Papcastle)
Brocavum
(Brougham)
Bravoniacum
(Kirkby Thore)
Vinovia
(Binchester)
Gabrosentum (Moresy)

Selgovae
Novantae
Hadrian's Wall
Antonine Wall
Ituna Aest. (Solway Firth)
Novantarum Prom.
(Mull of Galaway)

LONDINIUM; GERMANIC FRONTIERS

GERMANIC FRONTIERS WITH ROME

The Limes Germanicus, or Germanic Frontier, was a remarkable line of forts that operated between AD 83 and 260 as the division between the Roman Empire and the unsubdued Germanic tribes. At its height the line stretched from the North Sea at Katwijk in the Netherlands, down the Rhine, across the Taurus Mountains, and on to the Danube. The strength of the line varied according to location. The Limes were never able to prevent massed Germanic tribes from entering Roman territory. This was not the intention. The purpose of the limes was to give early warning of attack and to deter casual small-scale raids.

LONDINIUM

Londinium was established by the Romans soon after their invasion of AD 43. Initially it was an important trading centre, but after it was sacked and burned by Queen Boudica around AD 60, the city was rebuilt as a planned Roman town and by the end of the 1st century it had become Roman Britain's largest city and had replaced Colchester as capital. During the 2nd century the city had a population of 45,000 to 60,000, but after about AD 150 it suffered a fall in population, possibly due to plague, from which it never fully recovered. The famous Roman wall was built around the city sometime between 190 and 225.

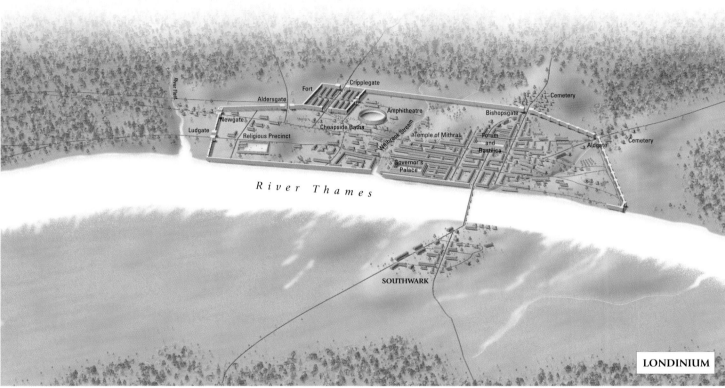

LONDINIUM

FIRST JEWISH REVOLT

FIRST JEWISH REVOLT AD 66–68

The Roman conquest of Israel and Egypt in the last century BC had brought many Jews into the Roman Empire. Although the majority stayed in Israel, a large number moved to Rome or to other places in the Roman Empire. The Romans always treated them with suspicion because they had a different religion and refused to worship the Roman emperor as a god. In general the Jews were allowed to continue to practice their religion, but by AD 66 hostility was growing, resulting in a revolt as the Jews tried to regain their independence. The Roman Emperor, Nero, sent his general Vespasian to put down the revolt.

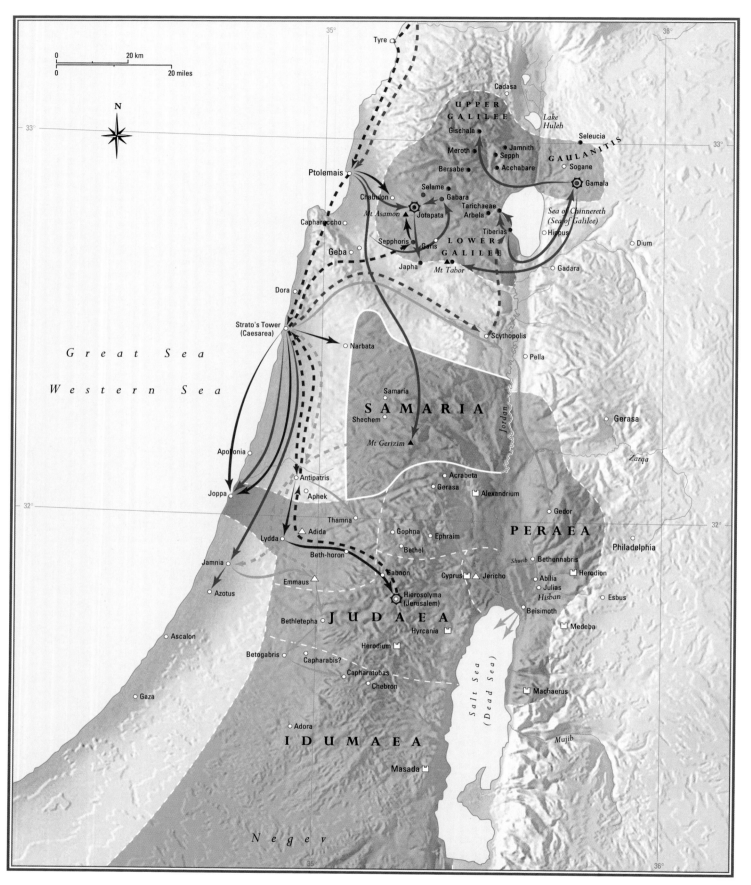

THE FIRST JEWISH REVOLT AD 66–68

- ◄-- Non-hostile troop movements
- ◄— Cestius Gallus AD 66
- ◄— AD 67
- ◄— AD 68
- ▨ Primarily Jewish population
- ▨ Primarily Samaritan population
- ▨ Rebel military district
- △ Major Roman camp
- ⌂ Hasmonaean or Herodian fortress used by rebels
- ⬡ Major siege
- • Site possibly fortified by rebels
- • Site probably fortified by rebels

JEWISH REVOLT 2

FIRST JEWISH REVOLT AD 69–70

After Nero committed suicide in 69, Vespasian became emperor and he left his son Titus to put down the Jewish revolt. Titus fought the Jews until he won. One of the last holdouts was the fortress of Masada. Here the Zealots, the last group of Jews, held out until the Romans built a great ramp up to the fortress, broke down the walls, and destroyed the city. Tradition has it that the Zealots then committed mass suicide rather than fall into Roman hands, but this is probably not true.

After years of ensuing suppression the Jews staged a second revolt in 132. After three years of struggle the Jews were once again defeated at the fortress of Betar in 135.

THE FIRST JEWISH REVOLT AD 69–70

- ◄--- Non-hostile troop movements
- ◄—— AD 69
- ◄—— AD 70
- ◄—— After AD 70
- ▨ Primarily Jewish population
- ▨ Primarily Samaritan population
- ▨ Rebel military district
- △ Major Roman camp
- ⌂ Hasmonaean or Herodian fortress used by rebels
- ⬡ Major siege
- • Site possibly fortified by rebels
- ● Site probably fortified by rebels

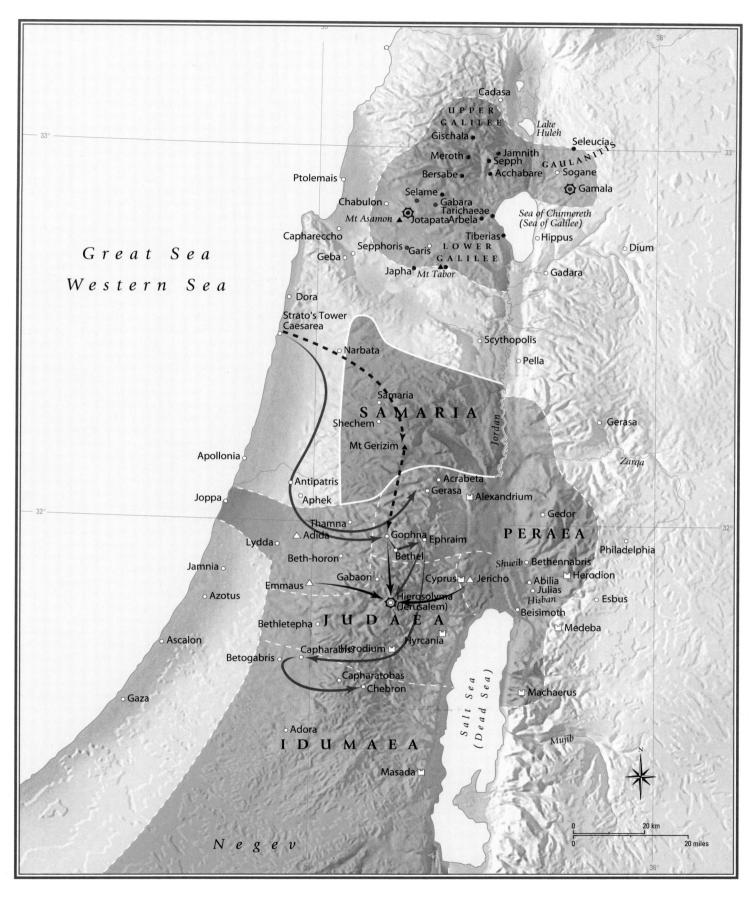

THE JEWISH DIASPORA

THE JEWISH DIASPORA
C. 1300 BC–AD 300
The diaspora is the name given to the scattering of the Jewish population throughout the world, often under duress. In 722 BC many were deported after the northern kingdom of Israel was conquered and in 588 BC Nebuchadnezzar deported a sizable proportion of the population to Babylon. By the time the Romans invaded in 63 BC there were a number of Jewish communities all around the Mediterranean. It is said that there were a million in Egypt and more than 7000 in Rome. Following the Great Jewish Revolt against the Romans in AD 66–70 and the Bar Kokhba Revolt in AD 132–135, there were mass deportations throughout the known world.

Following the Roman defeat of Jerusalem, the Jewish people spread throughout Babylonia and the Roman Empire

THE JEWISH DIAPSORA, C. 1300 B.C.E. – C. 300 C.E.

- Extent of the Roman Empire, c. 300 C.E.
- Kingdom of David, 10th century B.C.E.
- Kingdom of Israel, 931 – 722 B.C.E.
- Kingdom of Judah, 931 – 587 B.C.E
- Probable route of the Exodus, 13th century B.C.E.
- Route of Babylonian exile, 587 B.C.E.
- Jewish dispersion routes, c. 70 B.C.E. – c.300 C.E.

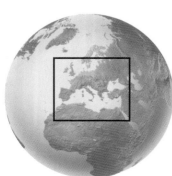

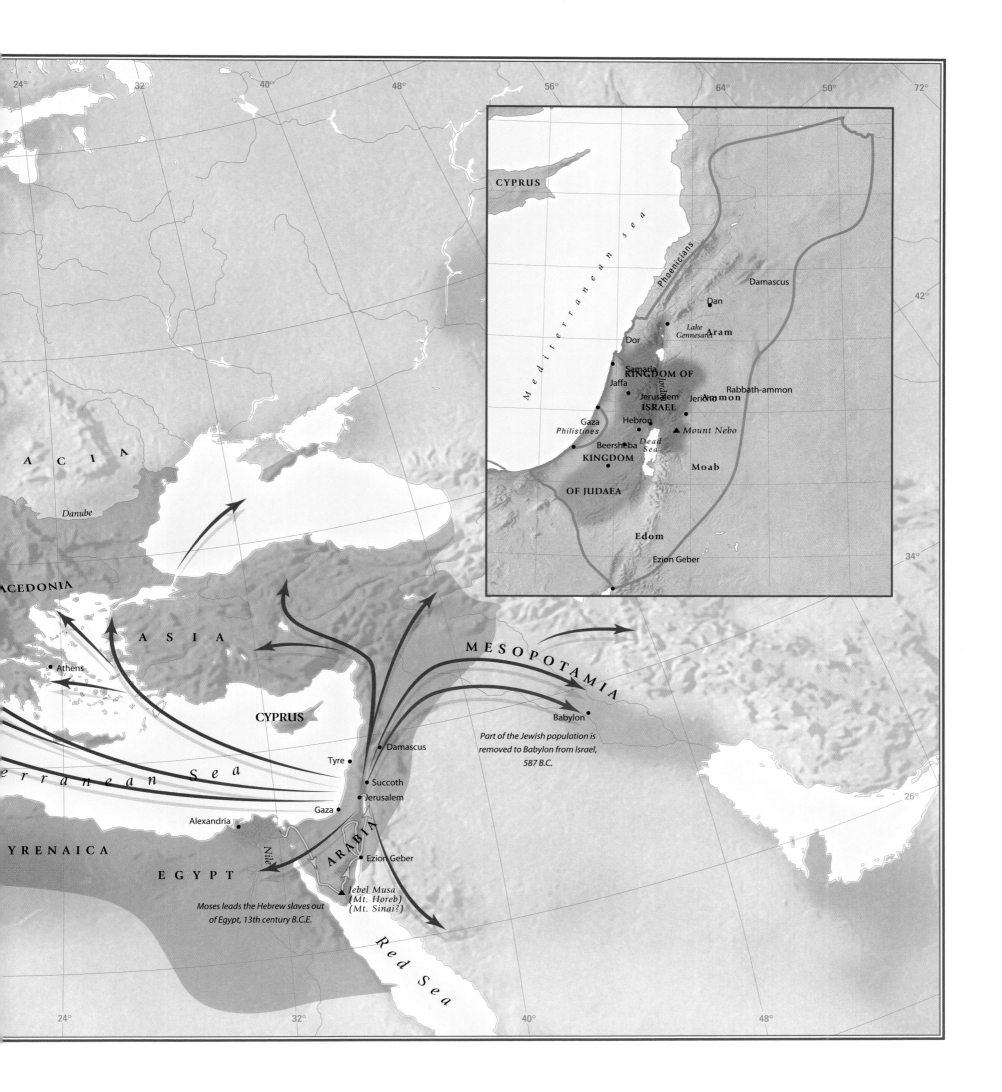

CYPRUS

Mediterranean sea

Phoenicians

Damascus

Dan

Lake Gennesaret **Aram**

Dor

Samaria

KINGDOM OF

Jaffa

Jordan

Jerusalem Jericho Rabbath-ammon

ISRAEL Ammon

Gaza Hebron

Philistines ▲ *Mount Nebo*

Beersheba *Dead Sea*

KINGDOM **Moab**

OF JUDAEA

Edom

Ezion Geber

ACIA

Danube

T H R A C I A

A S I A

• Athens

CYPRUS

erranean Sea

Tyre •

Damascus •

M E S O P O T A M I A

Babylon •

Part of the Jewish population is removed to Babylon from Israel, 587 B.C.

Succoth •

Jerusalem •

Gaza •

Alexandria •

YRENAICA

A R A B I A

E G Y P T

Nile

Ezion Geber •

Jebel Musa (Mt. Horeb) (Mt. Sinai?)

Moses leads the Hebrew slaves out of Egypt, 13th century B.C.E.

R e d S e a

83

THE SPREAD OF CHRISTIANITY

AD 45 – C. 300

THE SPREAD OF CHRISTIANITY

Following the death of Jesus Christ around AD 29, Christianity quickly spread through Rome's eastern provinces, aided by evangelists such as Saints Peter and Paul. By AD 50 a Christian community had developed in Rome, and in AD 64 Emperor Nero blamed them for the great fire that swept the city. In spite of this, Christianity continued to spread throughout the empire. For the next 240 years Christianity was either tolerated or persecuted, but relief eventually came when Emperor Constantine made it the state religion in 312. State-sponsored churches were built at St Peter's in Rome and over the holy places of other religions.

THE SPREAD OF CHRISTIANITY

- Christian by AD 45
- Christian by AD 100
- Christian by AD 185
- Christian by AD 325
- Roman Empire c. 300

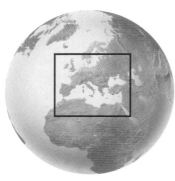

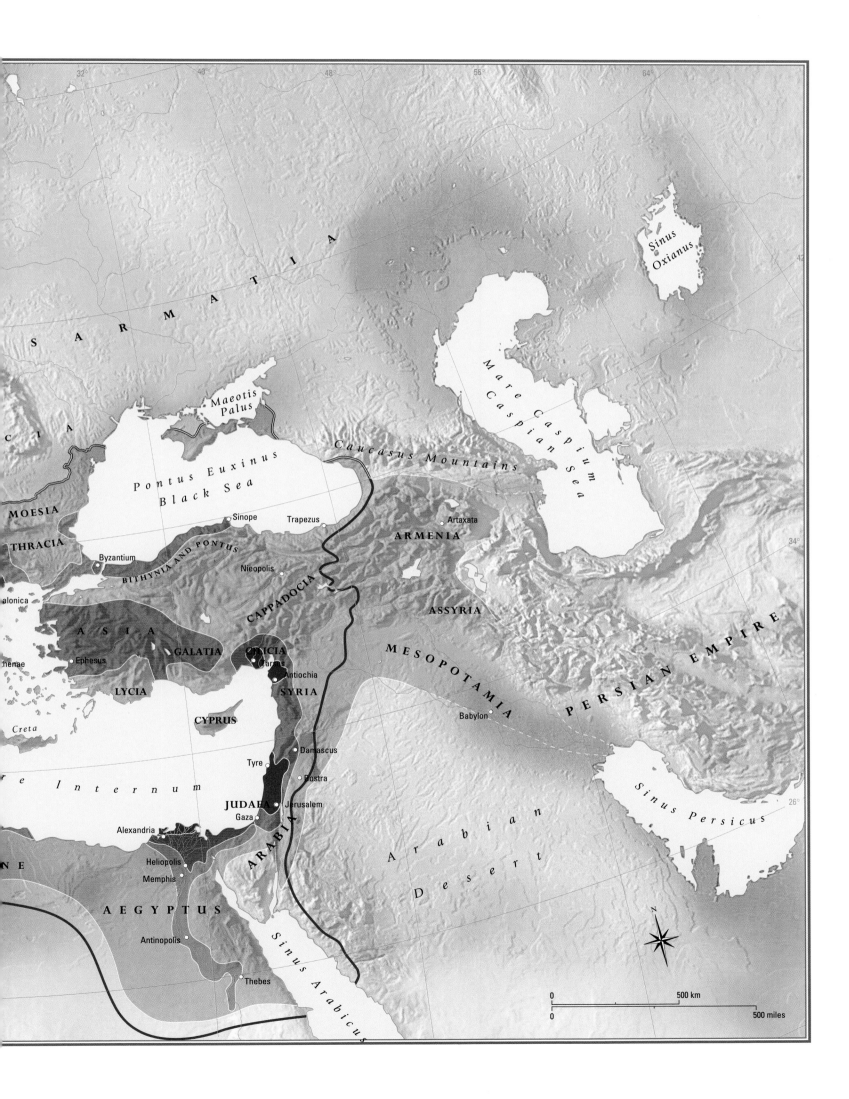

Sinus
Oxianus

Mare Caspium
Caspian Sea

S

S A R M A T I A

Maeotis
Palus

Caucasus Mountains

Pontus Euxinus
Black Sea

MOESIA

THRACIA

Byzantium

BITHYNIA AND PONTUS

Sinope

Trapezus

Artaxata

ARMENIA

Nieopolis

CAPPADOCIA

ASSYRIA

alonica

A S I A

GALATIA

henae

Ephesus

CILICIA
Tarsus

LYCIA

Antiochia

MESOPOTAMIA

PERSIAN EMPIRE

SYRIA

CYPRUS

Creta

Babylon

re   Internum

Damascus

Tyre

Bostra

Sinus Persicus

JUDAEA

Jerusalem

Gaza

ARABIA

Alexandria

Arabian

NE

Heliopolis

Memphis

A E G Y P T U S

Desert

N

Antinopolis

Thebes

Sinus Arabicus

0   500 km

0   500 miles

AD 101 – 117   THE DACIAN WARS

THE DACIAN WARS
These were two short wars between the Roman Empire and Dacia during the reign of Emperor Trajan. The Dacians had always presented a threat to the Roman Empire and in 101 Trajan prepared for a war against Dacia. This war lasted only for a few months and resulted in a heroic Roman victory. Before long the Dacans were again raiding Roman colonies across the Danube and this provoked a second war in 106. The Romans attacked the Dacian capital and burned it to the ground. The two wars were notable victories in Rome's expansionist campaign and Trajan became a true and honorable civil emperor.

THE DACIAN WARS
101–106

—— Frontier of Roman Empire 101

▨ Area annexed 105–06

● Dacian capital

● Roman province capital

○ Roman legionary base

First Dacian War

➤ Roman campaigns

➤ Dacian counter attack

Second Dacian War

➤ Roman campaigns

✕ Battle site

⌂ Site of Trajan's victory monument

THE PARTHIAN WARS

THE PARTHIAN WARS AD 114–117

The Parthian wars began as a result of an attempt by the Parthian king Osroes to impose his nephew as the next king of Armenia. Rome had held hegemony over Armenia for many years and had final authority in naming the king. Emperor Trajan moved east to restore order, reaching Armenia in 114. Osroes' nephew was deposed and the country was annexed as a Roman province. Trajan then moved south into Parthia capturing Babylon and Ctesiphon until he reached the Persian Gulf. On his way back to Rome, Trajan fell ill following a defeat at the desert fortress of Hatra. He died in Selinus in 117.

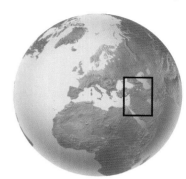

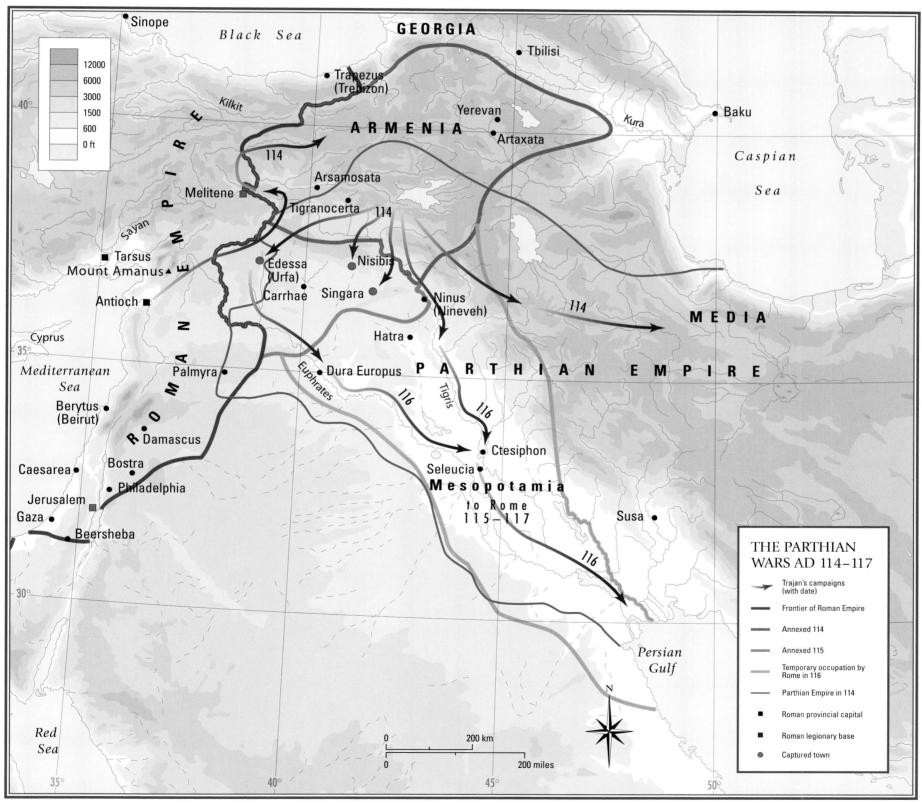

THE PARTHIAN WARS AD 114–117

→ Trajan's campaigns (with date)

— Frontier of Roman Empire

— Annexed 114

— Annexed 115

— Temporary occupation by Rome in 116

— Parthian Empire in 114

■ Roman provincial capital

■ Roman legionary base

● Captured town

EASTERN BORDERS

AD 114 – 360

EASTERN BORDERS 2ND AND 3RD CENTURIES AD

By the 2nd and 3rd centuries the Roman Empire was under almost constant pressure from the Persians. At the Battle of Edessa in 260 Emperor Valerian was captured by the Persians and was later brutally killed by them. The Romans asked the King of Palmyra for assistance in their fight against the Persians. He was very successful, but when he was assassinated his wife, Zenobia, assumed control. She scored spectacular victories and eventually proclaimed herself Queen of Egypt. This was too much for the Romans and she was captured and taken to Rome where she lived out the rest of her days.

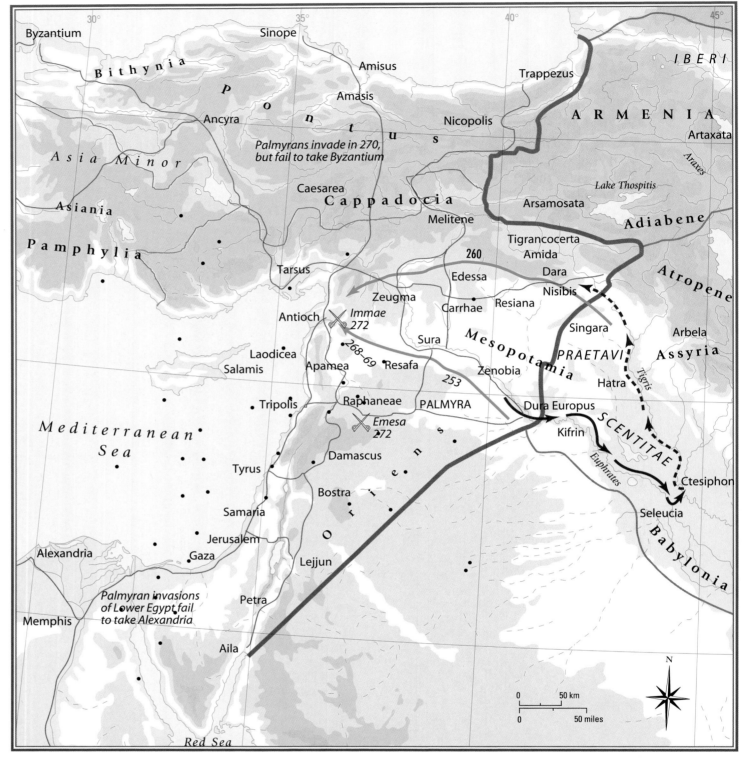

EASTERN BORDERS
2nd and 3rd Centuries AD

→ Persian raids

→ Julian's invasion of Persia AD 360

— Eastern border of Roman Empire c. AD 300

— Major trade route

THE SASSANIAN EMPIRE

THE SASSANIAN EMPIRE
The reign of the Sassanians
lasted from AD 224 to 651 and
they were the last native
dynasty to rule Persia before
the Arab conquest. The state
religion was Zoroastrianism
and no other religions were
tolerated. Christians were
persecuted and when the
Roman Empire became
Christian, persecution
increased. The conflict with
Rome began in 231 after the
Sassanians invaded Syria and
looted Antioch. In a second
war in 260 the Roman
emperor Valerian was defeated,
captured, and subsequently
tortured to death. Under
subsequent emperors the
Romans restored their fortunes
and in 298 the Sassanians had
to give up their territories in
northern Mesopotamia.

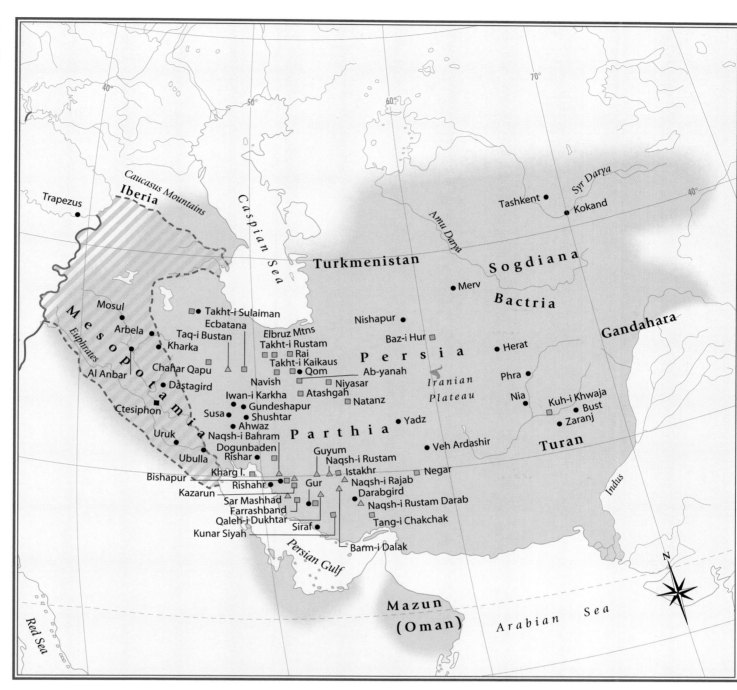

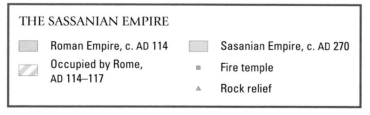

THE SASSANIAN EMPIRE

Roman Empire, c. AD 114

Occupied by Rome,
AD 114–117

Sasanian Empire, c. AD 270

Fire temple

Rock relief

AD 330

ROMAN CONTROLLED EGYPT c. AD 330

ROMAN CONTROLLED EGYPT c. AD 330

After the death of Cleopatra, Egypt became a Roman Province. Following their usual practice the Romans did not interfere with Egypt's internal affairs, although they tried to control the growth of Christianity that was spreading among the local population. In AD 324 Constantine made Christianity the official religion of the Roman Empire and established a new capital at Constantinople. The Roman Empire was split in two and Egypt became part of the Eastern Empire. Egypt continued to be a center of agriculture and commerce, but under the influence of Constantinople it gradually became more Greek and Asian.

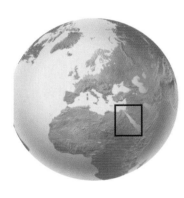

```
ROMAN
CONTROLLED EGYPT
c. AD 330

----    Desert route
```

Mediterranean Sea

Paratonium

Rosetta
Canopus
Alexandria
Buto
Hermupolis Parva
Naukratis
Sebannytos
Tanis
Pelusium

Jerusalem
Gaza
Raphia

AEGYPTUS

Terenuthis
Bubastis
Athribis
Leontopolis
Heliopolis
Memphis
Clysma

Wadi an-Natrun

LIBYA
INFERIOR

Saqqara

Karanis
Philoteras
Arsinoe
Aphroditopolis
Hawara
Abusir el-Melek
Heracleopolis Magna

PALAESTINA

Sinai

Petra

Aelana

Gulf of Suez

Gulf of Aqaba

HERCULIA

el-Hibe

el-Qasr
Bauit
Bahariyeh Oasis
El-Hays

Oxyrhynchos
Akoris

Antinoopolis
Tuna el-Gebel
Hermupolis Magna

Arab Desert

Farafra Oasis

Myos Hormos
Mons Porphyrites

Apollonis polis
THEBES
es-Salamuni
Panopolis

Mons Claudianus

Philoteras

Abydos
Kainopolis
Tentyris
Coptos

Leukos Limen

Deir el-Haggar
Qarat el-Muzawwakeh
Balat
Esbet
Bashindi
Gebel et-Teir
Hibis
Qasr al-Ghueita

Diospolis Magna
Kamuk
Thebes
Catopolis

Apollonopolis Magna

Nile

Mons Smaragdus

Kysis

Ombos

Kharga Oasis

Qubbet el-Hawa
Elephantine
Syene
Debod
Philae
Tizitzi
Talmis
Tutzis
Pselchis

Red Sea

Berenike

Karanog
Primius

Faras
Gebel Adda

Selima Oasis

Nile

N

Sedeinga

0   100 km
0   100 miles

ROMAN BRITAIN

ROMAN BRITAIN

Britain—or much of England and Wales, at least—was controlled by the Roman Empire between AD 43 and 410. The Romans brought many innovations with them, in the fields of urbanization, agriculture, industry, and architecture, leaving a lasting legacy that can still be seen today. One of the most obvious examples of this is the Roman roads, which were essential for the quick and efficient transportation of soldiers and supplies. As the map shows, many modern British highways follow the same routes as the original roads that were built nearly two thousand years ago.

ROMAN BRITAIN

- ■ Provincial capital
- ● Colonia
- ⌂ Legionary fortress
- ● Local capital
- ● Other major town
- ⋯⋯ Main Roman roads
- —— Roads where route is certain
- - - - Roads where route is uncertain
- ═══ Route of Roman road still in use

Antonine Wall

Hadrian's Wall

Dere Street

Liguvalium (Carlisle)

Coriosopitum (Corbridge)

Usurium Brigantum (Aldborough)

EBORACUM (YORK)

VI Legion

Petuaria (Brough-on-Humber)

A15

Segontium (Caernarfon)

Deva (Chester)

XX Legion

Aquae Amemetiae (Buxton)

Lindum Colonia (Lincoln)

B6403

A46

Venta Icemorum (Caistor-by-Norwich)

B5061 Watling Street

A38

Viroconium (Wroxeter)

A5

Ratae Coritanorum (Leicester)

Durobrivae (Water Newton)

Gariannonum (Burgh Castle)

Ermin Street

Magnis (Kenchester)

Ryknield St

B4455

Fosse Way

A5

A1198

Glevum Colonia (Gloucester)

A429

Akeman Street

Moridunum (Carmarthen)

Camulodunum (Colchester)

Verulamium (St Albans)

Caesaromagus (Chelmsford)

Isca Silvrum (Caerleon-on-Usk)

II Legion

Venta Silurum (Caerwent)

Corinium (Cirencester)

LONDINIUM AUGUSTA (LONDON)

Tamesis Flumen (Thames)

A2

Durovemum (Canterbury)

Rutupiae (Richborough)

Aquae Sulis (Bath)

A449

Calleva (Silchester)

A29

B2068

Dubrae (Dover)

A37

Lindinis (Ilchester)

Venta Belgarum (Winchester)

Noviomagus (Chichester)

Anderida (Pevensey)

Isca Dumnoniorum (Exeter)

Durnovaria (Dorchester)

N

AD 214 – 310

THE EMPIRE AD 214

ROMAN EMPIRE AD 214
By AD 214 the Roman Empire had reached its peak. It controlled vast areas around the Mediterranean and had borders of colossal length that had to be kept secure. This was the period of the Severan Dynasty, which lasted for about 40 years. Founded by Septimus Severus, the imperial court was dominated by formidable women. They arranged the succession of Alexander Severus, the last of the dynasty, and after he was assassinated there followed half a century of civil war and strife. The Pax Romana that had been established by Augustus some 200 years earlier, finally began to crumble.

THE CITY OF ROME C. AD 235–310

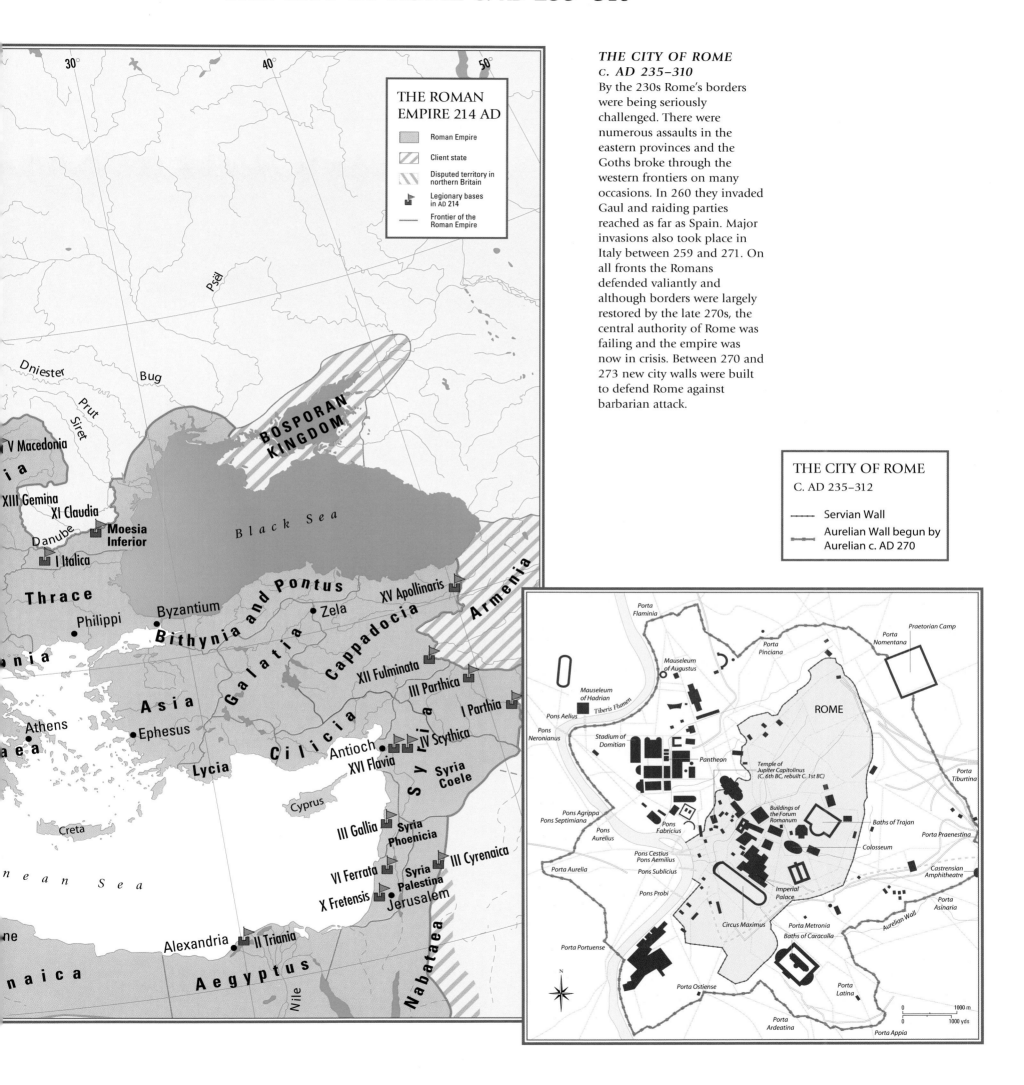

THE ROMAN EMPIRE 214 AD

Roman Empire

Client state

Disputed territory in northern Britain

Legionary bases in AD 214

Frontier of the Roman Empire

***THE CITY OF ROME
C. AD 235–310***

By the 230s Rome's borders were being seriously challenged. There were numerous assaults in the eastern provinces and the Goths broke through the western frontiers on many occasions. In 260 they invaded Gaul and raiding parties reached as far as Spain. Major invasions also took place in Italy between 259 and 271. On all fronts the Romans defended valiantly and although borders were largely restored by the late 270s, the central authority of Rome was failing and the empire was now in crisis. Between 270 and 273 new city walls were built to defend Rome against barbarian attack.

THE CITY OF ROME

C. AD 235–312

Servian Wall

Aurelian Wall begun by Aurelian c. AD 270

INVASIONS AND REBELLIONS AD 250–271

INVASIONS AND REBELLIONS AD 250–271

In the 3rd century the Roman Empire went through a period of crisis. In the east the emperor Valerian had been captured by Sassanid Persians and his son Gallienus had been left in shaky control. At the same time Goths were invading the northern borders in the east and Germanic tribes were invading the northern borders in the west. Gaul, Britain, and Hispania in the western part of the empire were feeling that Rome was neglecting them and they decided to form a breakaway province. This Gallic Empire was actually very successful, but after 13 years it was pulled back into the empire proper.

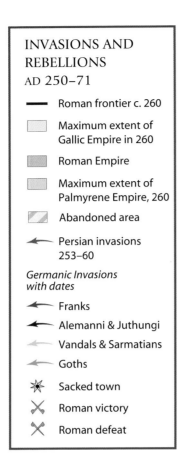

INVASIONS AND REBELLIONS AD 250–71

— Roman frontier c. 260

☐ Maximum extent of Gallic Empire in 260

▨ Roman Empire

☐ Maximum extent of Palmyrene Empire, 260

▨ Abandoned area

← Persian invasions 253–60

Germanic Invasions with dates

← Franks

← Alemanni & Juthungi

← Vandals & Sarmatians

← Goths

✳ Sacked town

⚔ Roman victory

⚔ Roman defeat

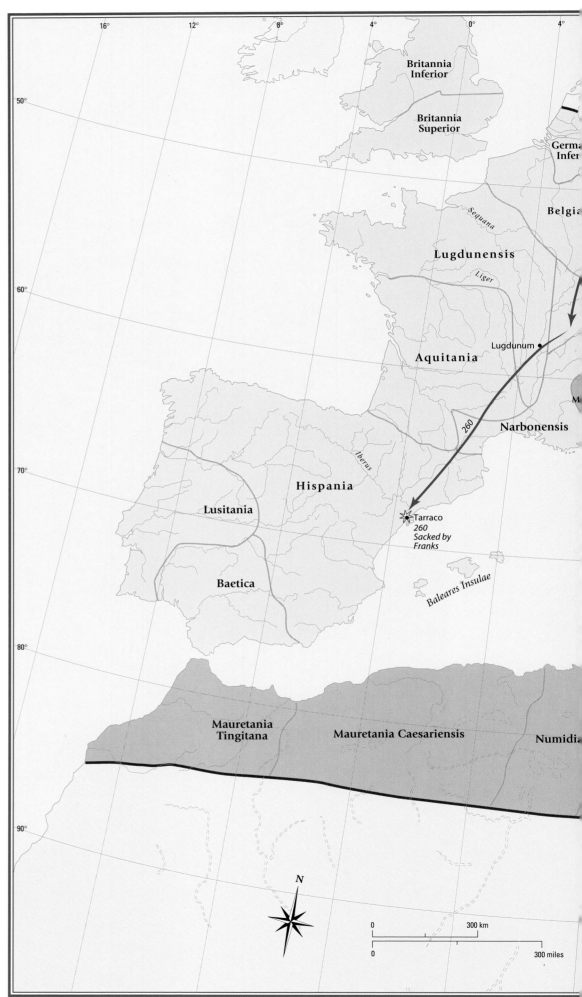

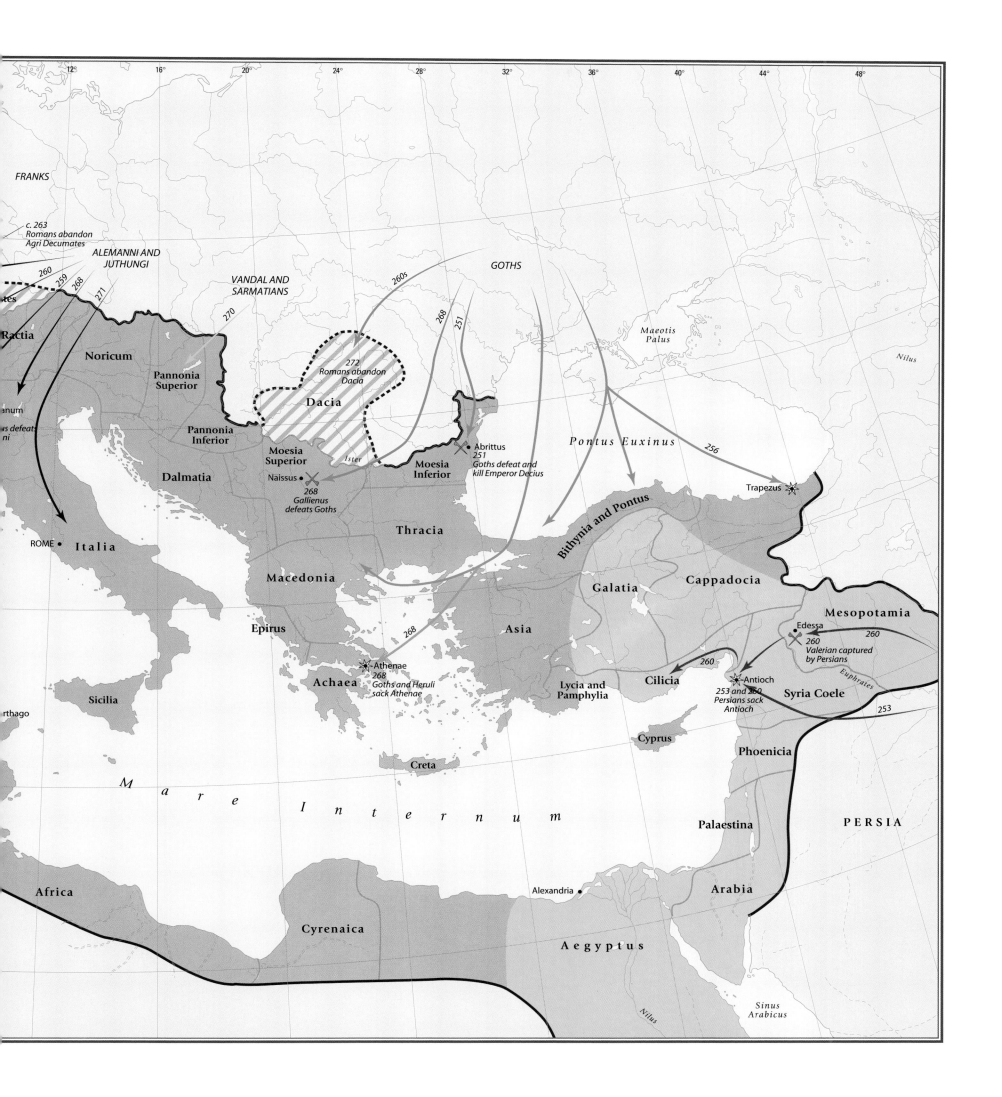

FRANKS

c. 263
Romans abandon
Agri Decumates

ALEMANNI AND
JUTHUNGI

VANDAL AND
SARMATIANS

GOTHS

260

259

268

271

270

260s

268

251

*Maeotis
Palus*

Nilus

Raetia

Noricum

Pannonia
Superior

Pannonia
Inferior

anum

s defeats
ni

272
Romans abandon
Dacia

Dacia

Ister

Moesia
Superior

Naissus ●

268
Gallienus
defeats Goths

Pontus Euxinus

256

Dalmatia

Moesia
Inferior

✕ ● Abrittus
251
Goths defeat and
kill Emperor Decius

Trapezus ☀

ROME ● Italia

Thracia

Bithynia and Pontus

Macedonia

Galatia

Cappadocia

Mesopotamia

Epirus

Asia

268

Edessa
●

260

260
Valerian captured
by Persians

Athenae ☀
268
Goths and Heruli
sack Athenae

Achaea

Lycia and
Pamphylia

Cilicia

260

☀ ● Antioch
253 and 260
Persians sack
Antioch

Syria Coele

Euphrates

253

Sicilia

rthago

Cyprus

Phoenicia

M   a   r   e   I   n   t   e   r   n   u   m

Creta

Palaestina

PERSIA

Africa

Cyrenaica

Alexandria ●

Arabia

A e g y p t u s

Nilus

*Sinus
Arabicus*

THE WEST BREAKS AWAY AD 260–273

THE WEST BREAKS AWAY C. 260–273

By the time of the Emperor Gallienus Rome was failing to retain the central power and authority that it once had. Many Romans, particularly those in the western provinces, found themselves drawn more to regional powers rather than to a distant emperor who was involved in dealing with rebellions in the east and north. In AD 260 Postumus, the governor of Lower Germany, led a rebellion and formed the Gallic Empire, which lasted for nearly 15 years. This region was prosperous and self-sufficient, but it was eventually reabsorbed into the Roman Empire by Aurelian after the battle of Châlons-sur-Marne.

THE WEST BREAKS AWAY c. 260–273

- Gallic Empire of Postumus, 261
- Gallic Empire of Tetricus, 271
- Roman Empire, 261
- Gallic mint
- • Capital of Gallic Empire
- Fortified land frontier
- River frontier
- Major road

Antonine Wall

Hadrian's Wall

G e r m a n i c u s
O c e a n u s

Eboracum

Britannia Inferior

Britannia Superior • Londinium

Postumus Assassinated after refusing to allow his troops to sack Mainz

Germania Inferior

Rhenus

Tetricus, last Gallic emperor, defeated by Aurelian's Roman forces

Colonia Agrippina

Durocatalauni •

Belgica

Mogontiacum

Sequana

• Lutetia

Augusta Treverorum

Lugdunensis

abandoned c. 263

Liger

Augusta Vindelicorum

O C E A N U S

• Limonum

Germania Superior

Raetia

April 260 altar records Roman victory over invading Juthungi c. 260 Raetia held by Postumus c. 262 Raetia recovered by Gollienus

Aquitania

Lugdunum •

Alpine Provinces

• Burdigala

Mediolanum •

Narbonensis

• Arelate

ITALIA

Tarraconensis

Iberus

• Narbo

Tagus

Lusitania

Tarraco •

Rome •

Olisipo •

• Toletum

Spanish provinces return to Roman allegiance

Baleares Insulae

Baetica

Sardinia

Corduba •

Gades •

• Carthago Nova

M a r e   I n t e r n u m

A   F   R   I   C   A

0 ____ 200 km
0 ____ 200 miles

PALMYRA AND THE EAST, AD 260–273

PALMYRA AND THE EAST 260-273

Palmyra is a very ancient city, said to have been founded by King Solomon. The Romans formally annexed it in AD 217 and gave it its name, which means 'city of palms'. In 260 the Persians overran several eastern Roman provinces and the Romans asked the King of Palmyra, Odaenathus, for assistance. He was very successful, but in 267 he was assassinated. His wife Zenobia assumed control, scored spectacular victories, annexed a number of Roman territories, and successfully invaded Egypt. This was too much for Emperor Aurelian and Zenobia's army was defeated in 273. Zenobia was led back to Rome in golden chains.

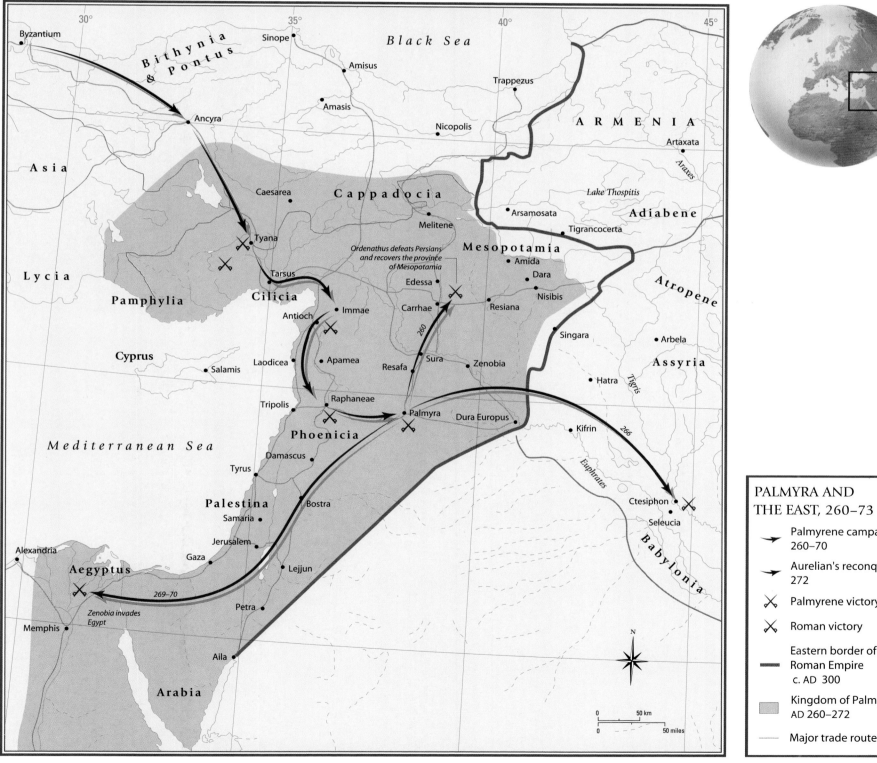

PALMYRA AND
THE EAST, 260–73

→ Palmyrene campaigns,
260–70

→ Aurelian's reconquest,
272

✕ Palmyrene victory

✕ Roman victory

━ Eastern border of
Roman Empire
c. AD 300

▦ Kingdom of Palmyra
AD 260–272

— Major trade route

DIOCLETIAN: THE EMPIRE REORGANISED

AD 284 – 310

Diocletian was Roman emperor from November 284 to May 305. He decided that the only future for the empire was to divide it in two. In 292 he devised a system of tetrarchy, or rule of four, where a senior emperor would rule the west and another would rule the east, and each would have a junior emperor called a Caesar. He chose the eastern half for himself and gave the western half to Maximian. Maximian divided his territory, making Constantius as his junior. Diocletian retired in 305 and persuaded Maximian to do the same. However, Maximian resumed his former position in 307 following a coup promoted by Maximian's son, who had been overlooked in the succession. Still powerful, Diocletian again persuaded Maximian to stand down. Despite doing so, Maximian tried again to take power in 310 before being captured by Constantius' son Constantine. He died soon after.

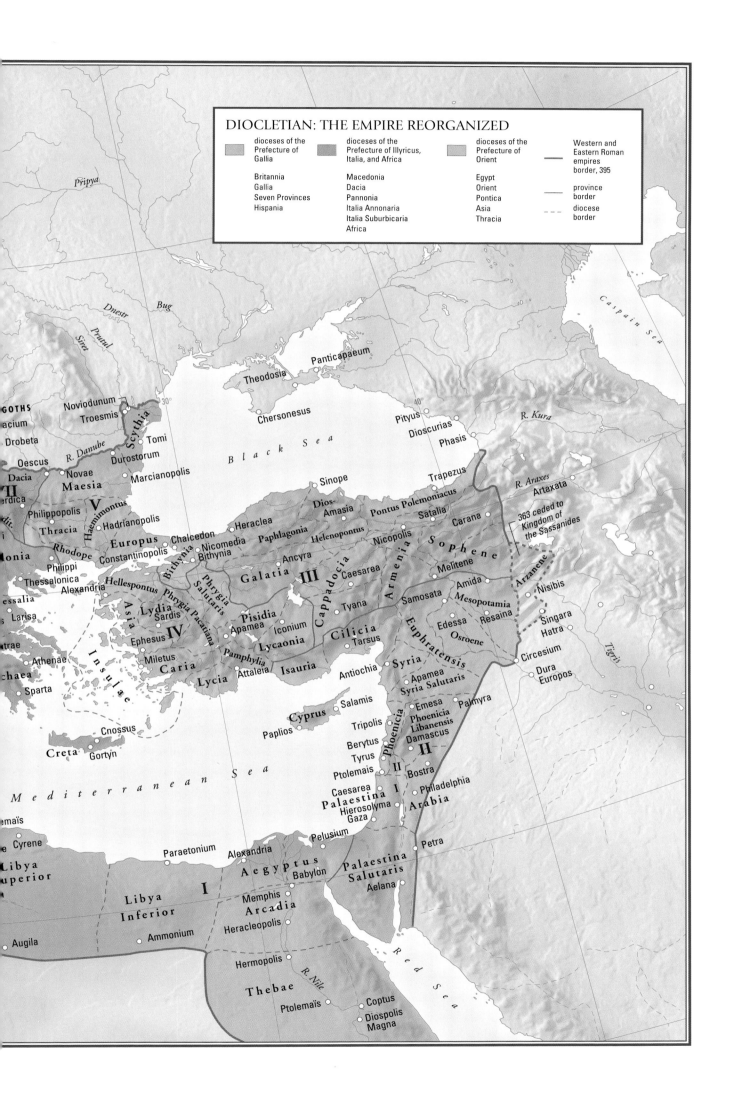

DIOCLETIAN: THE EMPIRE REORGANIZED

dioceses of the Prefecture of Gallia	dioceses of the Prefecture of Illyricus, Italia, and Africa	dioceses of the Prefecture of Orient

Western and Eastern Roman empires border, 395

province border

diocese border

Britannia
Gallia
Seven Provinces
Hispania

Macedonia
Dacia
Pannonia
Italia Annonaria
Italia Suburbicaria
Africa

Egypt
Orient
Pontica
Asia
Thracia

Pripya

Dnestr

Bug

Siret

Prutul

GOTHS
acium
Noviodunum
Troesmis
Scythia
30°
Tomi
Drobeta
Oescus
R. Danube
Durostorum
Dacia
Novae
Maesia
Marcianopolis
VII
erdica
Philippopolis
V
Haemimontus
dit.
Thracia
Hadrianopolis
Rhodope
Europus
Chalcedon
onia
Constantinopolis
Nicomedia
Bithynia
Philippi
Bithynia
Thessalonica
Alexandria
Hellespontus
essalia
Larisa
Asia
Lydia
Sardis
Phrygia Pacatiana
Phrygia Salutaris
chaea
Athenae
Ephesus
IV
Sparta
Insulae
Miletus
Caria
Lycia
Pamphylia
Attaleia
Isauria
Creta
Cnossus
Gortyn

Panticapaeum
Theodosia
Chersonesus

Black Sea

Caspain Sea

Pityus
Dioscurias
Phasis
R. Kura
Sinope
Trapezus
Artaxata
Dios-Amasia
Pontus Polemoniacus
Satalia
R. Araxes
Carana
Heraclea
Helenopontus
Nicopolis
363 ceded to Kingdom of the Sassanides
Paphlagonia
Ancyra
Galatia
III
Caesarea
Cappadocia
Sophene
Armenia
Melitene
Arzanene
Nisibis
Pisidia
Apamea
Iconium
Tyana
Samosata
Amida
Mesopotamia
Singara
Lycaonia
Cilicia
Edessa
Resaina
Hatra
Tarsus
Euphratensis
Osroene
Antiochia
Syria
Circesium
Apamea Syria Salutaris
Dura Europos
Cyprus
Salamis
Emesa
Phoenicia
Palmyra
Tripolis
Phoenicia Libanensis
Paplios
Berytus
Damascus
Tyrus
II
Ptolemaïs
II
Bostra
Caesarea
I
Philadelphia
Palaestina
Arabia
Hierosolyma
Gaza
Tigris

Mediterranean Sea

emaïs
Cyrene
Paraetonium
Alexandria
Pelusium
Petra
Libya Superior
Aegyptus
Babylon
Palaestina Salutaris
Libya Inferior
I
Memphis
Arcadia
Aelana
Augila
Ammonium
Heracleopolis
Hermopolis
R. Nile
Thebae
Red Sea
Ptolemaïs
Coptus
Diospolis Magna

AD 306 – 324   # THE RISE OF CONSTANTINE

RISE OF CONSTANTINE

Constantine's elevation to ruler of the Roman Empire began when his father Constantius was nominated as junior emperor under Maximian, whom he succeeded as Augustus of the western empire in 305. When Constantius died in 306 his soldiers proclaimed Constantine as his successor. This was in direct opposition to Maximentius, son of Maximian, who claimed his father's position. The two met at the Battle of the Milvian Bridge, which Constantine won. Constantine became ruler of the western empire. In 324 he reunited the whole empire and spread Christianity throughout its lands.

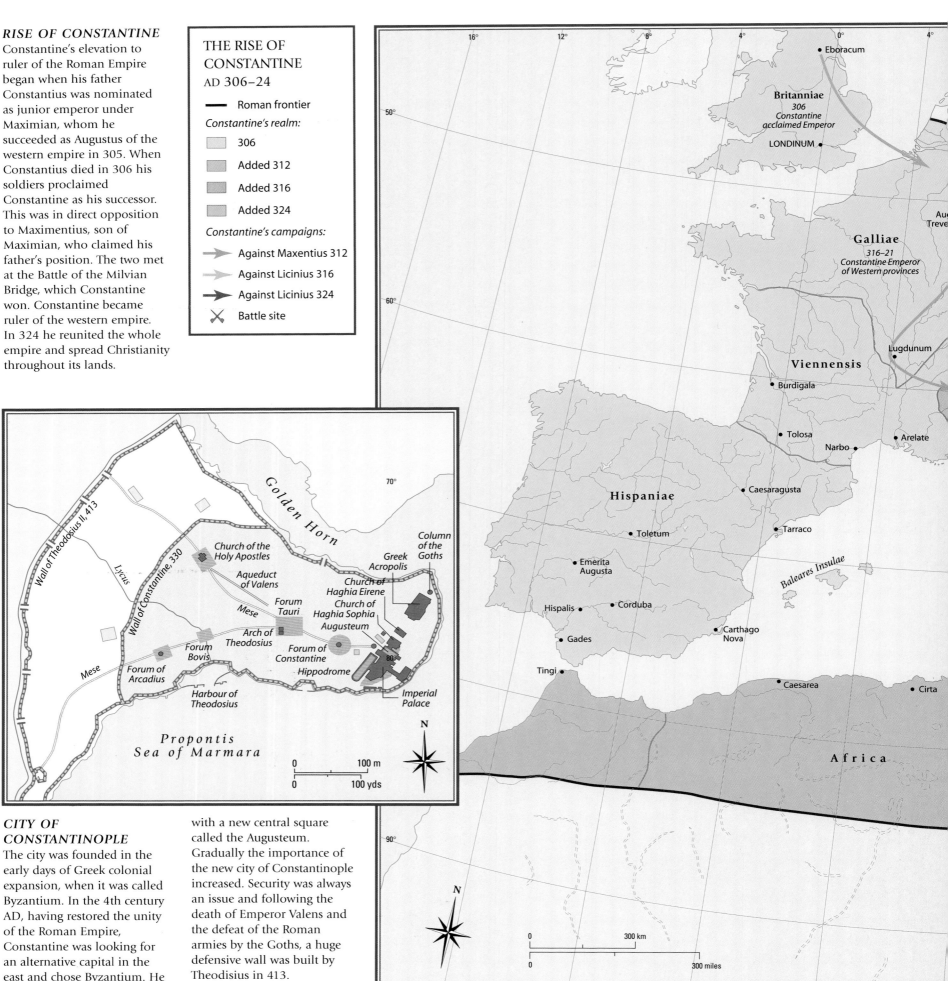

THE RISE OF CONSTANTINE
AD 306–24

—— Roman frontier

Constantine's realm:

☐ 306

☐ Added 312

☐ Added 316

☐ Added 324

Constantine's campaigns:

→ Against Maxentius 312

→ Against Licinius 316

→ Against Licinius 324

✕ Battle site

CITY OF CONSTANTINOPLE

The city was founded in the early days of Greek colonial expansion, when it was called Byzantium. In the 4th century AD, having restored the unity of the Roman Empire, Constantine was looking for an alternative capital in the east and chose Byzantium. He laid out and expanded city with a new central square called the Augusteum. Gradually the importance of the new city of Constantinople increased. Security was always an issue and following the death of Emperor Valens and the defeat of the Roman armies by the Goths, a huge defensive wall was built by Theodisius in 413.

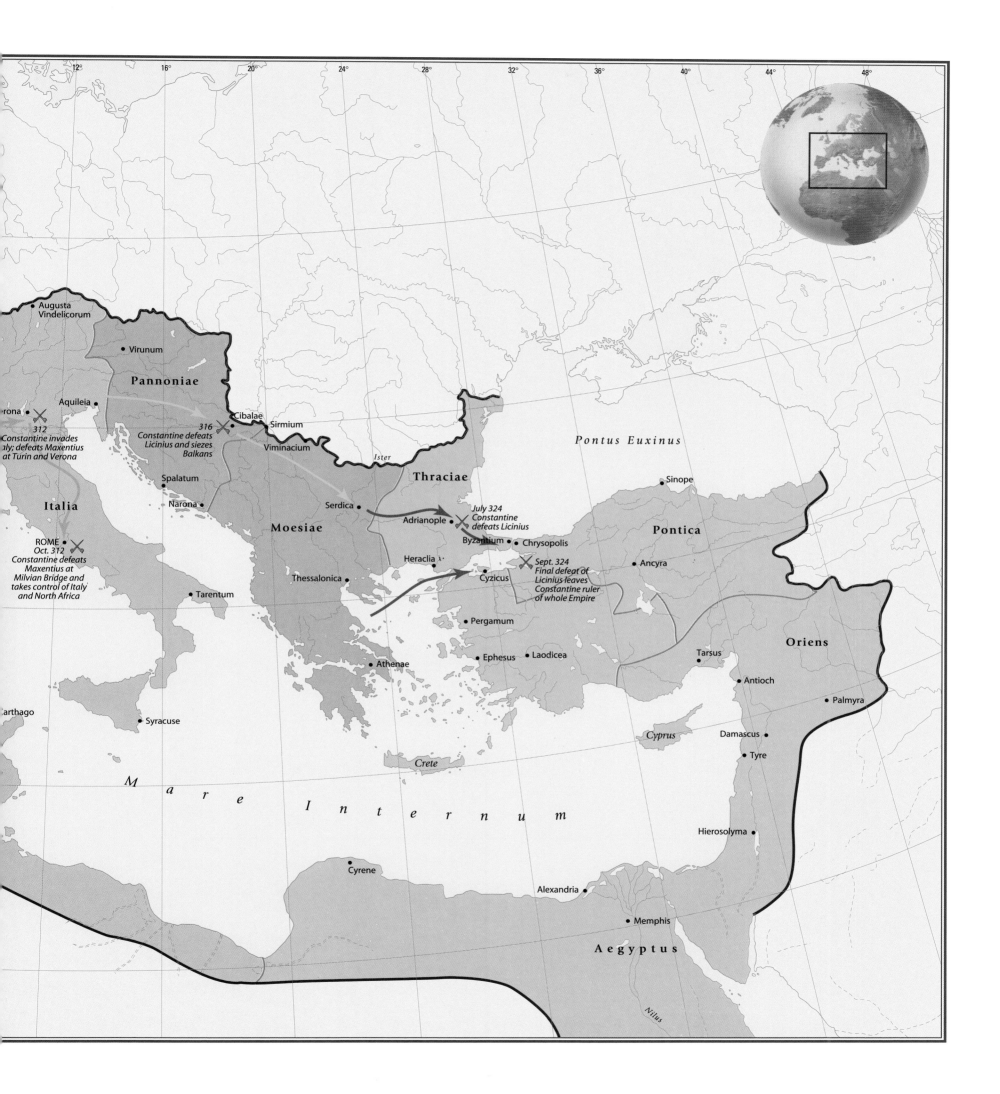

Augusta
Vindelicorum

Virunum

Pannoniae

Aquileia

rona

*312
Constantine invades
aly; defeats Maxentius
at Turin and Verona*

Cibalae

Sirmium

*316
Constantine defeats
Licinius and siezes
Balkans*

Viminacium

Italia

Spalatum

Narona

Ister

Thraciae

Pontus Euxinus

Sinope

Serdica

Moesiae

Adrianople

*July 324
Constantine
defeats Licinius*

Byzantium

Chrysopolis

Pontica

Ancyra

ROME
*Oct. 312
Constantine defeats
Maxentius at
Milvian Bridge and
takes control of Italy
and North Africa*

Thessalonica

Heraclia

Cyzicus

*Sept. 324
Final defeat of
Licinius leaves
Constantine ruler
of whole Empire*

Tarentum

Pergamum

Oriens

Tarsus

arthago

Syracuse

Athenae

Ephesus

Laodicea

Antioch

Palmyra

Cyprus

Damascus

Tyre

M   a   r   e   I   n   t   e   r   n   u   m

Crete

Hierosolyma

Cyrene

Alexandria

Memphis

Aegyptus

Nilus

THE ROMAN EMPIRE AD 395

AD 395

THE ROMAN EMPIRE AD 395

The Emperor Diocletian had divided the empire into a western half and an eastern half, and each half was further divided into two. The result was four Prefectures, which in turn were divided into three or four dioceses that were subdivided into administrative units. By 395 it was becoming difficult to defend the extremities of the empire and Britanniae's time as a Roman province was running out. The barbarians were at the door and the heart of the empire was under threat. Some legions had already been pulled back to defend Rome itself and within a few years Britanniae would be completely abandoned and

WESTERN DIVISION

Britannie
1. Valentia
2. Britannia II
3. Flavia Caesariensis
4. Britannia
5. Maxima Caesariensis

Galliae
1. Ludgunensis III
2. Ludgunensis II
3. Belgica II
4. Germania II
5. Ludgunensis Senonia
6. Ludgunensis I
7. Belgica I
8. Germania I
9. Maxima Sequanorum

Septum Provinciae
1. Aquitanica II
2. Aquitanica I
3. Novem Populi
4. Narbonensis I
5. Viennensis
6. Narbonensis II
7. Alpes Maritimae

Hispaniae
1. Gallaecia
2. Carthaginiensis
3. Tarraconensis
4. Lusitania
5. Baetica
6. Insulae Balearum
7. Tingitania

Africa
1. Mauretania Caesariensis
2. Mauretania Sitifensis
3. Numidia
4. Africa
5. Byzacena
6. Tripolitania

Italia
1. Alpes Cottiae
2. Aemilia
3. Raetia I
4. Raetia II
5. Liguria
6. Venetia et Histria
7. Flaminia et Picenum

Suburbicaria
1. Corsica
2. Sardinia
3. Tuscia et Umbria
4. Valeria
5. Picenum Suburbicarium
6. Roma
7. Campania
8. Samnium
9. Bruttii et Lucania
10. Apulia et Calabria
11. Sicilia

Pannonia (to ca.400); Illyricum (after ca. 400)
1. Noricum Ripense
2. Noricum Meditterraneum
3. Pannonia I
4. Valeria
5. Savia
6. Pannonia II
7. Dalmatia

EASTERN DIVISION

Dacia
1. Moesia I
2. Dacia Ripensis
3. Praevalitana
4. Dardania
5. Dacia Mediterranea

Macedonia
1. Epirus Nova
2. Macedonia
3. Epirus Vetus
4. Thessalia
5. Achaea
6. Creta

Thraciae
1. Moesia II
2. Scythia
3. Thracia
4. Haemimontus
5. Rhodope
6. Europa

Asiana
1. Hellespontus
2. Phrygia Pacatiana
3. Phrygia Salutaris
4. Asia
5. Lydia
6. Pisidia
7. Lycaonia
8. Caria
9. Pamphylia
10. Insulae
11. Lycia

Pontica
1. Bithynia
2. Honorias
3. Paphlagonia
4. Helenopontus
5. Pontus Polemoniacus
6. Galatia
7. Armenia I
8. Galatia Salutaris
9. Cappadocia II
10. Cappadocia I
11. Armenia II

Oriens
1. Isauria
2. Cilicia I
3. Cilicia II
4. Euphratensis
5. Mesopotamia
6. Syria
7. Osrhoene
8. Cyprus
9. Syria Salutaris
10. Phoenice
11. Phoenice Libanensis
12. Palaestina II
13. Arabia
14. Palestina I
15. Palestina Salutaris

Aegyptus
1. Libya Superior
2. Libya Inferior
3. Aegyptus
4. Augustamnica
5. Arcadia
6. Thebais

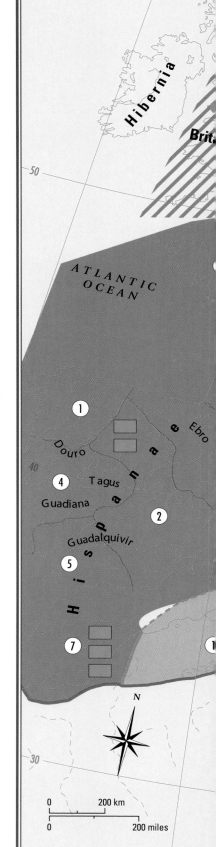

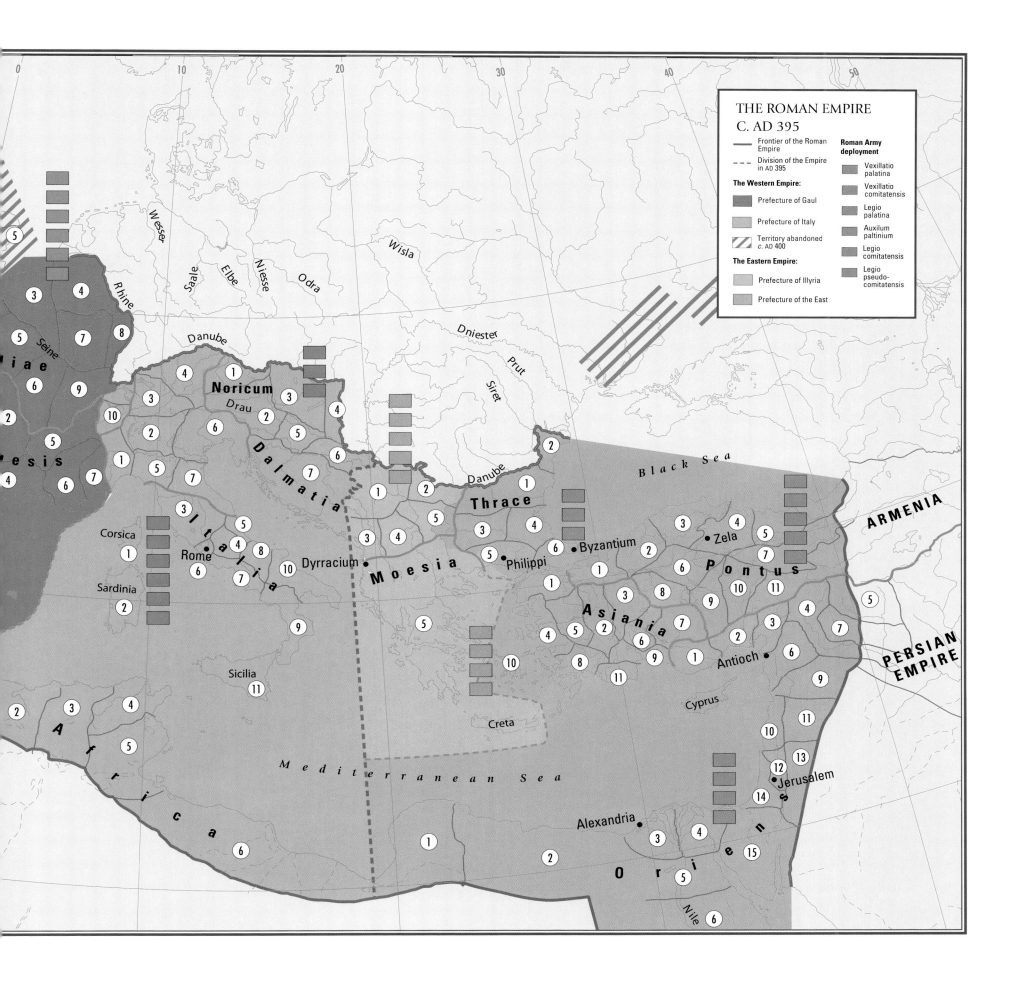

THE ROMAN EMPIRE
C. AD 395

Frontier of the Roman Empire	
Division of the Empire in AD 395	

The Western Empire:

Prefecture of Gaul

Prefecture of Italy

Territory abandoned c. AD 400

The Eastern Empire:

Prefecture of Illyria

Prefecture of the East

Roman Army deployment

Vexillatio palatina

Vexillatio comitatensis

Legio palatina

Auxilum paltinium

Legio comitatensis

Legio pseudo-comitatensis

GERMANIC KINGDOMS

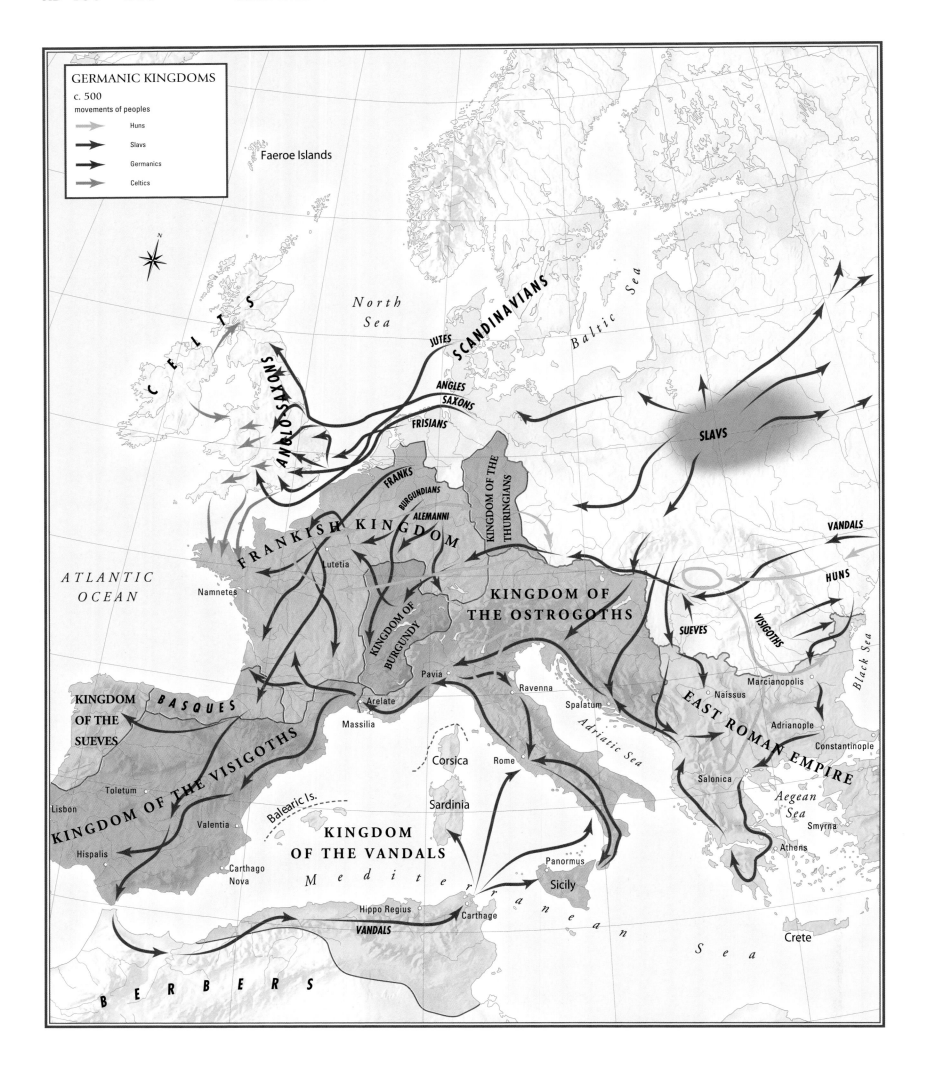

GERMANIC KINGDOMS
c. 500
movements of peoples

Huns
Slavs
Germanics
Celtics

Faeroe Islands

North Sea

Baltic Sea

CELTS

SCANDINAVIANS

JUTES

ANGLES

SAXONS

ANGLO-SAXONS

FRISIANS

SLAVS

FRANKS

BURGUNDIANS

ALEMANNI

KINGDOM OF THE THURINGIANS

VANDALS

FRANKISH KINGDOM

ATLANTIC OCEAN

Lutetia

Namnetes

KINGDOM OF BURGUNDY

KINGDOM OF THE OSTROGOTHS

HUNS

SUEVES

VISIGOTHS

Black Sea

Marcianopolis

Naissus

EAST ROMAN EMPIRE

KINGDOM OF THE SUEVES

BASQUES

Pavia

Ravenna

Spalatum

Adrianople

Constantinople

Arelate

Massilia

Adriatic Sea

Salonica

Aegean Sea

Smyrna

Toletum

KINGDOM OF THE VISIGOTHS

Corsica

Rome

Sardinia

Lisbon

Valentia

Balearic Is.

KINGDOM OF THE VANDALS

Mediterranean Sea

Panormus

Sicily

Athens

Hispalis

Carthago Nova

Hippo Regius

Carthage

Crete

VANDALS

BERBERS

ENEMY AT THE GATES

ENEMY AT THE GATES

By the 5th century, the Roman Empire was in a very parlous state. As more resources were needed to defend Rome itself, these were pulled back from the furthest outposts, such as Britain. The result was that invaders, such as the Saxons, who had been waiting for just such an opportunity, promptly, took advantage of the situation. One by one invaders overtook various regions in the empire. Some stayed as nominal allies of Rome, while some just sat back and waited for the rich pickings that they were sure would come their way.

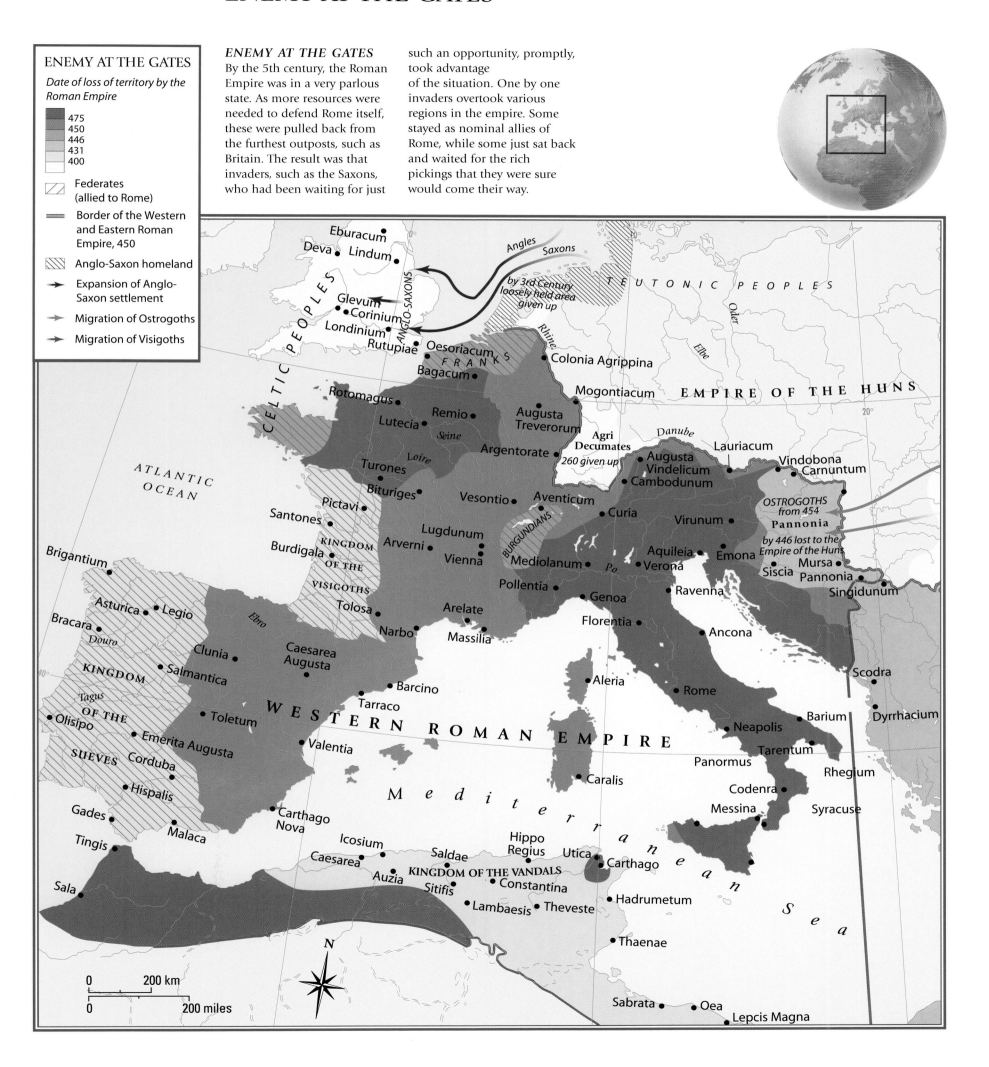

ENEMY AT THE GATES

Date of loss of territory by the Roman Empire

- 475
- 450
- 446
- 431
- 400

Federates (allied to Rome)

Border of the Western and Eastern Roman Empire, 450

Anglo-Saxon homeland

Expansion of Anglo-Saxon settlement

Migration of Ostrogoths

Migration of Visigoths

AD 527 – 565

EMPIRE OF JUSTINIAN

THE EMPIRE OF JUSTINIAN

Justinian had a great dream to reunite the lands of the old Roman Empire. It was an ambitious idea, but ultimately unrealistic. Although he never fought himself, his armies succeeded in recovering large stretches of land around the western Mediterranean basin that had been lost earlier. As a Christian Roman emperor he considered it his divine duty to restore the Roman Empire to its ancient boundaries. He achieved lasting fame through his judicial law reforms. Even more would probably have been achieved if there had not been an outbreak of plague in 542. Justinian caught it, but recovered.

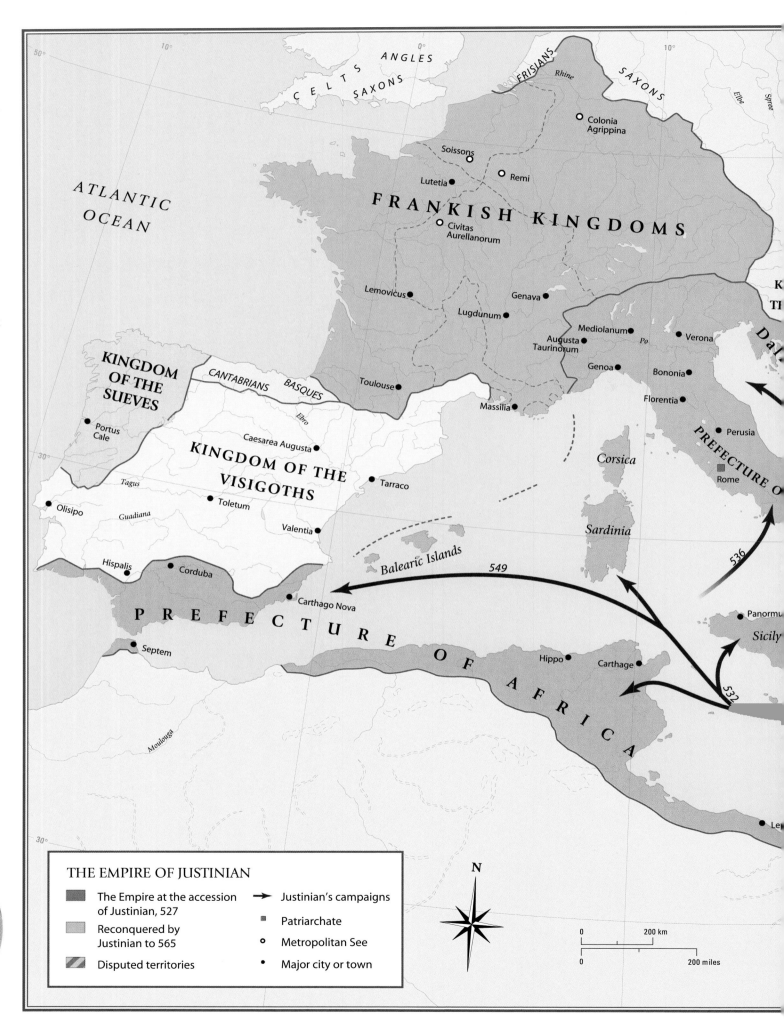

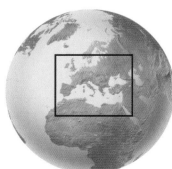

THE EMPIRE OF JUSTINIAN

▪ The Empire at the accession of Justinian, 527	→ Justinian's campaigns
▪ Reconquered by Justinian to 565	▪ Patriarchate
▨ Disputed territories	○ Metropolitan See
	● Major city or town

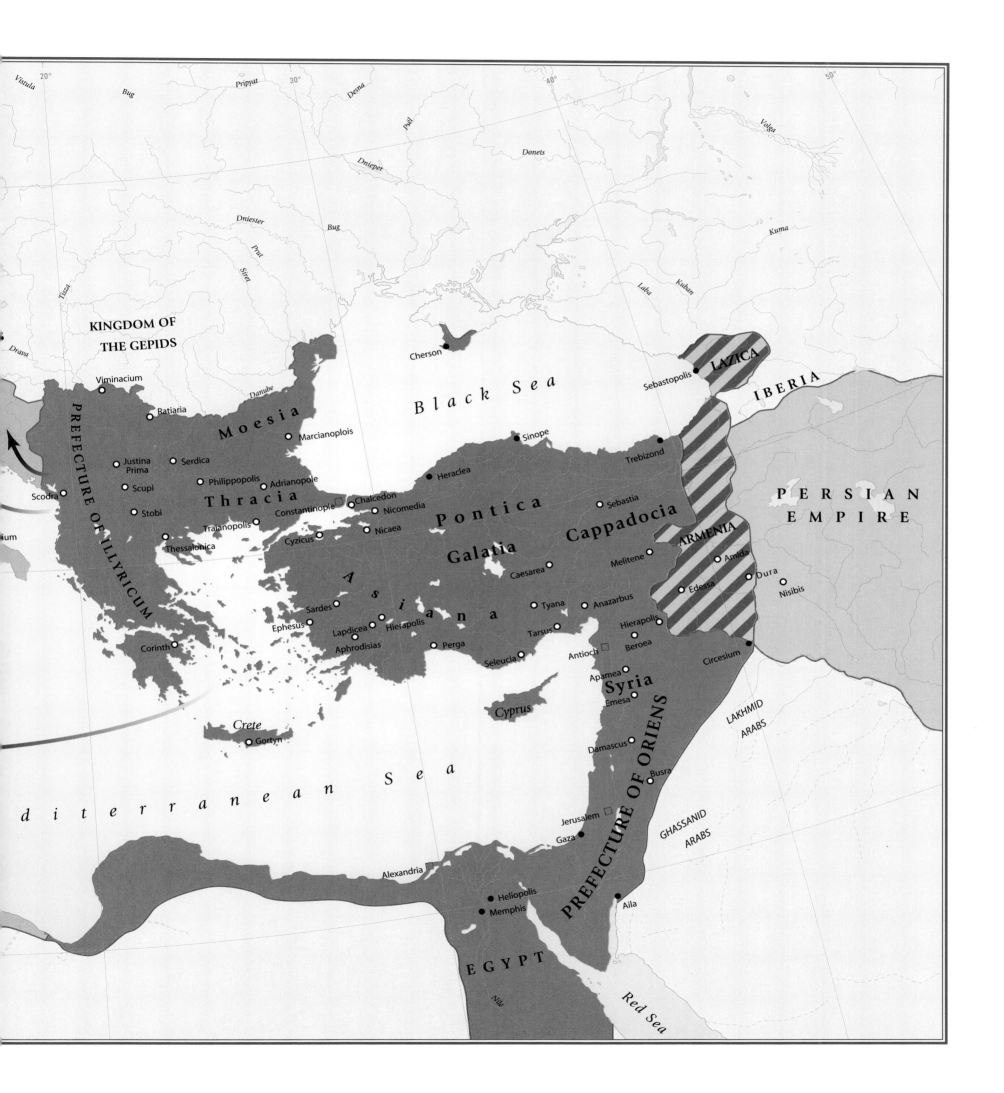

KINGDOM OF
THE GEPIDS

Black Sea

LAZICA

IBERIA

Cherson

Sebastopolis

Viminacium

PREFECTURE OF ILLYRICUM

Moesia

Ratiaria

Marcianoplois

Sinope

Trebizond

Justina
Prima

Serdica

Thracia

Philippopolis

Adrianople

Heraclea

Sebastia

P E R S I A N
E M P I R E

Scupi

Scodra

Stobi

Traianopolis

Chalcedon

Constantinople

Nicomedia

Pontica

Cappadocia

Melitene

ARMENIA

Amida

Dura

Thessalonica

Cyzicus

Nicaea

Galatia

Caesarea

Edessa

Nisibis

A
s
i
a
n
a

Sardes

Tyana

Anazarbus

Ephesus

Lapdicea

Hierapolis

Hierapolis

Aphrodisias

Perga

Tarsus

Beroea

Corinth

Seleucia

Antioch

Apamea

Syria

Circesium

Cyprus

Emesa

LAKHMID
ARABS

Crete

Gortyn

Damascus

Busra

PREFECTURE OF ORIENS

M e d i t e r r a n e a n   S e a

Jerusalem

GHASSANID
ARABS

Gaza

Alexandria

Aila

Heliopolis

Memphis

EGYPT

Nile

Red Sea

1453

THE FALL OF CONSTANTINOPLE

THE FALL OF CONSTANTINOPLE
The fall of Constantinople in May 1453 brought an end to the political independence of the millennium-old Byzantine Empire. By now all that was left were a few Greek monarchies. Most importantly it accelerated the scholarly exodus of Byzantine Greeks, who had introduced Classical Greek studies to the European Renaissance. In addition it made an important contribution to Ottoman political stability and its subsequent expansion in the Eastern Mediterranean and the Balkans. The date is also regarded by many as marking the end of the Middle Ages.

THE FALL OF
CONSTANTINOPLE
562–1430

extent of the
Byzantine empire

565
814
1095
1328
1430

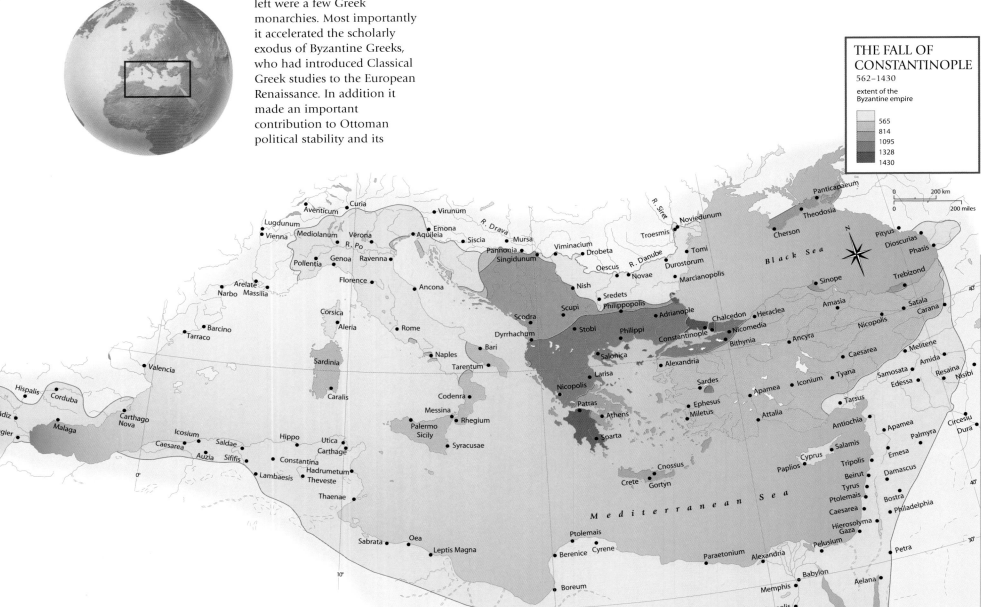

PART 5

INDIA

*I*NDIA SAW THE RISE AND FALL OF SEVERAL civilizations, the earliest known being that in the Indus Valley (c. 2750 BC) where there were large settlements at Harappa and Mohenjo-Daro. These peoples traded with Bahrain, Persia, and Afghanistan, and depended on agriculture grown on alluvial soil from the flooding Indus. The next major culture was the Mauryan. Founded by Chandragupta, an official in Magadha, it defeated Syrian Seleucid invaders. The dynasty reached its greatest extent under Asoka, a monarch who spread Buddhist principles throughout his territories. The empire collapsed soon after his death in 232 BC. Another major state was the Gupta (AD 320–535), created by Chandragupta I. The dynasty expanded its original Magadha lands to cover northern India, with a virtual client state in Vakataka. The Gupta era comprised Hindu classical civilization, which continued until Muslim conquest. The arts flourished with Bhoja (c. 1018–1060) writing books on astronomy, poetics, and architecture, while a Chalukya King, Kumarapda (1143–1172) converted to and evangelized Jainism. Muslim invasions in the 12th-century saw the establishment of a Delhi Sultanate. The last sultan, Mohammad ibn Tuhgluq, persecuted Hindus and Buddhists causing rebellion and territorial secessions. The sultanate was crushed by Timur at Panipat (1398).

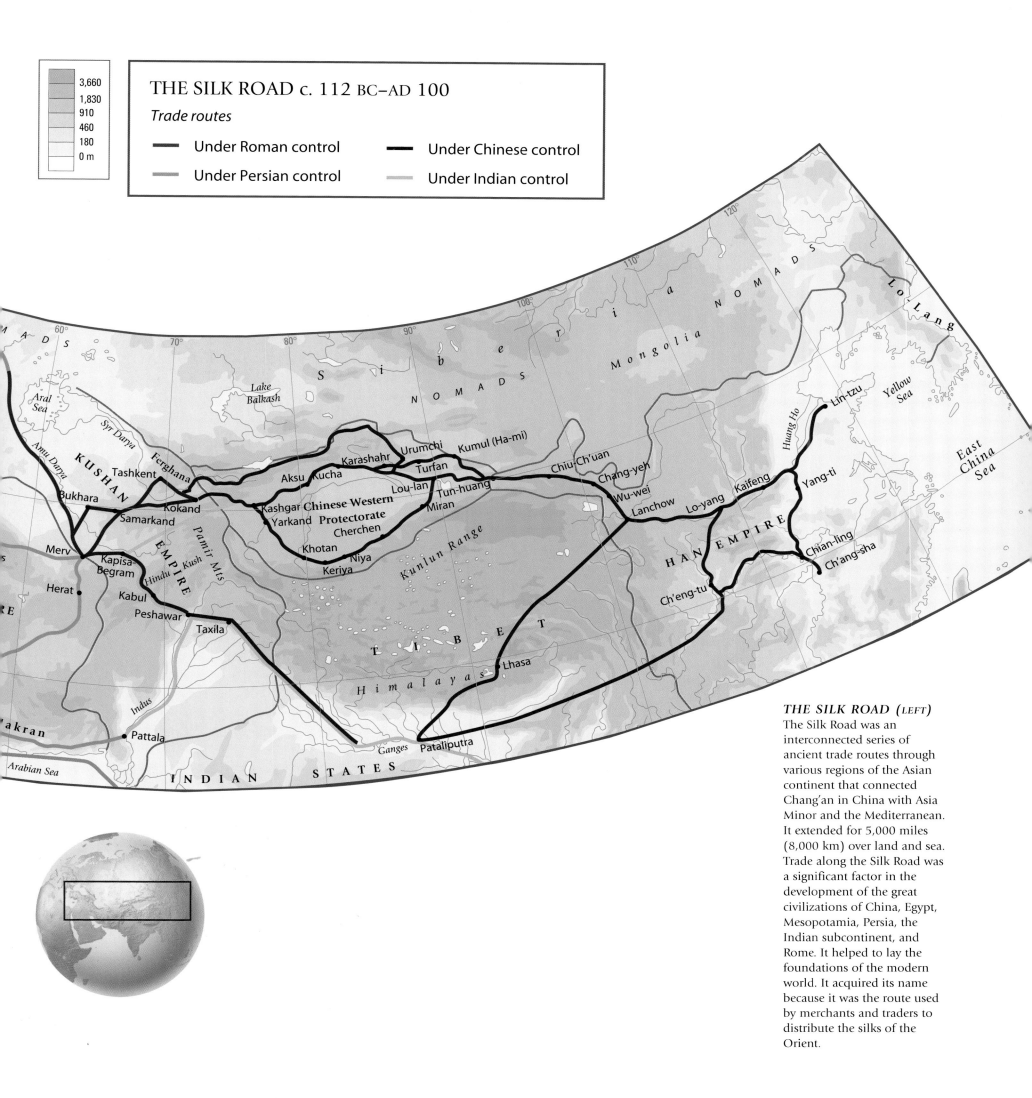

THE SILK ROAD c. 112 BC–AD 100

Trade routes

—— Under Roman control   —— Under Chinese control

—— Under Persian control   —— Under Indian control

3,660
1,830
910
460
180
0 m

Aral
Sea

Syr Darya

KUSHAN

Amu Darya

Bukhara

Kokand

Samarkand

Merv

Kapisa-
Begram

EMPIRE

Herat

Kabul
Hindu Kush

Peshawar

Taxila

Indus

Pattala

Arabian Sea

'akran

Tashkent

Ferghana

Aksu Kucha

Kashgar

Yarkand

Khotan

Keriya

Niya

Pamir Mts.

Lake
Balkash

S   i   b   e   r   i   a

NOMADS

Karashahr

Urumchi

Turfan

Lou-lan

Miran

Cherchen

Chinese Western
Protectorate

Kunlun Range

TIBET

Himalayas   Lhasa

Ganges   Pataliputra

INDIAN   STATES

Kumul (Ha-mi)

Tun-huang

NOMADS

Mongolia

Chiu-Ch'uan

Chang-yeh

Wu-wei

Lanchow

Ch'eng-tu

Huang Ho

Lin-tzu

Yellow
Sea

Lo-Lang

East
China
Sea

Yang-ti

Chian-ling

Ch'ang-sha

Lo-yang   Kaifeng

HAN   EMPIRE

THE SILK ROAD (LEFT)

The Silk Road was an
interconnected series of
ancient trade routes through
various regions of the Asian
continent that connected
Chang'an in China with Asia
Minor and the Mediterranean.
It extended for 5,000 miles
(8,000 km) over land and sea.
Trade along the Silk Road was
a significant factor in the
development of the great
civilizations of China, Egypt,
Mesopotamia, Persia, the
Indian subcontinent, and
Rome. It helped to lay the
foundations of the modern
world. It acquired its name
because it was the route used
by merchants and traders to
distribute the silks of the
Orient.

AD 2

THE HAN EMPIRE

THE HAN EMPIRE
The reign of the Han Dynasty of China lasted for about 400 years from 206 BC to AD 220. It is commonly considered within China to have been one of the greatest periods in Chinese history. During this dynasty China officially became a Confucian state and there was much prosperity. Agriculture, handicrafts, and commerce all flourished and the population reached 55 million. As with all civilizations, trade was vital. Many major trade routes developed, both within China and externally through the route known as the Silk Road.

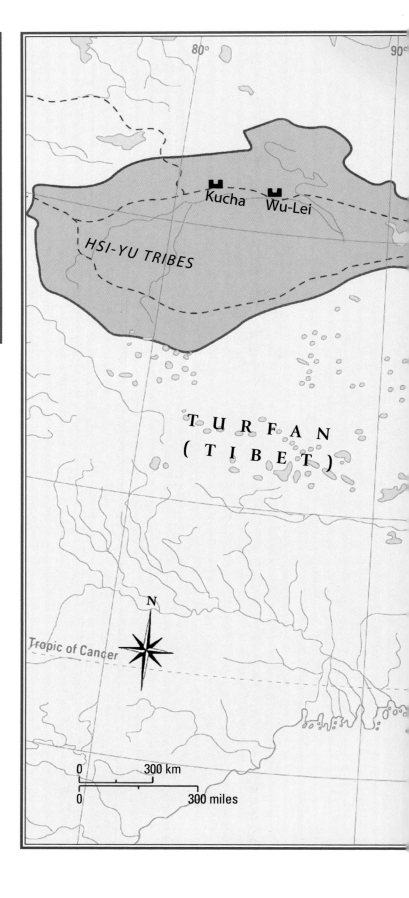

THE HAN EMPIRE AD 2

- ■ Principality
- ■ Commandery
- ■ Protectorate
- ▨ Fluctuating Han control
- --- Province boundary
- ᨆᨆ Great Wall
- ≡≡≡ Road or major trade route
- • Major trading city
- ⊔ Fort
- — Northern limit of wheat cultivation
- — Northern limit of rice cultivation

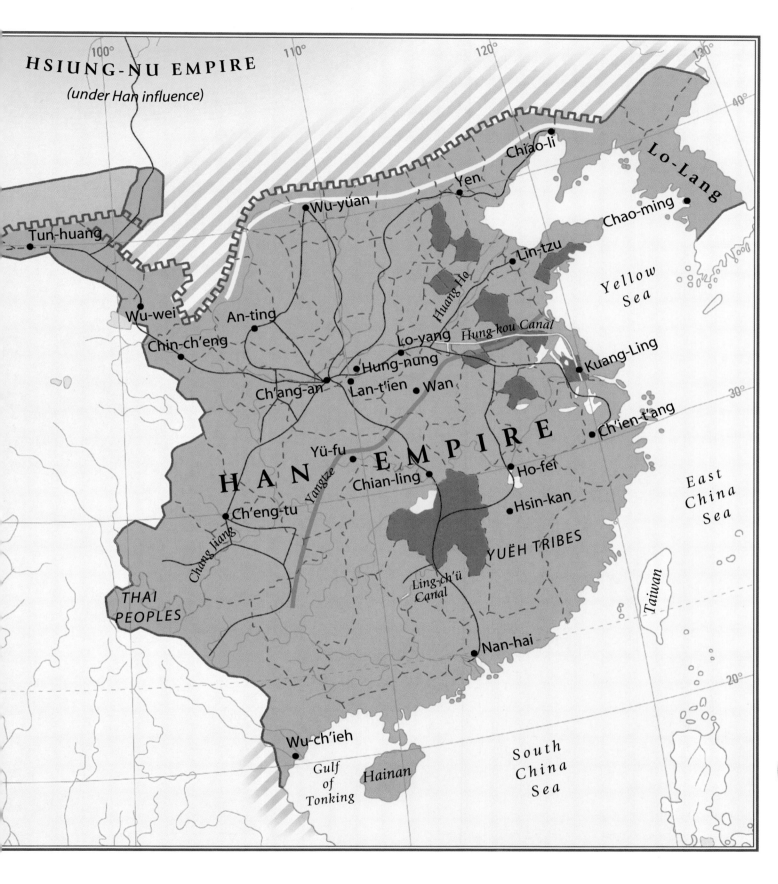

HSIUNG-NU EMPIRE

(under Han influence)

Tun-huang

Wu-wei

Chin-ch'eng

An-ting

Wu-yüan

Yen

Chiao-li

Lo-Lang

Chao-ming

Lin-tzu

Yellow Sea

Huang Ho

Lo-yang

Hung-kou Canal

Hung-nung

Ch'ang-an

Lan-t'ien

Wan

Kuang-Ling

Ch'ien-t'ang

H A N · E M P I R E

Yü-fu

Yangtze

Chian-ling

Ho-fei

Hsin-kan

East China Sea

Ch'eng-tu

Chang Jiang

YUËH TRIBES

Taiwan

THAI PEOPLES

Ling-ch'ü Canal

Nan-hai

Wu-ch'ieh

Gulf of Tonking

Hainan

South China Sea

AD 220 – 280

THREE KINGDOMS

THREE KINGDOMS

The end of the Han Dynasty saw China return to a long period of disunity and strife. It began with the Three Kingdoms, ruled by the Wei, the Wu, and the Shu, each of whom was trying to reunite China under its own leadership. The Wei eventually conquered the Shu in 263. A militant Wei leader, Wu Ti, became emperor and founded the Chin Dynasty. He defeated the Wu in 280, which ended the Three Kingdoms period and reunited China.

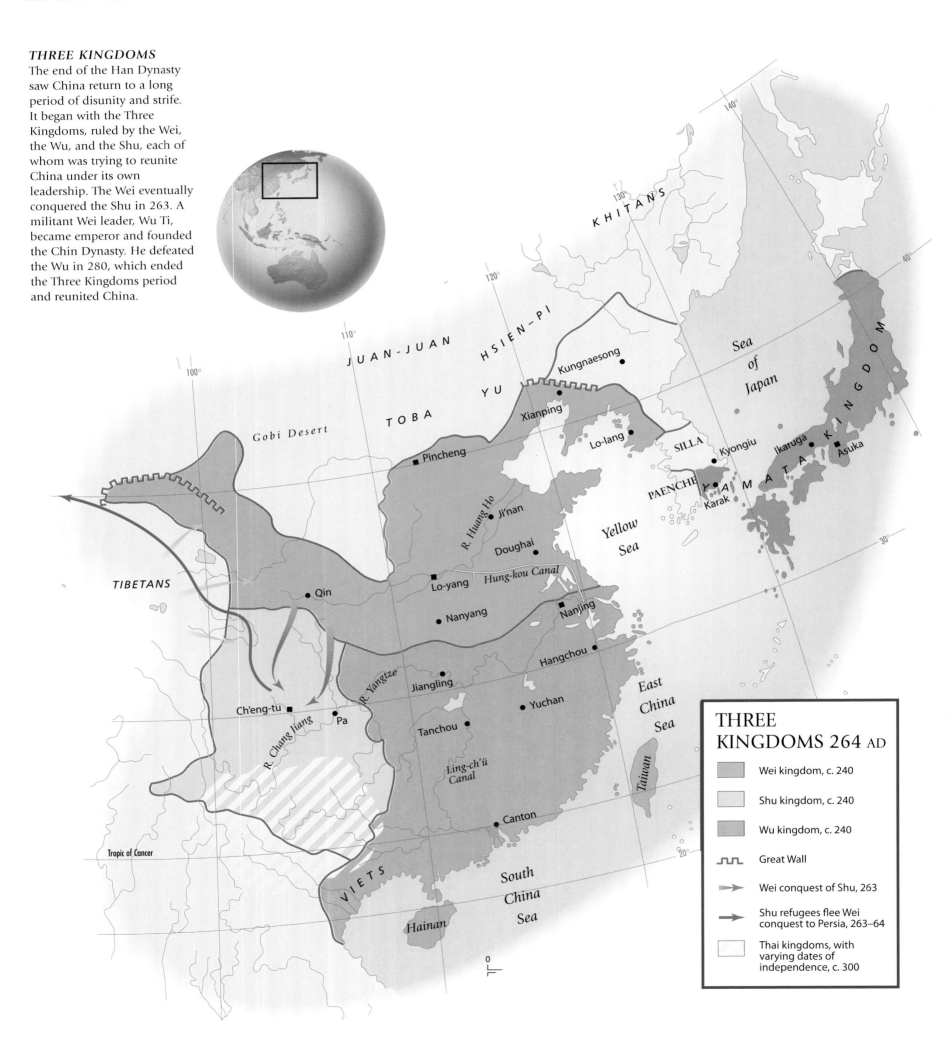

THREE KINGDOMS 264 AD

	Wei kingdom, c. 240
	Shu kingdom, c. 240
	Wu kingdom, c. 240
⊓⊔	Great Wall
→	Wei conquest of Shu, 263
→	Shu refugees flee Wei conquest to Persia, 263–64
	Thai kingdoms, with varying dates of independence, c. 300

CONFUCIUS IN CHINA 550 BC

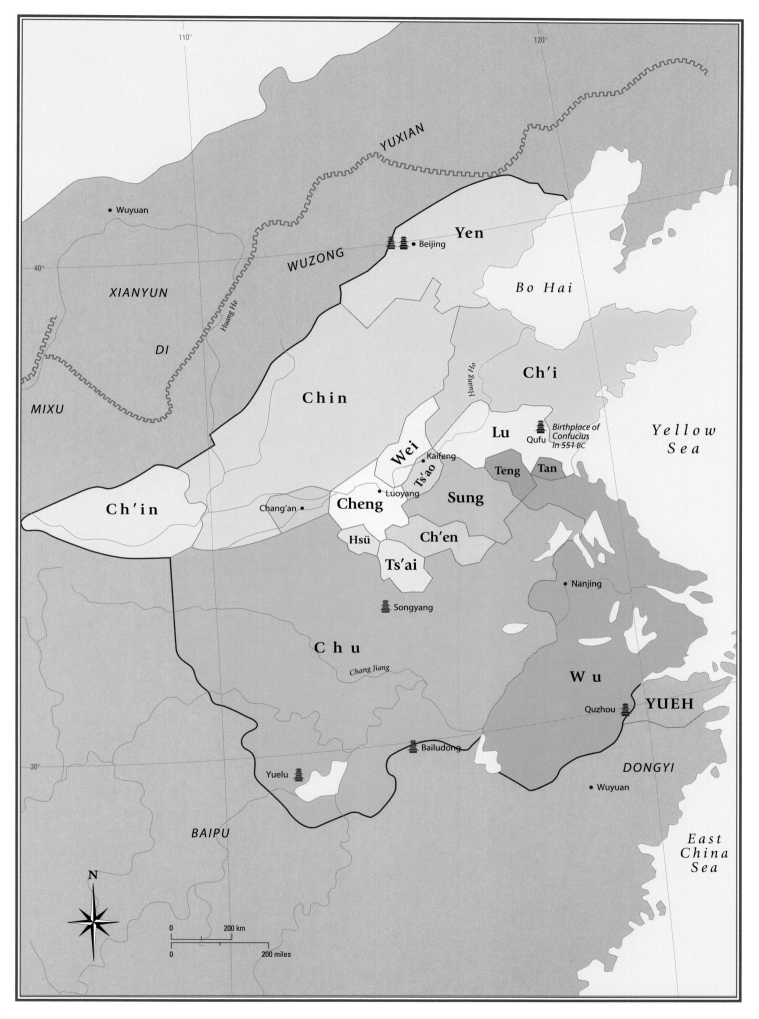

According to tradition Confucius was born in 551 BC. There are various legends about his early life, but at some point he set out on a journey or series of journeys around the small kingdoms of northeast and central China. Confucius presented himself as a "transmitter who invented nothing." He placed great emphasis on the importance of study. He also championed strong family loyalty, ancestor worship, respect for elders by their children, and the family as a basis for an ideal government. One of his favorite principles was not to do to others what you would not like done to yourself.

CONFUCIUS IN CHINA 550 BC

- 🛕 Confucian Temple
- 🛕 Confucian academy
- • Capitals of China from 4th Century BC
- — Zhou China border
- ⊓⊔ Wall of China
- ▨ States with Confucian influence
- *MIXU* Barbarian tribe

THE SUI AND T'ANG DYNASTIES

1206 – 1259

THE SUI AND T'ANG DYNASTIES

The Sui and T'ang dynasties are often discussed together. The Sui extended the Grand Canal, built granaries around their three capitals, and fortified the Great Wall. They attacked Korea four times but were always defeated. Their dynasty collapsed and was succeeded by the T'ang, who improved trade routes by building more canals and improved the administrative systems. They also began a program of land reforms that gave land back to the peasants. This move led to an increase in the rice crop and produced a higher tax revenue. Horses were very important and played a large part in T'ang empire building, since cavalry was the only way to defeat marauding nomads. The T'ang made inroads into large parts of Asia and captured most of the Korean peninsula. The T'ang also produced China's only empress, Wu Chao, who usurped the throne in 690. Her reign led to a brief period of instability until the male line was restored.

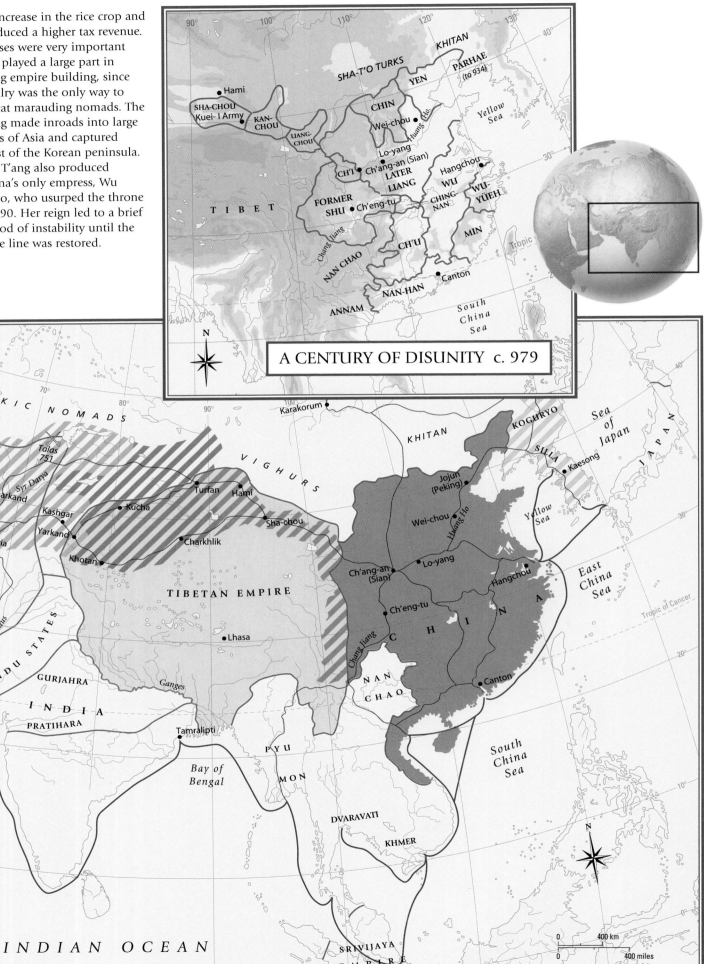

A CENTURY OF DISUNITY c. 979

THE T'ANG EMPIRE
c. 700

- Chinese Empire under the T'ang dynasty
- T'ang protectorate, 645–763
- T'ang protectorate, 659–69
- T'ang protectorate, 668–76
- Abbasid caliphate, c. 751
- Tibetan Empire, c. 800
- Road or trade route
- Sea trade route
- Battle

THE EMPIRE OF THE GREAT KHAN

A CENTURY OF DISUNITY (LEFT)

The end of the T'ang Dynasty saw the Chinese empire fractured once more into five dynasties in the north and ten kingdoms in the south. Despite the political disunity trade flourished through tea exports and the development of porcelain. The new skill of printing played an important role in providing books for the education of the populace and in the production of a new system of paper money. However, Buddhism suffered a sharp decline as temples were closed and monks were forced back to a secular lifestyle.

THE EMPIRE OF THE GREAT KHAN

Kublai Khan was the grandson of Genghis Khan. He was the last Great Khan of the Mongol Empire and the first Emperor of the Chinese Yuan Dynasty. He succeeded his elder brother in 1260 and immediately set about crushing any opposition. The empire was divided into four khanates, each ruled by a separate khan and overseen by Kublai Khan himself, who controlled Mongolia and eventually the whole of

China. The empire reached its greatest extent in 1279 with Kublai's conquest of the Song Dynasty of China. He maintained stability throughout the whole region and died in 1294 at the age of 79.

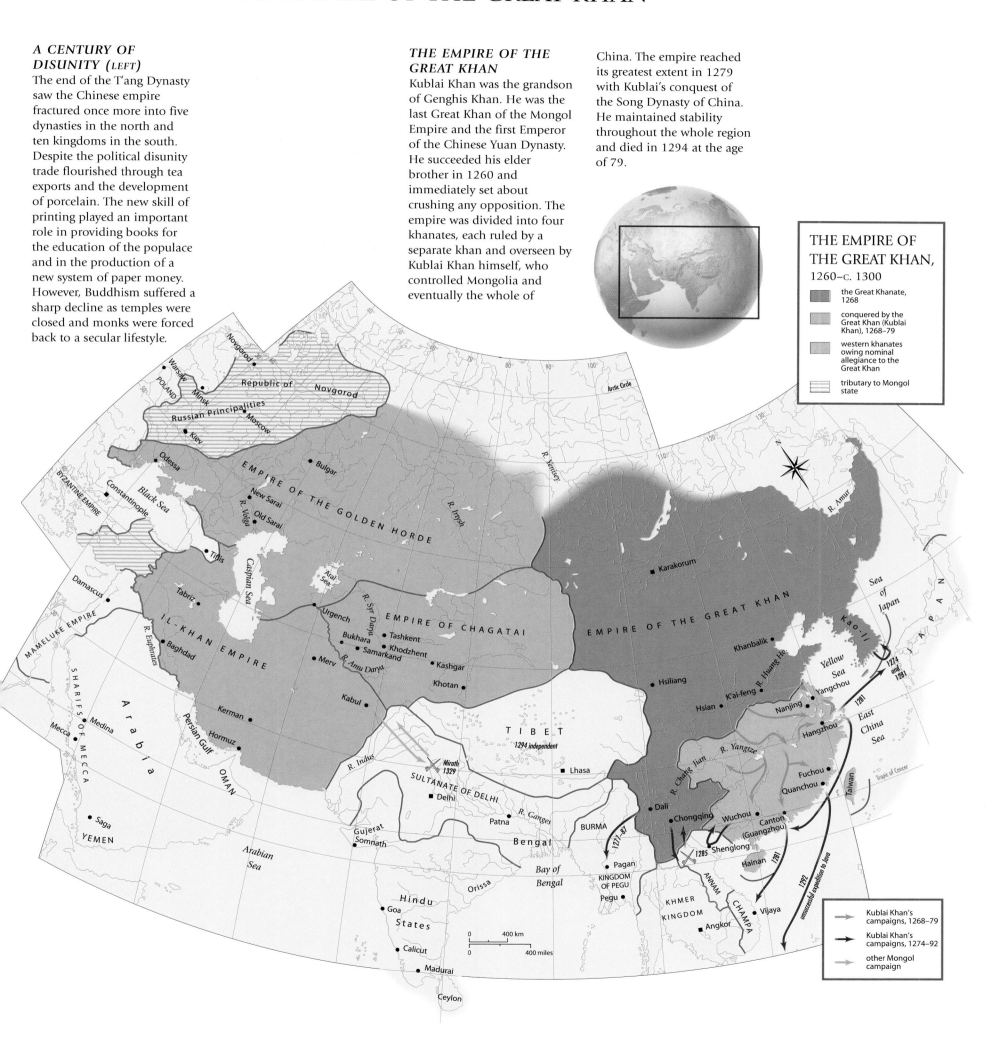

THE EMPIRE OF THE GREAT KHAN, 1260–c. 1300

- the Great Khanate, 1268
- conquered by the Great Khan (Kublai Khan), 1268–79
- western khanates owing nominal allegiance to the Great Khan
- tributary to Mongol state

→ Kublai Khan's campaigns, 1268–79
→ Kublai Khan's campaigns, 1274–92
→ other Mongol campaign

MONGOL CONQUESTS

MONGOL CONQUESTS

Genghis Khan founded the Mongol Empire in 1206 after he had united the Mongol tribes. He became one of the most significant and successful military leaders in history. In Mongolia he is regarded as the father of the nation, but elsewhere he is seen as a ruthless and bloodthirsty conqueror who was responsible for wars of aggression and destruction that resulted in the violent deaths of tens of millions of people. Although he died in 1227, under his sons and grandsons the empire continued to grow, eventually stretching from the Sea of Japan to the Black Sea.

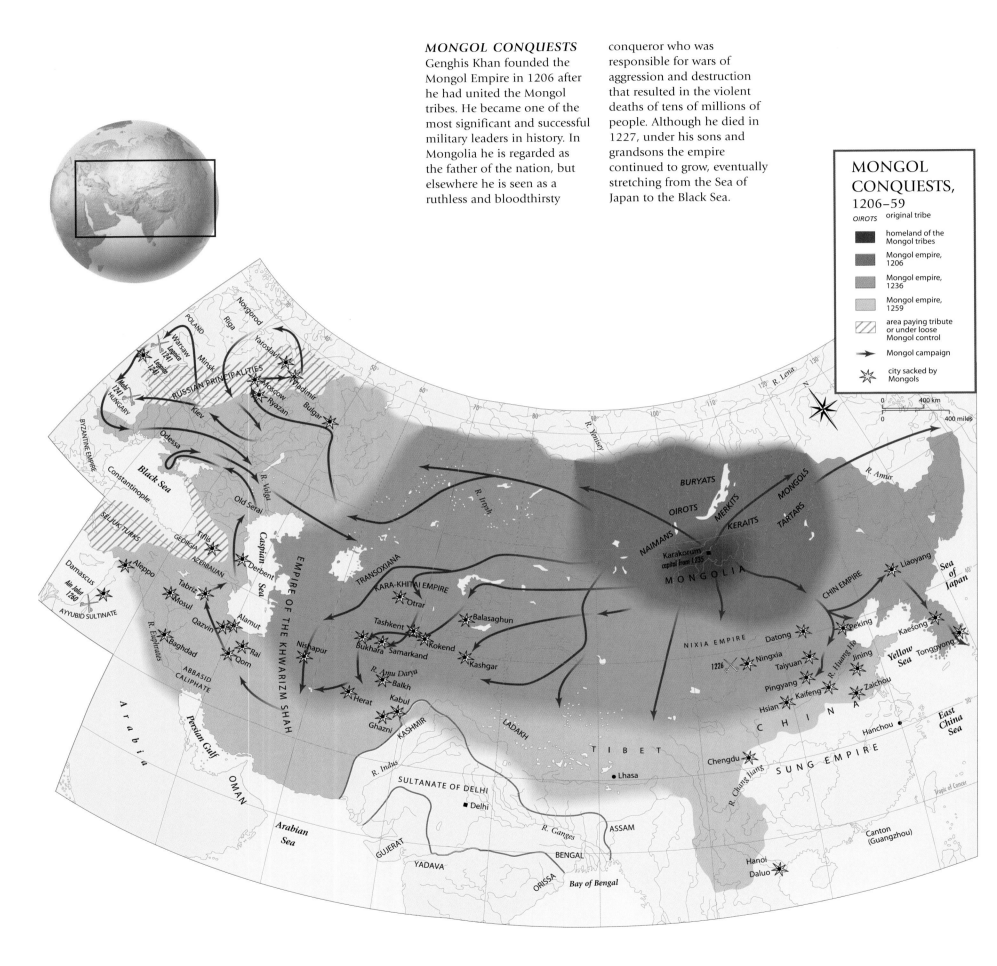

MONGOL CONQUESTS, 1206–59

OIROTS original tribe

- homeland of the Mongol tribes
- Mongol empire, 1206
- Mongol empire, 1236
- Mongol empire, 1259
- area paying tribute or under loose Mongol control
- → Mongol campaign
- ✶ city sacked by Mongols

0 400 km
0 400 miles

PART 7

JAPAN

THE ORIGINS OF JAPAN ARE SHROUDED IN mystery. Socially, the inhabitants were organised into clans, a large group of these (*uji*) would be ruled by a clan chief (*uji-no-kami*) who also acted as a priest. The imperial clan, the Yamato, gradually established suzerainty over much of central and western Japan, and even parts of Korea, thereby forming a conduit for Chinese ideas and civilisation, Korean immigrants, and Buddhism. Chinese politics demanded the centralisation of power in imperial hands and the Yamato copied this, extending their lands and authority. Buddhism was supported by the powerful Soga clan, which dominated the imperial court even to

the extent of murdering emperors, thereby ensuring the unimpeded spread of their chosen faith. While Empress Suiko (AD 593–628) ruled using Chinese political methods, her heir, Crown Prince Sh'toku, established Buddhism fully and issued the Seventeen Article Constitution (604). Relations were established with T'ang China. Meanwhile, the Soga kingmaker, Iruka, was assassinated to remove Soga influence over the imperial family. The future Emperor Tenchi (661–672) led a coup d'état aided by Nakatomi Kamatari, founder of the new Fujiwara clan. The demise of the Soga led to a cycle of far-reaching reforms in the Taika (great change) period

600 – 1500 SHINTOISM IN JAPAN

SHINTOISM IN JAPAN 600–1500

Shintoism is the native religion of Japan and was once its state religion. After World War II Shinto lost its status as the state religion of Japan. Many of the old Shinto traditions have been dropped and most of those that remain no longer have any religious significance. For around a thousand years Shinto happily existed in combination with Buddhism, but in 1868 this practice was banned. Shinto became the official religion and the Emperor was worshipped as a god. Shintoism and patriotism became intertwined and became more pronounced as time progressed.

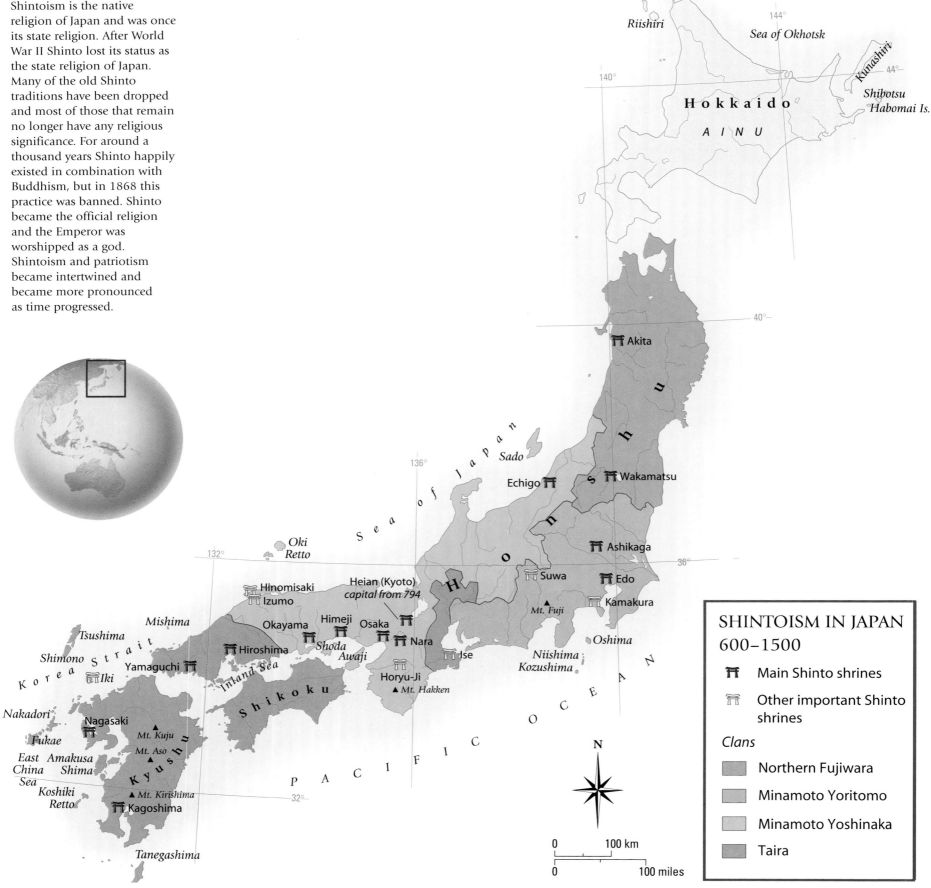

SHINTOISM IN JAPAN 600–1500

⛩ Main Shinto shrines

⛩ Other important Shinto shrines

Clans

Northern Fujiwara

Minamoto Yoritomo

Minamoto Yoshinaka

Taira

0   100 km
0   100 miles

THE TAIKA REFORMS IN JAPAN 646–710

TAIKA REFORMS

In AD 646 the emperor Kotoku began a series of top-down reforms to Japanese society, government, land, and laws. They began with land reform based on Confucian ideas and philosophies from China, but the true aim of the reforms was to bring about greater centralization and to enhance the power of the imperial court, which was also based on Chinese governmental structure. Students and envoys were sent to China to learn about the system of Chinese writing, its literature, religion, and architecture and even its dietary habits. The impact of these reforms can still be seen in Japanese cultural life after 1350 years.

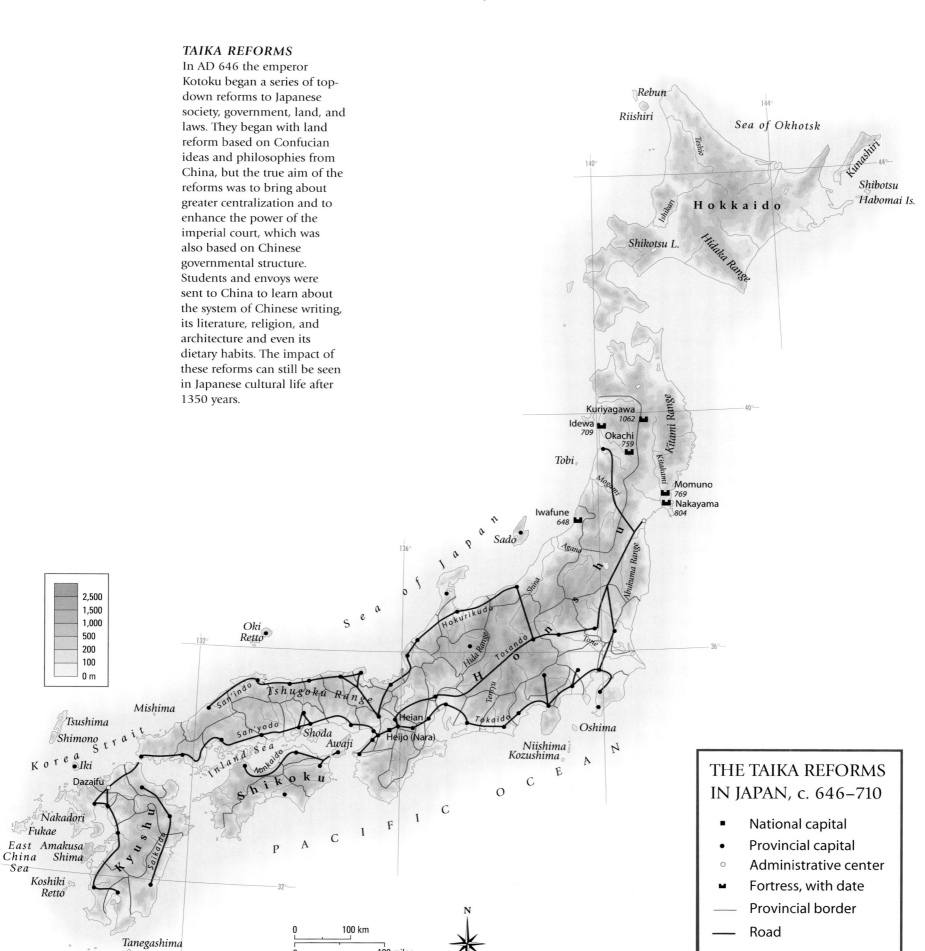

THE TAIKA REFORMS
IN JAPAN, c. 646–710

- ■ National capital
- ● Provincial capital
- ○ Administrative center
- ⚏ Fortress, with date
- — Provincial border
- — Road

C. 794 – 1185 — WARRIOR JAPAN

WARRIOR JAPAN

Among the worst failures of the Taika reforms of the 640s were land and taxation reforms that resulted in the impoverishment of many farmers, who then had to sell their properties and become tenants of larger landowners. Many of these aristocratic landowners had tax immunity, as did Buddhist monasteries. As a result, political power gradually shifted from central government to large independent landowners, many of whom hired samurai to protect their properties. A growing warrior class emerged, with a number of warlords, leading to national conflict as they wrestled for supremacy. Eventually Minamoto Yoritomo succeeded as leader of Japan and was appointed Shogun.

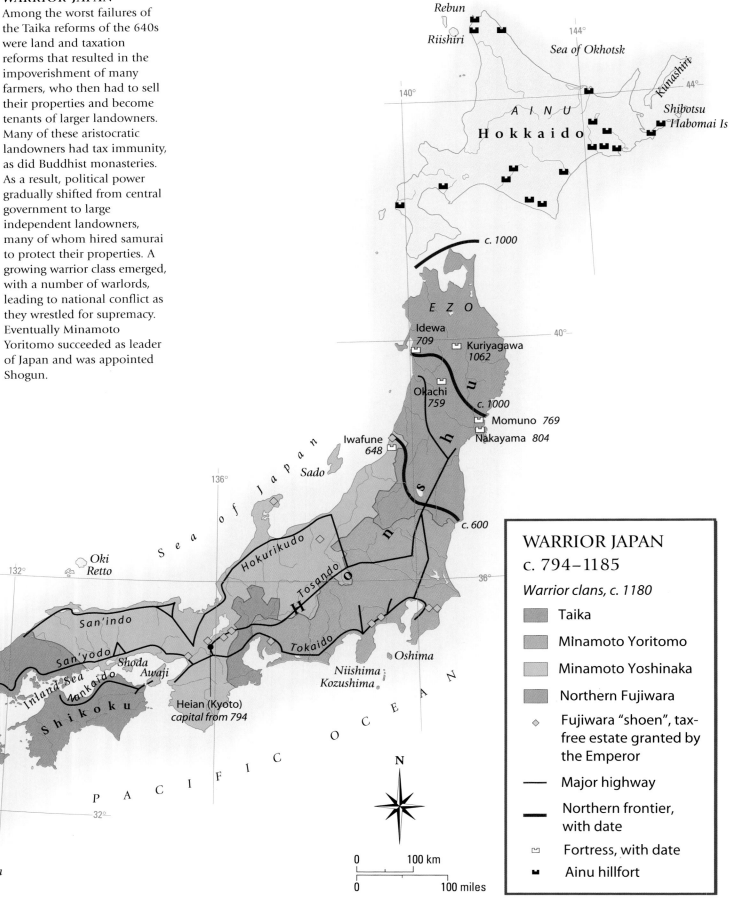

WARRIOR JAPAN
c. 794–1185

Warrior clans, c. 1180

- Taika
- MInamoto Yoritomo
- Minamoto Yoshinaka
- Northern Fujiwara
- ◇ Fujiwara "shoen", tax-free estate granted by the Emperor
- —— Major highway
- —— Northern frontier, with date
- ⊡ Fortress, with date
- ◾ Ainu hillfort

PART 8

CENTRAL AND SOUTHERN AMERICA

MESOAMERICA GAVE BIRTH TO A VARIETY OF societies who used the surpluses from their sophisticated agricultural systems to convert subsistence villages into urban civilizations. These were generally characterized by monuments and towns such as Teotihuacán, with its plazas and temples surmounting large platforms reached by stairs. The societies developed hieroglyphics, calendar calculations, and ritual ballgames but metalware was absent until AD 800. Among the important cultures were the Olmecs, Toltecs, Maya, and Zapotec, which developed remarkable religious architecture and empires controlled by force. Events concerning leaders and conquests were often represented by stone carvings. Possibly, the most significant civilization was the Maya, lasting from c. 250 BC–AD 1519. Elsewhere, the Valley of Mexico was home not just to the impact of Toltec culture but to the Aztecs, skilled agricultural and hydraulic engineers whose farming techniques sustained a large urban population and an army. The Andean civilizations are popularly remembered through tourism to Incan Machu Pichu. Cultures existed on the coasts (the Caral) and in the Chavín and Moche societies, often noted for their mummification practices. Later civilizations included the Nazca and Huari, followed by the Chimú with their metropolis at Chanchan. The most noticeable Andean state was the Inca, which had a hierarchical society ruled by the absolutist Sapa Inca.

CULTURE LEVELS IN CENTRAL AND SOUTH AMERICA

6000-1500BC

CULTURES OF CENTRAL AND SOUTH AMERICA

Culture and civilization have always gone hand in hand with quality of resources to sustain them. If the community was settled in a rich agricultural area or an area with plentiful natural resources, it would tend to be wealthy. On the other hand, if it was a community of hunter-gatherers who existed by subsistence, the likelihood would be a poorer level of civilization. South and Central America developed a number of important civilizations over a considerable period of time. These were mainly concentrated in the Central America strip and down the west coast of South America between the Pacific and the Andes Mountains.

CULTURES IN SOUTH AMERICA

- high civilization empires
- theocratic and militaristic chiefdoms
- tropical forest farm villages
- desert farm villages
- nomadic hunting, fishing, and gathering peoples

CULTURES OF CENTRAL AND SOUTH AMERICA

CULTURAL AREAS OF MESOAMERICA

Mesoamerica, literally "middle America," was inhabited by a number of complex indigenous pre-Columbian cultures. These exhibited a range of common cultural characteristics. Several well-known Mesoamerican cultures include the Olmec, Teotihuacán, the Maya and the Aztec. As different cultures developed they were forced to adapt themselves to their environment. In Central Mexico, for example, with its high cool valleys and low rainfall, irrigation schemes were developed. Oaxaca is a mountainous area that has been occupied since prehistoric times. Excavations have uncovered ancient remains that are about 3500 years old.

EARLY CIVILISATIONS – PERU

The Chavin culture, dating from around 900 BC, has long been regarded as the first civilisation of South America. It spread throughout the Andean region, leaving behind its distinctive stone sculptures. By around 200 BC the Chavins had declined, to be replaced by more localised cultures, notably the Moches to the north and the Nazcas to the south. In about the fifth century AD the centre of Andean civilisation moved from the coastal area up into the highlands, leading to the growth of a new empire that preceded the Inca and to the creation of cities such as Tiahuanaco on the banks of Lake Titicaca on the Peru-Bolivia border.

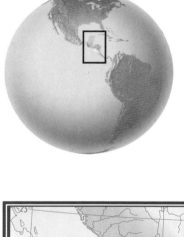

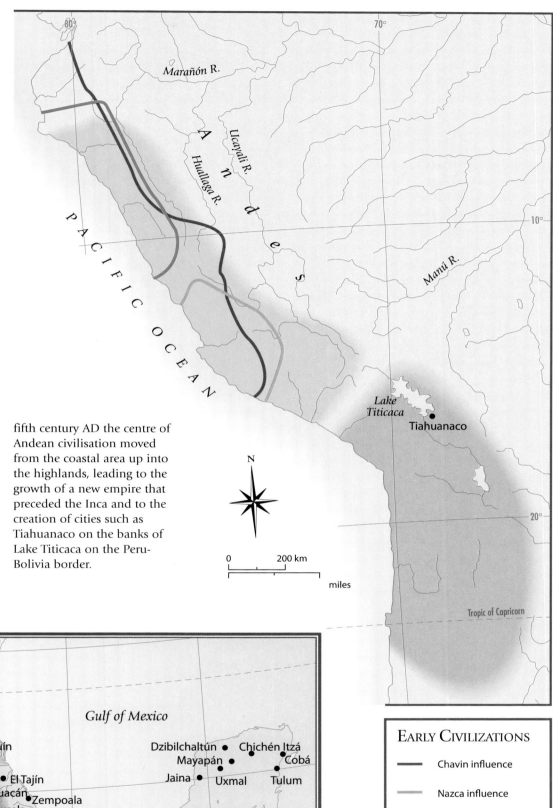

CULTURAL AREAS IN MESOAMERICA

- Northeast frontier
- Northwest frontier
- Western Mexico
- Central Mexico
- Puebla-Oaxaca Highlands
- Oaxaca
- Coastal zones
- Maya Lowlands
- Maya Highlands

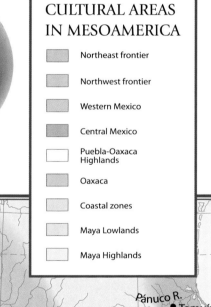

EARLY CIVILIZATIONS

- Chavin influence
- Nazca influence
- Moche influence
- Huari empire
- Tiahuanacan empire, AD 500–1000

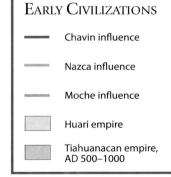

1200 BC – AD 1500 OLMEC CIVILIZATION

OLMEC CIVILISATION
The Olmec civilization was the earliest civilization in Central America and possibly the earliest civilization in the whole of the Americas. Originally they lived in the Gulf Coast region of southern Mexico, but soon expanded into what is now Guatemala. Olmec society was very simple. Elite people lived in small urban areas, while common people lived in rural areas. Since the Olmec were predominately agricultural people, it was the common people who effectively supported the elite. They were the first civilization to build pyramids. Around 300 BC the civilization suddenly vanished and nobody has ever been able to give a reason why.

THE MAYA (RIGHT)
The first Maya settlements were established on the Pacific coast around 1800 BC, but in the pre-Classic period important sites were established at El Mirador in the southern Maya lowlands an at Dzibilchaltun in the north.

The Classic Period AD 300–900
The Classic Period saw a peak in large-scale construction and urbanization. This mainly took place in the lowland regions, where there was a period of significant artistic and intellectual development. An agriculturally intensive city-centered empire developed, consisting of numerous independent city-states. In the central lowlands these include well-known cities such as Tikal, Palenque, and Copan. There were also large population centres in the north, such as Oxintok and Uxmal. The most notable monuments of this time were the pyramids. These were built in Mayan religious centers and close to the palaces of their leaders.

The Postclassical Period AD 900–1500
During the 8th and 9th centuries the Mayan centers in the southern lowlands went into a decline, but the Mayan cities of the Yucatan continued to flourish. Maypan ruled all of Yucatan until a revolt in 1450. After the revolt the region degenerated into a group of competing city-states until the Spanish eventually conquered the peninsula.

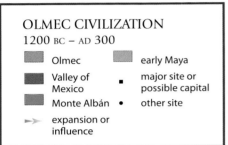

OLMEC CIVILIZATION
1200 BC – AD 300

- Olmec
- Valley of Mexico
- Monte Albán
- early Maya
- ■ major site or possible capital
- • other site
- → expansion or influence

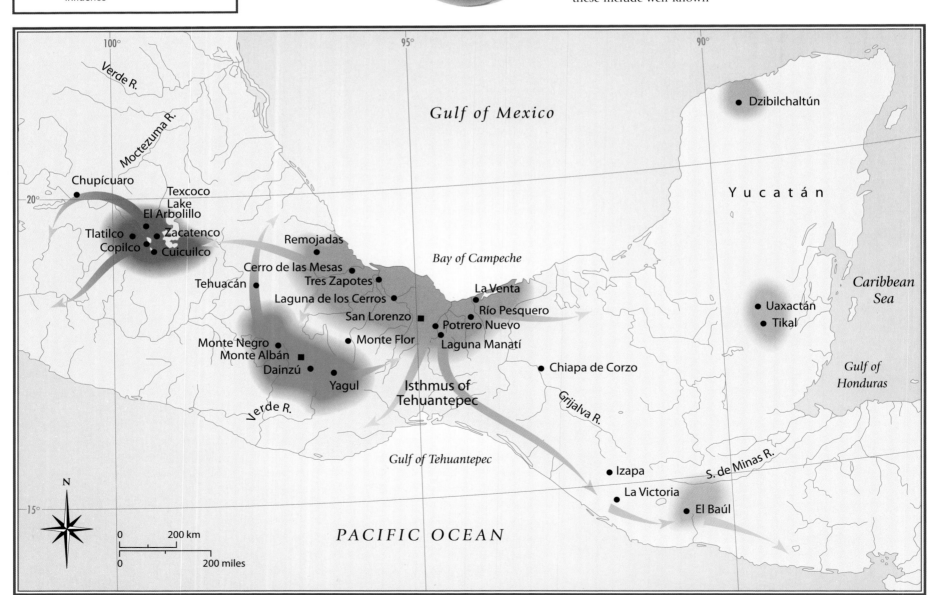

THE MAYA AD 150 – 1200

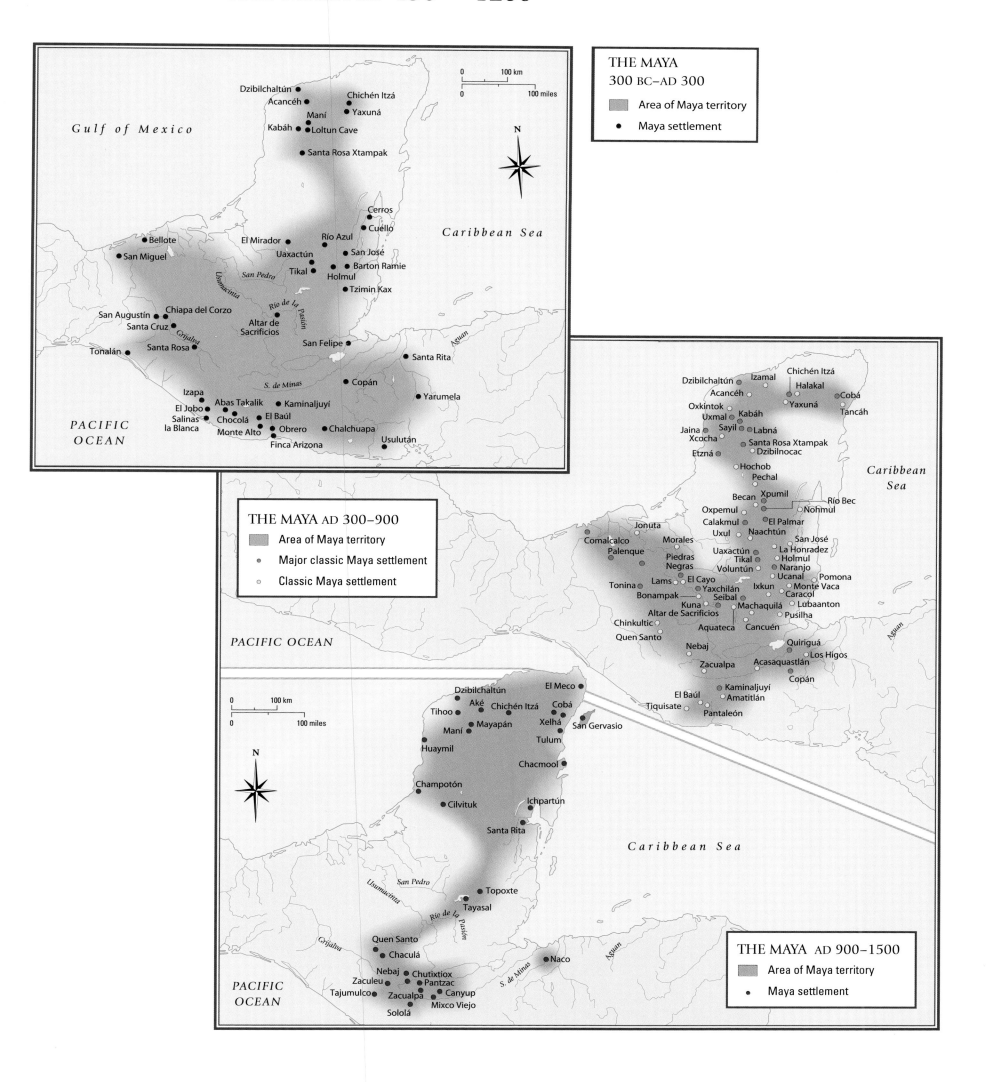

THE MAYA
300 BC–AD 300
Area of Maya territory
● Maya settlement

0   100 km
0   100 miles

Gulf of Mexico

Dzibilchaltún
Acancéh
Maní
Chichén Itzá
Yaxuná
Kabáh
Loltun Cave
Santa Rosa Xtampak

Caribbean Sea

N

Cerros
Cuéllo
Bellote
El Mirador
Río Azul
San José
Uaxactún
Barton Ramie
Tikal
Holmul
San Miguel
Tzimin Kax
San Pedro
Usumacinta
Río de la Pasión
Chiapa del Corzo
San Augustín
Santa Cruz
Grijalva
Altar de Sacrificios
Tonalán
Santa Rosa
San Felipe
Aguan
Santa Rita
S. de Minas
Copán
Izapa
Yarumela
El Jobo
Abas Takalik
Kaminaljuyí
Salinas
la Blanca
Chocolá
El Baúl
Monte Alto
Obrero
Chalchuapa
Finca Arizona
Usulután
PACIFIC
OCEAN

THE MAYA AD 300–900
Area of Maya territory
● Major classic Maya settlement
○ Classic Maya settlement

PACIFIC OCEAN

Dzibilchaltún
Izamal
Chichén Itzá
Acancéh
Halakal
Oxkintok
Yaxuná
Cobá
Uxmal
Kabáh
Tancáh
Jaina
Sayil
Labná
Xcocha
Santa Rosa Xtampak
Etzná
Dzibilnocac
Hochob
Caribbean
Sea
Pechal
Becan
Xpumil
Río Bec
Oxpemul
Calakmul
El Palmar
Nohmul
Jonuta
Uxul
Naachtún
Comalcalco
Morales
San José
Palenque
Uaxactún
La Honradez
Piedras
Tikal
Holmul
Negras
Voluntún
Naranjo
Tonina
Lams
El Cayo
Ucanal
Pomona
Bonampak
Yaxchilán
Ixkun
Monte Vaca
Kuna
Seibal
Caracol
Chinkultic
Altar de Sacrificios
Machaquilá
Lúbaanton
Quen Santo
Aquateca
Cancuén
Pusilha
Nebaj
Quiriguá
Los Hígos
Zacualpa
Acasaquastlán
Copán
El Baúl
Kaminaljuyí
Tiquisate
Amatitlán
Pantaleón
Aguan

THE MAYA AD 900–1500
Area of Maya territory
● Maya settlement

0   100 km
0   100 miles

N

Dzibilchaltún
El Meco
Aké
Chichén Itzá
Cobá
Tihoo
Mayapán
Xelhá
Maní
San Gervasio
Huaymil
Tulum
Chacmool
Champotón
Cilvituk
Ichpartún
Santa Rita
Caribbean Sea
San Pedro
Usumacinta
Topoxte
Río de la Pasión
Tayasal
Grijalva
Quen Santo
Chaculá
Nebaj
Chutixtiox
Naco
Zaculeu
Pantzac
S. de Minas
Tajumulco
Zacualpa
Canyup
Mixco Viejo
Sololá
PACIFIC
OCEAN
Aguan

TEOTIHUACÁN EMPIRE; TEOTIHUACAN CITY

AD 150 – 1200

TEOTIHUACÁN CITY

At its height in between AD 150 and 450 Teotihuacán was the largest city in the Americas. It was situated approximately 25 miles northeast of present-day Mexico City, covered an area of 11.5 square miles, and probably housed more than 150,000 people, although some estimates put the number as high as 250,000. Many buildings in the city had great religious significance. Human sacrifice was widely practiced and as the city expanded it is thought that ritual sacrifice took place to dedicate all new buildings in order to ensure their prosperity.

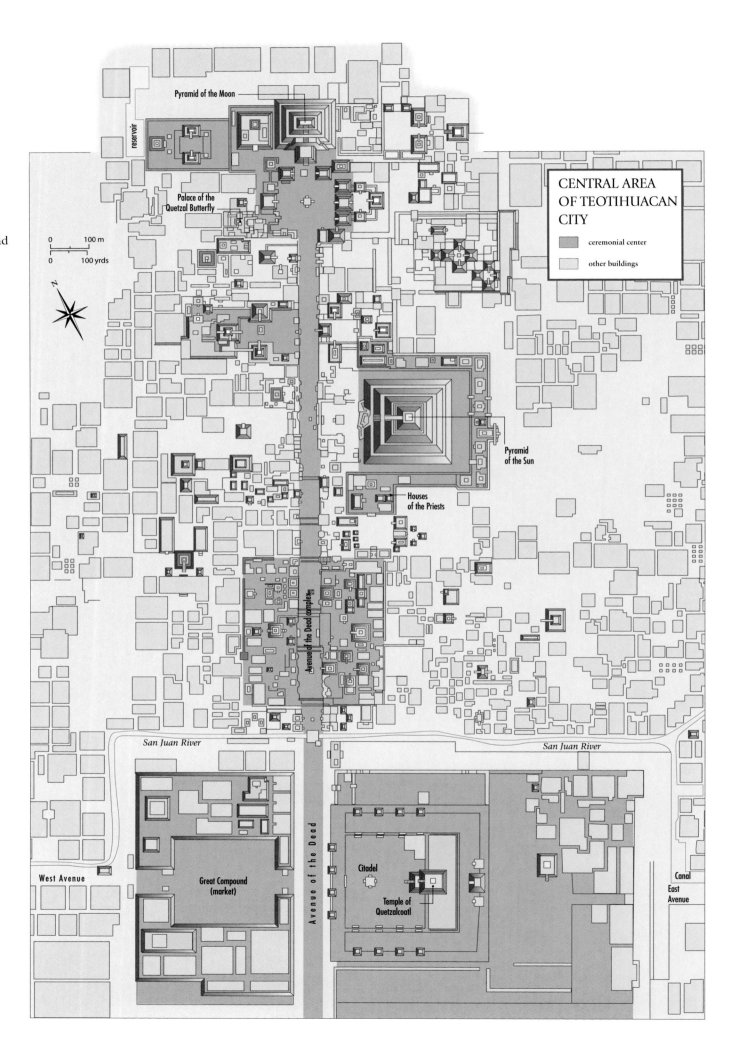

CENTRAL AREA OF TEOTIHUACAN CITY

ceremonial center

other buildings

Pyramid of the Moon

reservoir

Palace of the Quetzal Butterfly

0   100 m
0   100 yrds

N

Pyramid of the Sun

Houses of the Priests

Avenue of the Dead complex

San Juan River

San Juan River

West Avenue

Great Compound (market)

Avenue of the Dead

Citadel

Temple of Quetzalcoatl

Canal

East Avenue

THE TOLTEC STATES

THE TOLTEC STATES

The Toltecs invaded what is now Central Mexico in about 1050. They built an empire that dominated the entire region and was to spread its influence to very distant areas. The empire's capital Tula, was transformed into a great city with a population of about 40,000. Although rainfall was low, irrigation systems enabled the development of agriculture. Warfare was important, along with human sacrifice of prisoners, but the Toltecs were also skilled craftsmen and their influence spread through trade as well as by conquest. In 1170 the Chichimecs moved in from the north, heralding the destruction of the Toltec Empire.

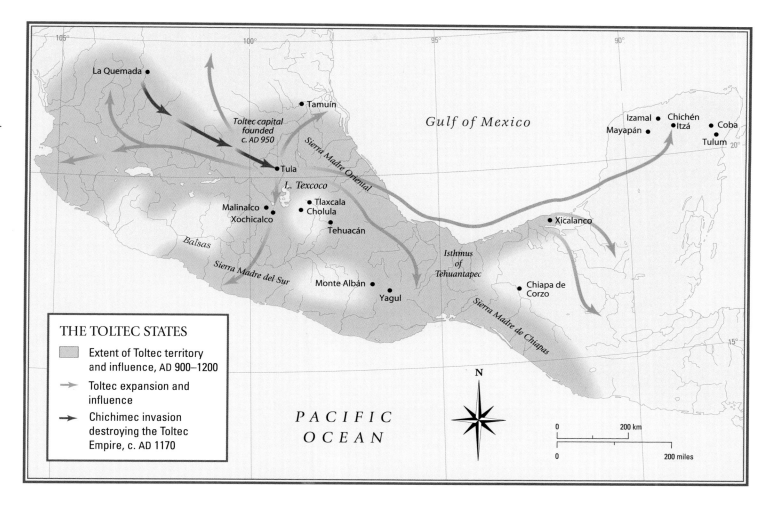

THE TOLTEC STATES

- Extent of Toltec territory and influence, AD 900–1200
- Toltec expansion and influence
- Chichimec invasion destroying the Toltec Empire, c. AD 1170

TEOTIHUACÁN EMPIRE
(BOTTOM RIGHT)

Centered on the city of Teotihuacán , the Teotihuacán Empire played an important role in the pre-Columbian life of Central America. The city was enormous and life appeared to be based on trade that took place throughout the Central American region. The city was famed for its industry and there were many potters, jewelers, and other craftsmen. In particular Teotihuacan was known for the production of obsidian artifacts. Obsidian is a naturally occurring glass that is found within the margins of volcanic lava flows. Although conquest contributed to the expansion of the empire, there is a notable absence of any fortifications or military structures in the city.

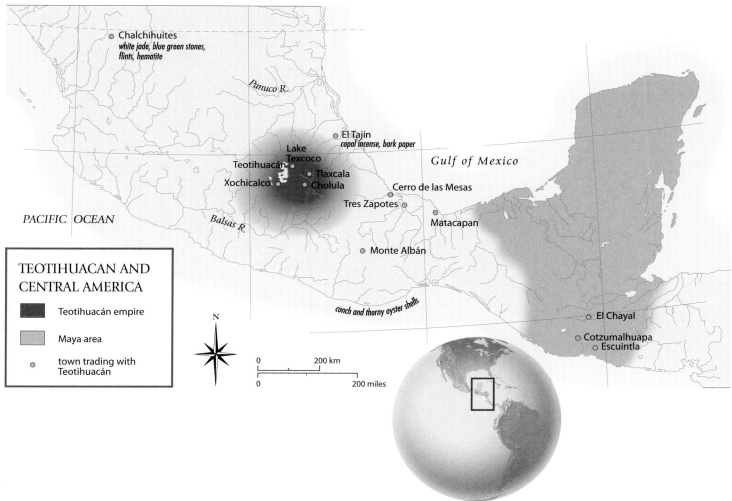

TEOTIHUACAN AND CENTRAL AMERICA

- Teotihuacán empire
- Maya area
- town trading with Teotihuacán

1200 – 1519   EARLY AZTEC EMPIRE

EARLY AZTEC EMPIRE

The two primary architects of the Aztec Empire were the half-brothers Tlacaelel and Moctezuma. Tlacaelel worked behind the scenes, reforming the Aztec state and religion. He is also credited with rewriting the history of the Aztec people and promoting the belief that Aztecs were always a powerful and mythic nation. One component of this reform was the institution of ritual war, where constant sacrifices had to be made to keep the sun moving across the sky. As trade developed the area of influence increased, usually by conquest, but most areas within the empire were organized as self-governing city-states.

THE RISE OF THE AZTEC EMPIRE AD 1200–1500

Aztec is a term used to describe certain peoples who lived in Central America before the arrival of Columbus. Their true origin is uncertain, but it appears that they arrived at Chapultepec from somewhere to north of the Valley of Mexico in or around the year 1248. With their two principal allies, the people of Texcoco and Tlacopan, during the 14th, 15th and 16th centuries they built an extensive empire that came to dominate the Valley of Mexico and extended its power to both the Gulf of Mexico and the Pacific shore. The empire collapsed after the Spanish invasion of 1519.

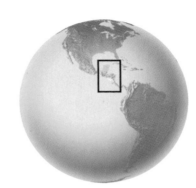

THE CONQUEST OF THE AZTEC EMPIRE

This took place between 1519 and 1521 after Hernán Cortés, the Spanish conquistador, had landed in Mexico's Yucatan peninsula and formally claimed the territory for the Spanish crown. Initially the Aztecs offered little resistance to the Spanish. In September 1519 Cortés arrived in Tlaxcala. This was an independent state within the Aztec Empire and its rulers were enthusiastic, since they saw the Spanish as an ally against the Aztecs. Cortés then marched on to Cholula, which he destroyed and killed more than 3,000 of its inhabitants. Finally in November Cortés reached the capital, Tenochtitlán. The king was captured and the empire subsequently fell.

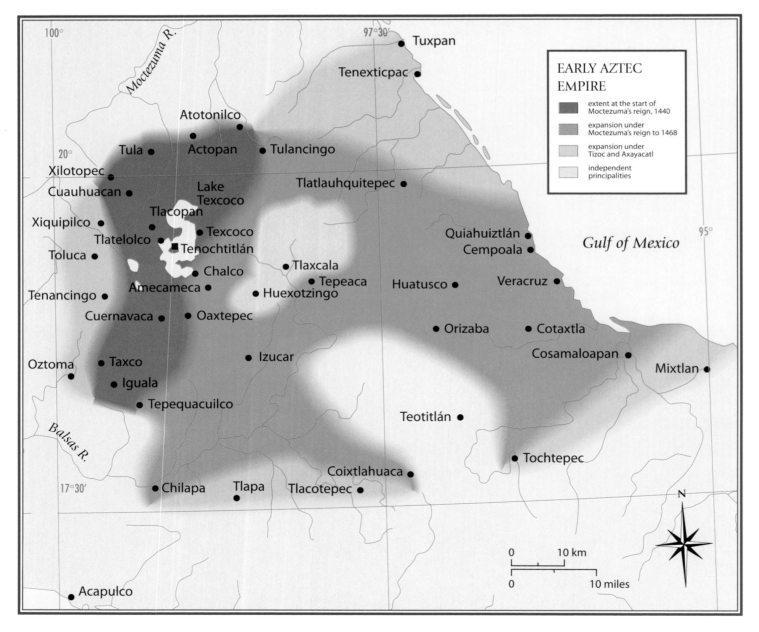

EARLY AZTEC EMPIRE

- extent at the start of Moctezuma's reign, 1440
- expansion under Moctezuma's reign to 1468
- expansion under Tizoc and Axayacatl
- independent principalities

THE RISE OF THE AZTEC EMPIRE; THE CONQUEST OF THE AZTEC EMPIRE

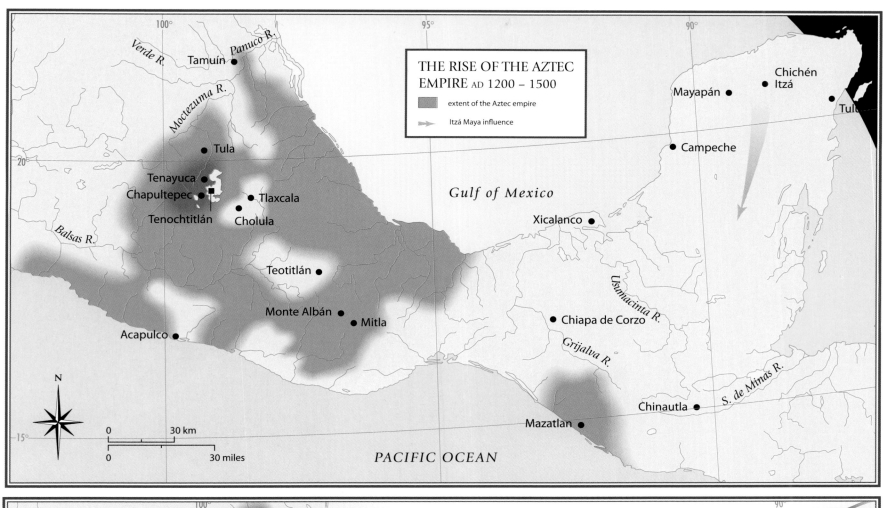

THE RISE OF THE AZTEC
EMPIRE AD 1200 – 1500

extent of the Aztec empire

Itzá Maya influence

Verde R.

Tamuín

Panuco R.

Moctezuma R.

Tula

Tenayuca

Chapultepec

Tenochtitlán

Tlaxcala

Cholula

Balsas R.

Teotitlán

Monte Albán

Mitla

Acapulco

Gulf of Mexico

Chichén Itzá

Mayapán

Tulu

Campeche

Xicalanco

Usumacinta R.

Chiapa de Corzo

Grijalva R.

Chinautla

S. de Minas R.

Mazatlan

PACIFIC OCEAN

N

0   30 km

0   30 miles

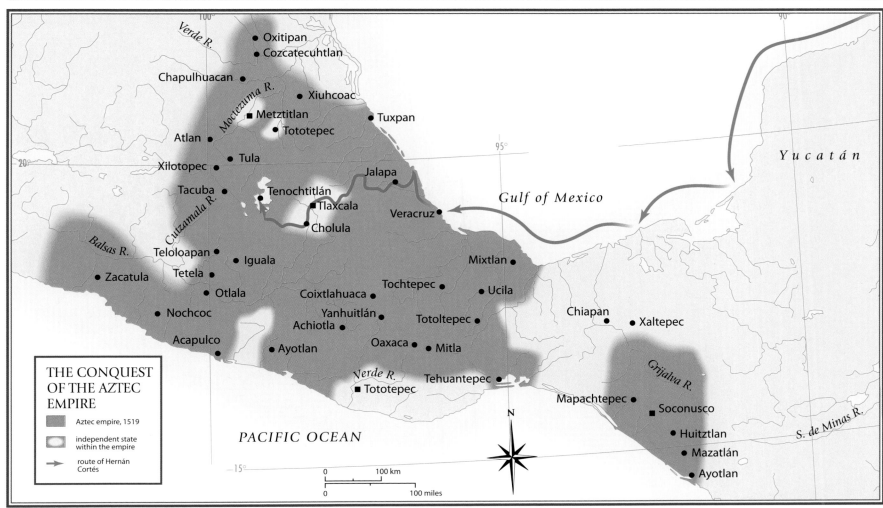

THE CONQUEST
OF THE AZTEC
EMPIRE

Aztec empire, 1519

independent state
within the empire

route of Hernán
Cortés

Verde R.

Oxitipan

Cozcatecuhtlan

Chapulhuacan

Moctezuma R.

Xiuhcoac

Metztitlan

Tototepec

Tuxpan

Atlan

Xilotopec

Tula

Jalapa

Tacuba

Tenochtitlán

Cutzamala R.

Tlaxcala

Cholula

Veracruz

Balsas R.

Teloloapan

Iguala

Mixtlan

Zacatula

Tetela

Tochtepec

Ucila

Otlala

Coixtlahuaca

Nochcoc

Yanhuitlán

Totoltepec

Achiotla

Acapulco

Oaxaca

Mitla

Ayotlan

Verde R.

Tehuantepec

Tototepec

PACIFIC OCEAN

Gulf of Mexico

Yucatán

Chiapan

Xaltepec

Grijalva R.

Mapachtepec

Soconusco

Huiztlan

Mazatlán

Ayotlan

S. de Minas R.

N

0   100 km

0   100 miles

139

CHIMU PRIOR TO INCA EXPANSION

THE CHIMU IN PERU

The Chimu civilization was founded in the Moche valley of Peru, later spreading into adjacent valleys. In its latter stages the maximum extent of the empire covered about 620 miles of coastline up to the Ecuadorean border. Its culture was famous throughout South America and its engineers were expert at road building, irrigation canal construction, and city development. The capital, Chan-Chan was the largest city ever built in ancient Peru. The empire's wealth depended on its sophisticated irrigation systems. Although the south was defended by a large fortress at Paramonga, it was from the north that the Incas invaded in 1466.

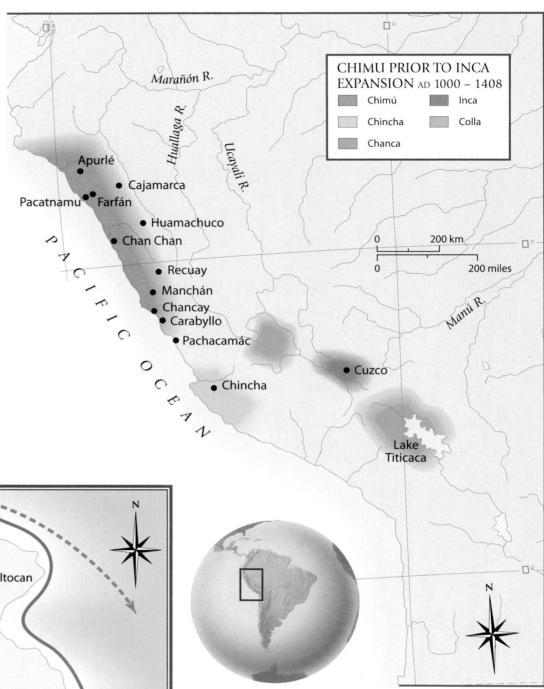

CHIMU PRIOR TO INCA
EXPANSION AD 1000 – 1408

- Chimú
- Chincha
- Chanca
- Inca
- Colla

CORTÉS'S CONQUEST OF TENOCHTITLÁN

In November 1519 Cortés and his men finally reached Tenochtitlán, the island capital of the Aztecs. This city was one of the largest in the world with an estimated population somewhere between 60,000 and 300,000. The only European city larger than Tenochtitlán was Constantinople. Initially it seems that Cortés was welcomed with great pomp, but later the population rebelled against the Spaniards. In 1521 Cortés laid siege to the city and it finally fell on 13th August 1521, by which time it was almost totally destroyed and thousands were already dead from a smallpox outbreak that had been brought by the Spaniards.

CUZCO AND THE INCA EMPIRE

CUZCO AND THE INCA EMPIRE

Cuzco was the capital of the Inca Empire. It is in the middle of the Andes and is more than 11,000 feet above sea level. To the Incas it was a divine place, the center of the empire and the center of the world. It was divided into four to correspond with the empire's four provinces, with a road leading to each. Local leaders were obliged to build houses in the city, and to live there for part of the year, but only in the quarter of the city corresponding to the part of the empire in which they had territory. The Spanish conquistadors looted and destroyed the city.

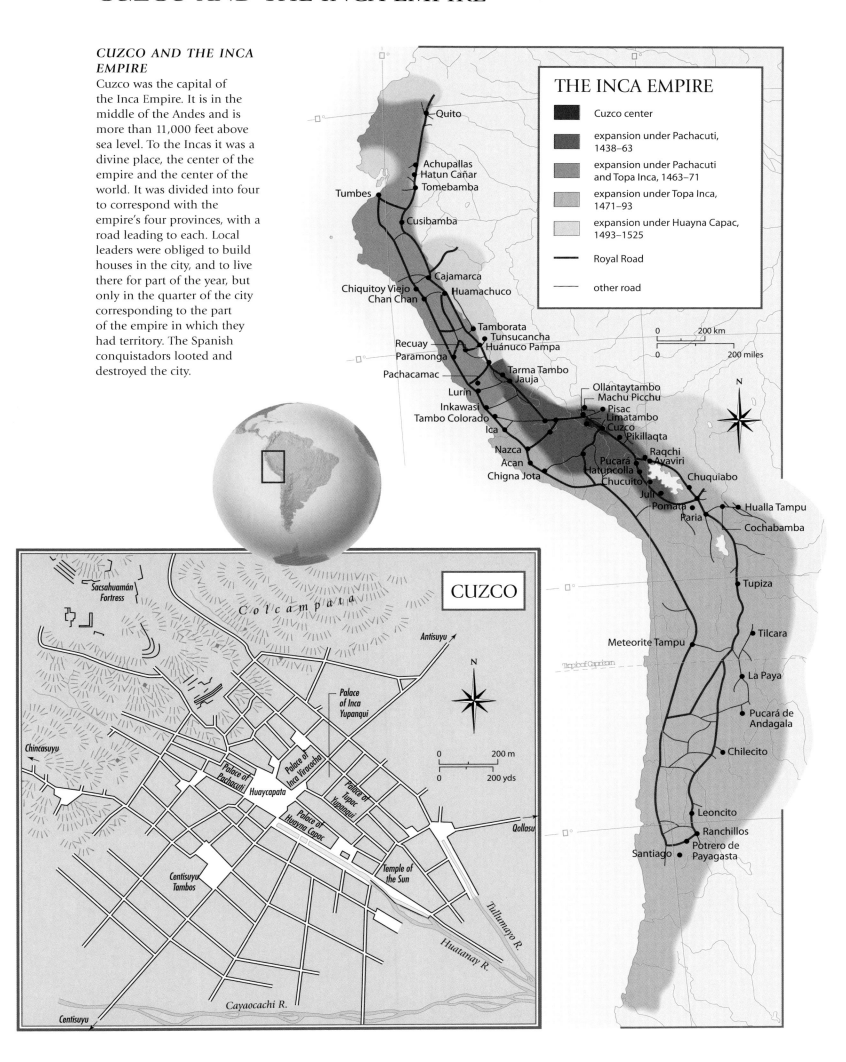

THE INCA EMPIRE

- Cuzco center
- expansion under Pachacuti, 1438–63
- expansion under Pachacuti and Topa Inca, 1463–71
- expansion under Topa Inca, 1471–93
- expansion under Huayna Capac, 1493–1525
- Royal Road
- other road

0   200 km
0   200 miles

Quito

Achupallas
Hatun Cañar
Tomebamba
Tumbes

Cusibamba

Cajamarca
Chiquitoy Viejo   Huamachuco
Chan Chan

Tamborata
Recuay   Tunsucancha
Paramonga   Huánuco Pampa
Pachacamac
Tarma Tambo
Jauja
Lurin   Ollantaytambo
Inkawasi   Machu Picchu
Tambo Colorado   Pisac
Ica   Limatambo
Cuzco
Pikillaqta
Nazca   Raqchi
Acan   Pucará   Ayaviri
Chigna Jota   Hatuncolla
Chucuito   Chuquiabo
Juli
Pomata   Hualla Tampu
Paria
Cochabamba

Tupiza

Meteorite Tampu   Tilcara

La Paya

Pucará de
Andagala

Chilecito

Leoncito
Ranchillos
Santiago   Potrero de
Payagasta

CUZCO

Sacsahuamán
Fortress

Colcampata

Antisuyu

Chincasuyu

Palace of
Inca Yupanqui

Palace of
Inca Viracocha
Palace of
Pachacuti   Palace of
Huaycapata   Tupac
Yupanqui
Palace of
Huayna Capac

Centisuyu
Tambos   Temple of
the Sun

Qollasu

0   200 m
0   200 yds

Tullumayo R.

Huatanay R.

Cayaocachi R.

Centisuyu

THE END OF THE INCA EMPIRE

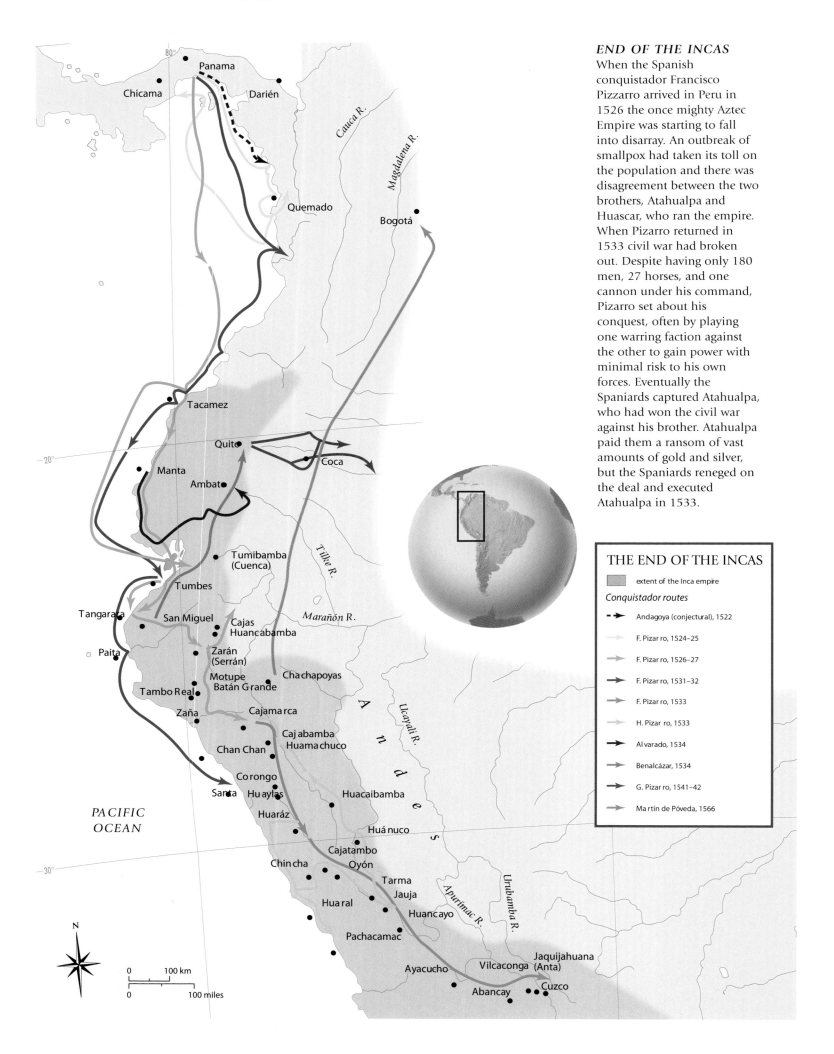

END OF THE INCAS

When the Spanish conquistador Francisco Pizarro arrived in Peru in 1526 the once mighty Aztec Empire was starting to fall into disarray. An outbreak of smallpox had taken its toll on the population and there was disagreement between the two brothers, Atahualpa and Huascar, who ran the empire. When Pizarro returned in 1533 civil war had broken out. Despite having only 180 men, 27 horses, and one cannon under his command, Pizarro set about his conquest, often by playing one warring faction against the other to gain power with minimal risk to his own forces. Eventually the Spaniards captured Atahualpa, who had won the civil war against his brother. Atahualpa paid them a ransom of vast amounts of gold and silver, but the Spaniards reneged on the deal and executed Atahualpa in 1533.

THE END OF THE INCAS

- extent of the Inca empire

Conquistador routes

- Andagoya (conjectural), 1522
- F. Pizarro, 1524–25
- F. Pizarro, 1526–27
- F. Pizarro, 1531–32
- F. Pizarro, 1533
- H. Pizarro, 1533
- Alvarado, 1534
- Benalcázar, 1534
- G. Pizarro, 1541–42
- Martín de Póveda, 1566

PART 9

NORTH AMERICA

THE NORTHERN NATIVE AMERICANS possess a rich cultural and linguistic diversity, more so than Europe in the 1500s, although many of the languages are now extinct. Linguistic classifications are various, seeking to relate groups and trace tribal histories. One important group were the Mississippian mound builders, flourishing between AD 750 and 1500, while spreading along the Mississippi and its tributaries. The mounds were surmounted by buildings housing priest-leaders with a supreme ruler akin to the Great Sun of the Natchez. The mound at Cahokia, Illinois, is 100 feet high, covers 78,000 square yards, and the town held about 20,000–40,000 people. The settlements were often surrounded by a fortified palisade and a ditch. The Mississippians were linked into an extensive trade and communication network that imported freshwater pearls, Great Lake copper, Ohio flint, and Arkansas quartz, as well as shark and alligator teeth. The north–south Mississippi trade route was tied to the trade systems of the Pacific, Gulf, and Atlantic coasts. Goods were generally moved by canoe, whether frame or dugout, or by dog sledge. Connections from the Plains to California had several routes, one through passes around Lake Tahoe, and another in the north along the Klamath River Valley to the Sacramento, then to San Francisco Bay.

SIX BASIC NATIVE AMERICAN LANGUAGES

1000 BC – AD 1700

SAPIR'S THESIS: SIX BASIC NATIVE AMERICAN LANGUAGES

- ■ Eskimo-Aleut
- ▢ Na-dene
- ▢ Macro Algonquian
- ▢ Macro Siouan-Hokan
- ▢ Penutian
- ■ Aztec-Tanoan

SIX BASIC NATIVE AMERICAN LANGUAGES
In 1929 Edward Sapir proposed a classification of North American native languages that broke them down into six basic groups. To the north were the Eskimo-Aleut group, which included Inuit and natives of the Aleutian Islands who inhabited the coastal area of Alaska and northern Canada. Further inland were the Na-dene group, with peoples such as the Athabascans. In the centre were the Algonquian, comprising many of the Plains tribes, while west of the Rockies were the Penutians.

A large group to the south comprised the Siouan-Hokans, with famous tribes such as the Sioux and the Iroquois. Finally in the south-west lived a group that Sapir called the Aztec-Tanoan.

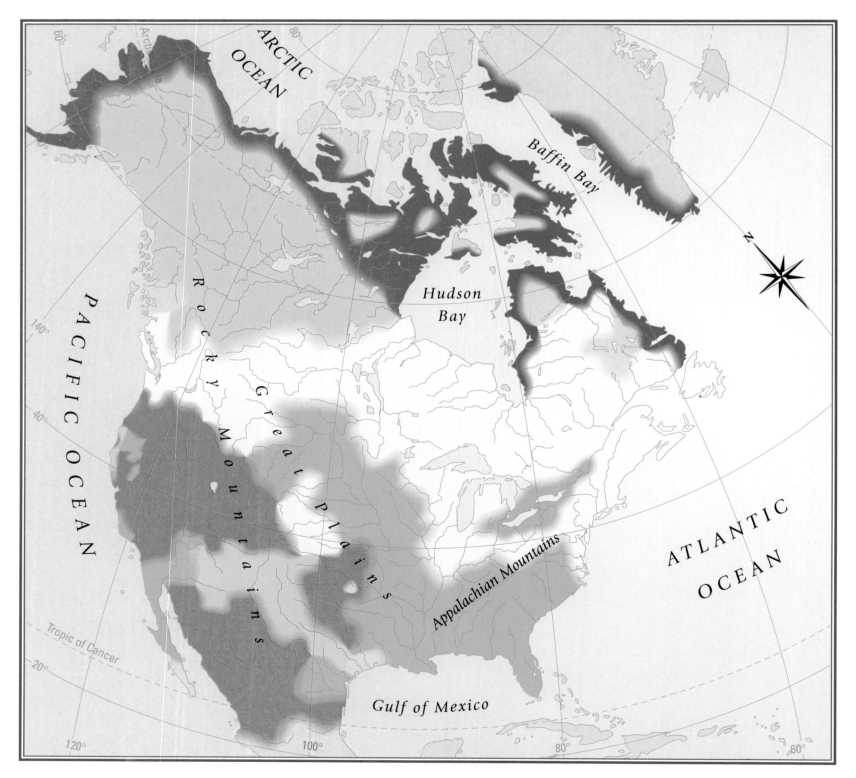

THE MOUND BUILDERS

THE MOUND BUILDERS
There were two phases of mound building in early American cultures. The first were the Woodlanders of about 1000 BC, subsistence dwellers who gradually evolved a system of gathering and storing natural food resources as well as planting small garden crops. In later centuries they extended into pottery, minerals, and other goods that they could barter for food. They built a number of earthworks, such as those at Adena and Hopewell, to bury their dead.

The Mississippians were a later culture dating from about AD 700, who lived on the banks of the Mississippi River. Their mounds were often used ceremonially and usually had a building on top. Periodically these buildings would be razed to the foundations, the earthwork built up, and a new structure

---

ADENA, HOPEWELL, AND MISSISSIPPIAN MOUNDS

▲ Major Adena or Hopewell mounds, 1000 BC–AD 1000

▲ Major Mississippian mounds, AD 700–1700

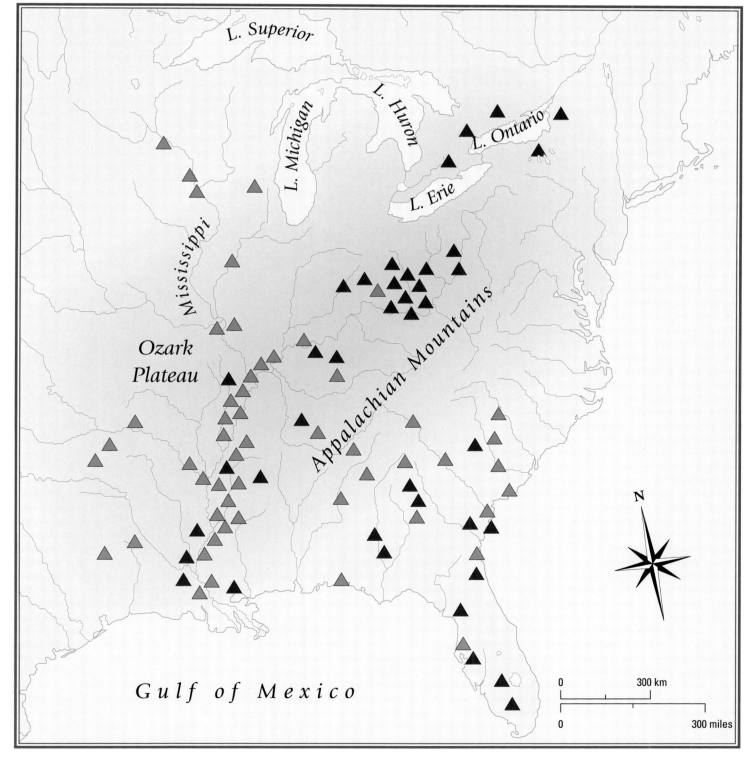

C. 1762

COLONIAL AMERICA

COLONIAL AMERICA
By 1700 large areas of eastern North America had been colonized by the English and the French. Spain also held large areas, chiefly in Central and South America, and there was some Russian influence along the western coast. However, vast areas of the central mid-west, western states and Canada remained unoccupied. Even in settled areas humans were relatively few in number. The distinctive economic, religious, and cultural character of the various settler nations was reflected in the way in which they lived their lives. Each built different types of houses, grew different crops, and held different values. Even within the same nationalities, groups held different religious views that shaped the governance and lifestyle of their communities.

Hudson Bay

Fort Albany · Fort Rupert

Ft. St Charles
Ft. St Pierre
Ft. Michipicton
Lake Superior

Plains of Abraham 1759 · Québec
Fort Beauséjour
Louisbourg 1745 and 1758
Halifax

Montréal

Fort Edward Augustus
Lake Michigan
Lake Huron
Fort George
Ft. Oswego
Boston

Fort St Joseph
Ft. Niagara
Ft. Presque Isle
Lake Erie
Ft. Duquesne
New York

Fort Beauharnais

Ft. Pickawillany
1755
Fort Necessity
Philadelphia
Baltimore

Fort Orléans
Richmond

Fort Chartres

Mississippi
New Bern
Wilmington

Fort Augusta
1742
Ft. King George
Georgetown
Charleston
Savannah

Atlantic Ocean

Fort Rosalie · Fort Condé
St Augustine

New Orleans
1740, 1743

Gulf of Mexico

N

0 — 400 km
0 — 400 miles

COLONIAL NORTH AMERICA C.1762

European territorial claims, 1750

- ▉ British
- ▉ French
- ▉ Spanish
- ✕ battle
- 🏰 British fort
- 🏰 French fort

PART 10

AFRICA

Africa has witnessed numerous civilizations, the most significant being those of Carthage, Nubian Cush, and Songhay. Carthage was originally (500 BC) a Phoenician settlement but became independent, acquiring an empire by founding Mediterranean colonies and taking over Phoenician settlements. Eventually, the imperium included the North African coast from Morocco to the Egyptian border, Sardinia, Malta, the Balearics, and parts of southern Spain and Sicily. When the Egyptian New Kingdom collapsed, an independent state of Nubia (850 BC) emerged with a capital at Napata. Expeditions were launched into Egypt, conquering land for a time. When faced with an expansionist Assyrian Empire invading Egypt, the Napatan Kingdom moved its heart to Meroë. The Cushite state survived until its decline in the 1st century AD when it faced the rise of the Kingdom of Aksum, an Ethiopian highland state. The Aksumite army crushed Nubia in 350 AD. The Songhay Empire in sub-Saharan Africa was founded in the 15th century by Sonni Ali. He and his successor, Askia Mohammed Turre, spread Islam and acquired Mali as a tributary state. The empire's power expanded into the Hausa states and Bornu Kanem, as well as over the Tuareg of Taskedda and Air. They also captured the lucrative salt deposits at Taghaxa.

THE DEVELOPMENT OF AFRICAN AGRICULTURE

4000BC – AD 1000

DEVELOPMENT OF AGRICULTURE

The area of earliest livestock domestication in Africa roughly coincides with the area of the present Sahara. Following the end of the last ice age from about 8000 to 6000 BC, low-pressure weather formations over the collapsing ice sheets to the north led to damp conditions in the area. Gradually the Sahara began to dry out and by about 2500 BC the monsoon line, which had pulled in cool wet air from the ocean, moved south and desert took over. Further south the opportunities for agriculture were poor, restricted either by tropical rain forest or desert.

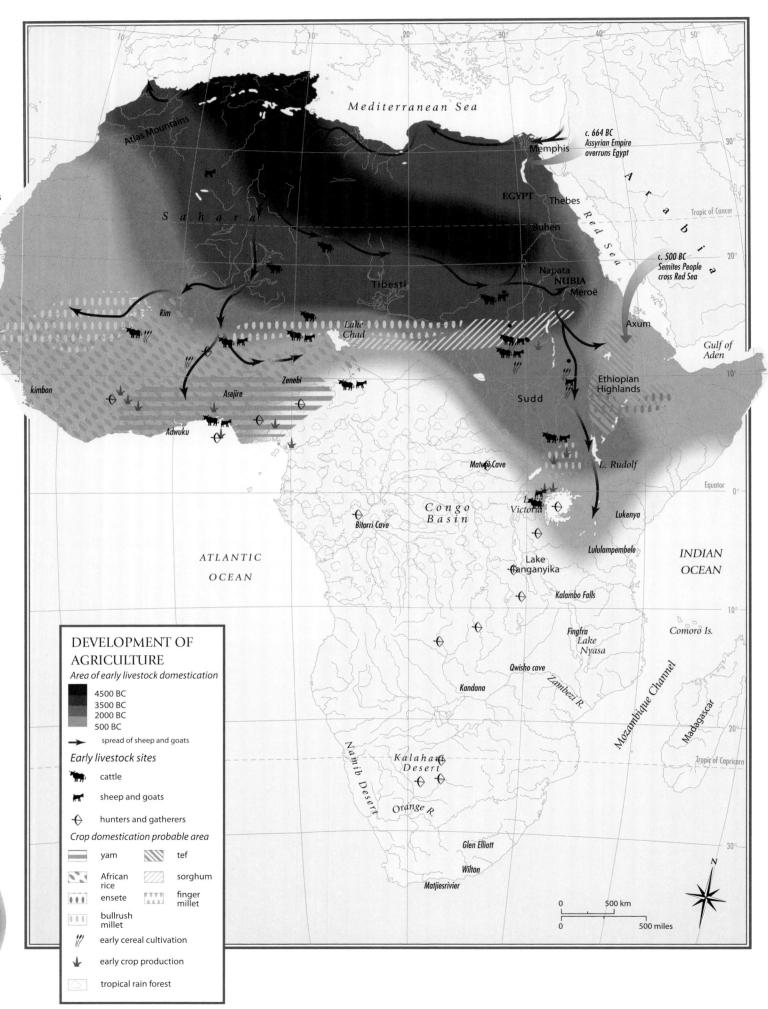

DEVELOPMENT OF AGRICULTURE

Area of early livestock domestication

- 4500 BC
- 3500 BC
- 2000 BC
- 500 BC

→ spread of sheep and goats

Early livestock sites

- cattle
- sheep and goats
- hunters and gatherers

Crop domestication probable area

- yam
- African rice
- ensete
- bullrush millet
- tef
- sorghum
- finger millet

- early cereal cultivation
- early crop production
- tropical rain forest

Map labels:
Mediterranean Sea · Atlas Mountains · Sahara · Memphis · c. 664 BC Assyrian Empire overruns Egypt · EGYPT · Thebes · Red Sea · Arabia · Tropic of Cancer · Buhen · Tibesti · Napata · NUBIA · Meroë · c. 500 BC Semites People cross Red Sea · Rim · Lake Chad · Axum · Gulf of Aden · kimbon · Zenebi · Asejire · Ethiopian Highlands · Sudd · Adwuku · Matupi Cave · L. Rudolf · Lukenya · Bitorri Cave · Congo Basin · L. Victoria · Equator · Lululampembele · INDIAN OCEAN · ATLANTIC OCEAN · Lake Tanganyika · Kalambo Falls · Comoro Is. · Fingira Lake Nyasa · Qwisho cave · Kandana · Zambezi R. · Mozambique Channel · Madagascar · Namib Desert · Kalahari Desert · Orange R. · Glen Elliott · Wilton · Matjiesrivier · Tropic of Capricorn

0 — 500 km
0 — 500 miles

ABBASAID EMPIRE; FATMID NORTH AFRICA

THE ABBASID EMPIRE C.850

The Abbasid Empire was the second of the two Sunni dynasties of the Arab Empire. It seized power in 750 and shifted the capital from Damascus to Baghdad, where it flourished for two centuries, before the rising power of the Turkish army, which the Abbasids had themselves created, brought about their

decline. At its height it controlled vast areas, including a huge swathe of North Africa, but vast areas are notoriously difficult to control and there were a number of incursions from the east. By the mid-9th century the Abbasids had lost control of North Africa, with the lands divided up between the Idrisids, Aghlabids, the Tulunids, and Ikshidids.

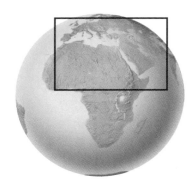

FATIMID NORTH AFRICA TO C. 1000

The Fatimids, (descendants of Fatima, prophet Muhammad's daughter), occupied and ruled Egypt from 969. The Fatimids initially gained control of the north African coast as far west as Morocco. In 973 the Fatimid Caliphe, Al-Mu'izz, moved the capital from the Maghrib to Cairo, and in doing so he lost control of the

western part of his state. The Fatimid Caliphate (a mode of governance that is based on Islamic political unity), now based in Egypt, went on to build up a large trading empire, at its peak consisting of North Africa, Sicily, Palestine, Lebanon, Syria, the Red Sea coast of Africa and Yemen. Its currency, the Fatimid dinar minted in gold, was imported across the Sahara from the states of Western Africa. On the death of the last Fatimid Caliphe in 1171, Salah al-Din, known to the West as Saladin, took power, founding the Ayyubid dynasty.

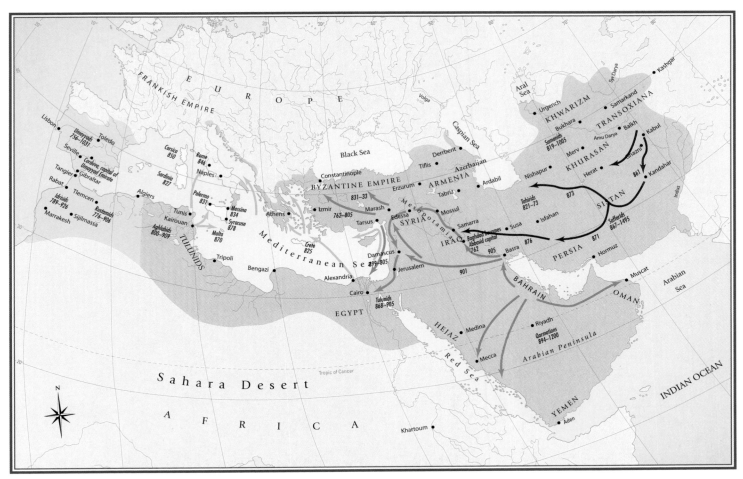

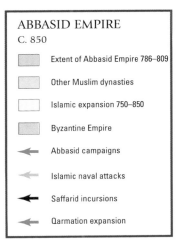

ABBASID EMPIRE
C. 850

- Extent of Abbasid Empire 786–809
- Other Muslim dynasties
- Islamic expansion 750–850
- Byzantine Empire
- Abbasid campaigns
- Islamic naval attacks
- Saffarid incursions
- Qarmation expansion

FATIMID NORTH AFRICA TO c. 1000

- Fatimid caliphate at its maximum extent, c. 1000
- Breakaway principalities, with date
- Movement of Arab peoples (Banu Hilal and Banu Sulayman), c. 1000
- Fatimid caliphate, c. 1055
- Sulayman and Hilal attacks, encouraged by the Fatimids

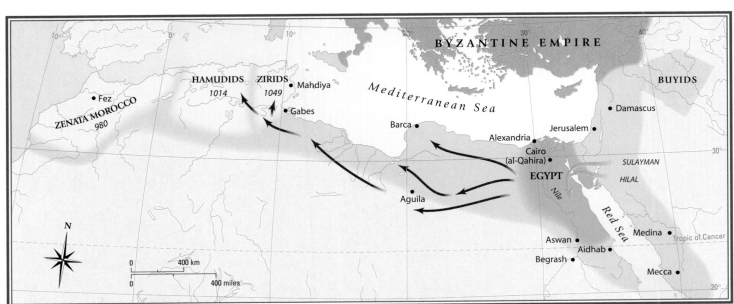

500 BC – AD 1000 AFRICA 500 BC–AD 600

AFRICA 500 BC–AD 600
The Iron Age came to Africa in the 6th century BC, but from earliest times Africans had been skilled at working with metal. Iron had the great advantage of being harder than other metals at that time. Once sharpened it kept a good edge and was useful for both tools and weapons. There was also a great population movement. The Bantu originated in west-central Africa and they gradually moved east and south. Prior to 200 BC most people south of the Sahara lived as hunter-gatherers, but after that time they moved toward the keeping of domesticated animals.

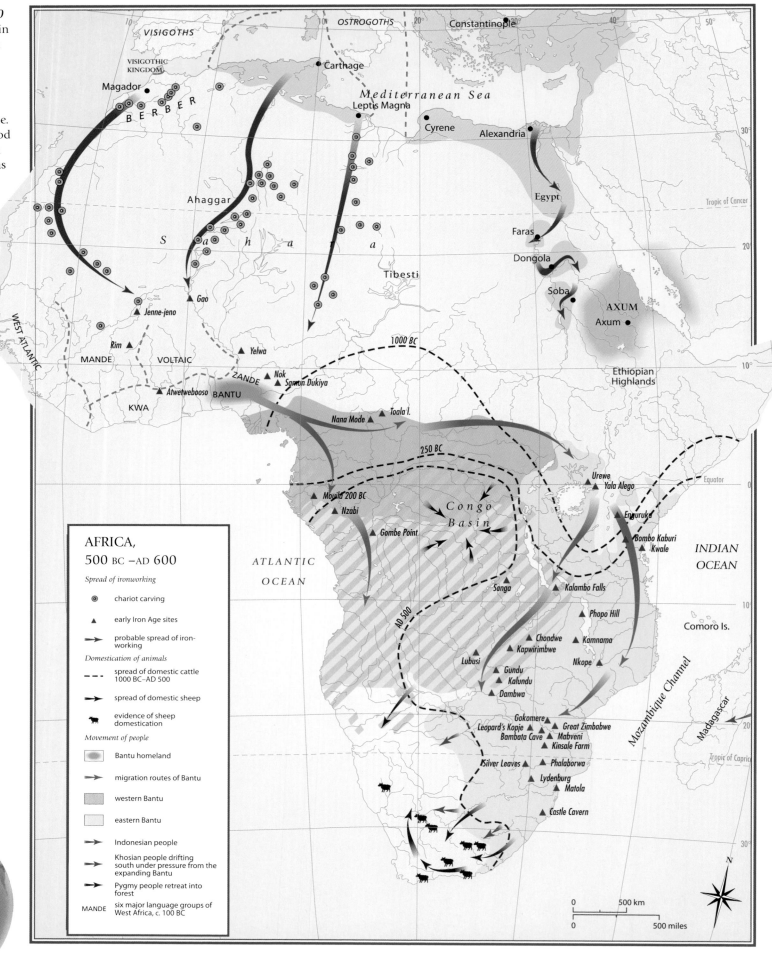

AFRICA,
500 BC –AD 600

Spread of ironworking

⊙ chariot carving

▲ early Iron Age sites

→ probable spread of iron-working

Domestication of animals

- - - spread of domestic cattle 1000 BC–AD 500

→ spread of domestic sheep

🐑 evidence of sheep domestication

Movement of people

☁ Bantu homeland

→ migration routes of Bantu

☐ western Bantu

☐ eastern Bantu

→ Indonesian people

→ Khosian people drifting south under pressure from the expanding Bantu

→ Pygmy people retreat into forest

MANDE six major language groups of West Africa, c. 100 BC

AFRICAN LANGUAGES

AFRICAN LANGUAGES AD 1000

Bantu is the general term for more than 400 different ethnic groups in Africa from Cameroon to South Africa who are united by a common language family. It is thought that the language originated in Nigeria and by AD 1000 had reached modern-day Zimbabwe and South Africa. To the north, the Muslims had conquered Egypt in 646 and spread rapidly across northern Africa. Trade routes developed and cities and kingdoms arose that were primarily Arab speaking. In these regions, because Arabic was dominant, many Africans began to use the Arabic alphabet to write their own languages.

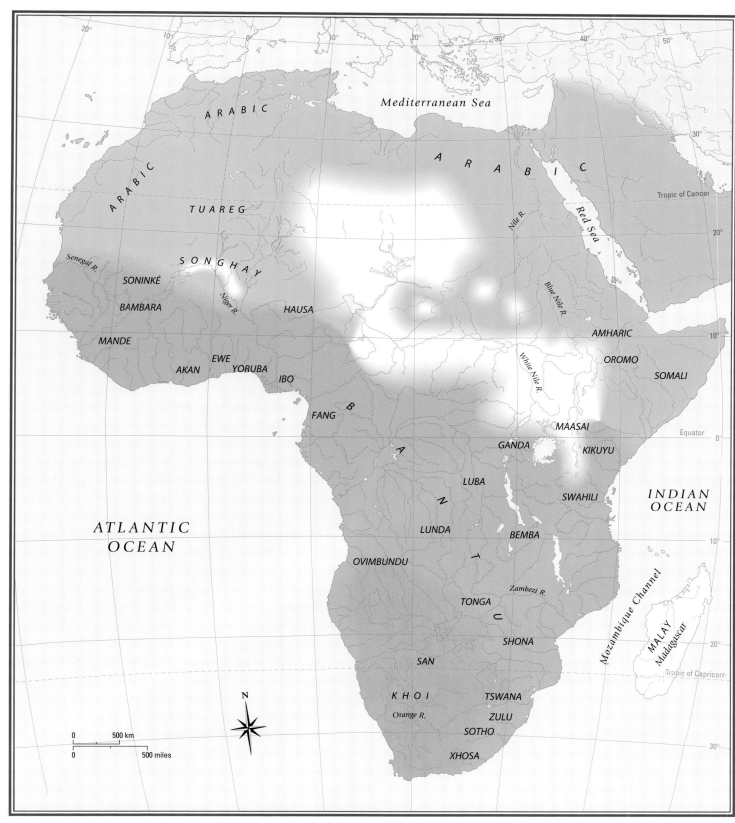

AFRICAN LANGUAGES AD 1000

- Niger-Kordofanian (inc. Bantu)
- Nilo-Saharan
- Afro-Asiatic
- Khoisan
- Not known

SONGHAY EMPIRE C. 1540

**SONGHAY EMPIRE
C. 1540**
This was a precolonial African state centered on eastern Mali. From the early 15th to the late 16th centuries Songhay was one of the largest African empires in history, owing its immense wealth to trade throughout the Arab world. The Songhay Empire absorbed the declining Mali Empire that was centered on Timbuktu and had once dominated the region. As with all such civilizations, having a strong leader led to development and a weak leader led to decline. In its early day the Songhay's strong leadership had created enormous expansion but by the 1590s, following a defeat by Morocco, the empire simply broke up.

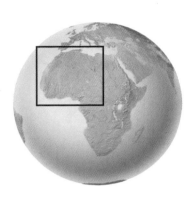

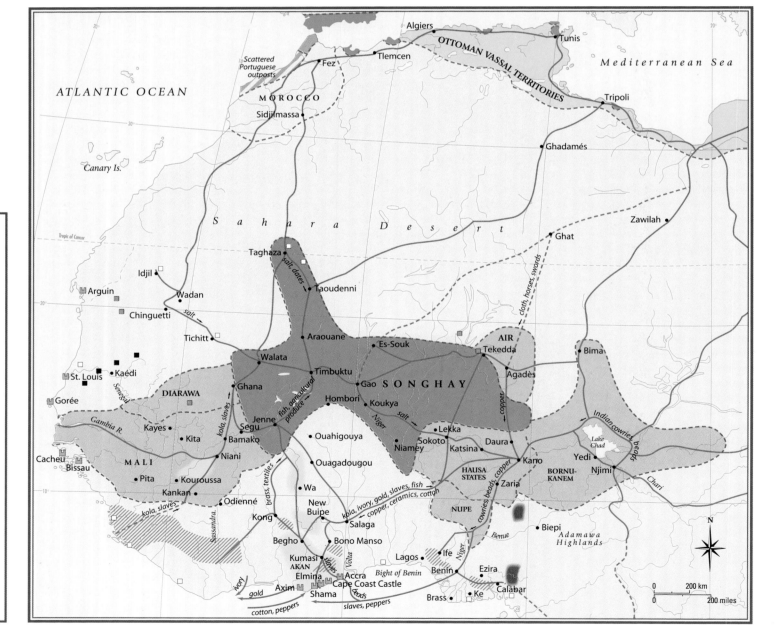

PART 11

CLASSICAL INHERITANCE

The classical age, especially Greece and Rome, has left a legacy in so many fields, noticeably in law and philosophy. The empire of Charlemagne became a major inheritor of this legacy when he was crowned Emperor of the Romans in AD 800 by Pope Leo III. Other political legacies were the Holy Roman Empire, and the eastern Byzantine Empire until Constantinople was captured by the Ottomans (1453). Other obvious aspects of the classical tradition can be seen in the restrained, carefully ordered architecture of recent centuries. Whether viewing the US White House or the Palladian Kedleston Hall in England, the use of columns and pediments is testimony to the past.

US President Thomas Jefferson proposed Greek and Roman styles for the University of Virginia when it was being built in 1825. Likewise, he believed classical styles were represented in American democracy with its various checks and balances, legal system, and accountability, all found in the Roman Republic. Settlements and college names, too, show a link with the past, with many places in America having names such as Athens, Rome, Ithaca, and Sparta. Meanwhile, old Roman roads such as the English Fosse Way between Lincoln and Exeter are still used, while the world holds Olympic Games every four years.

FRANCIA
990 – 1167

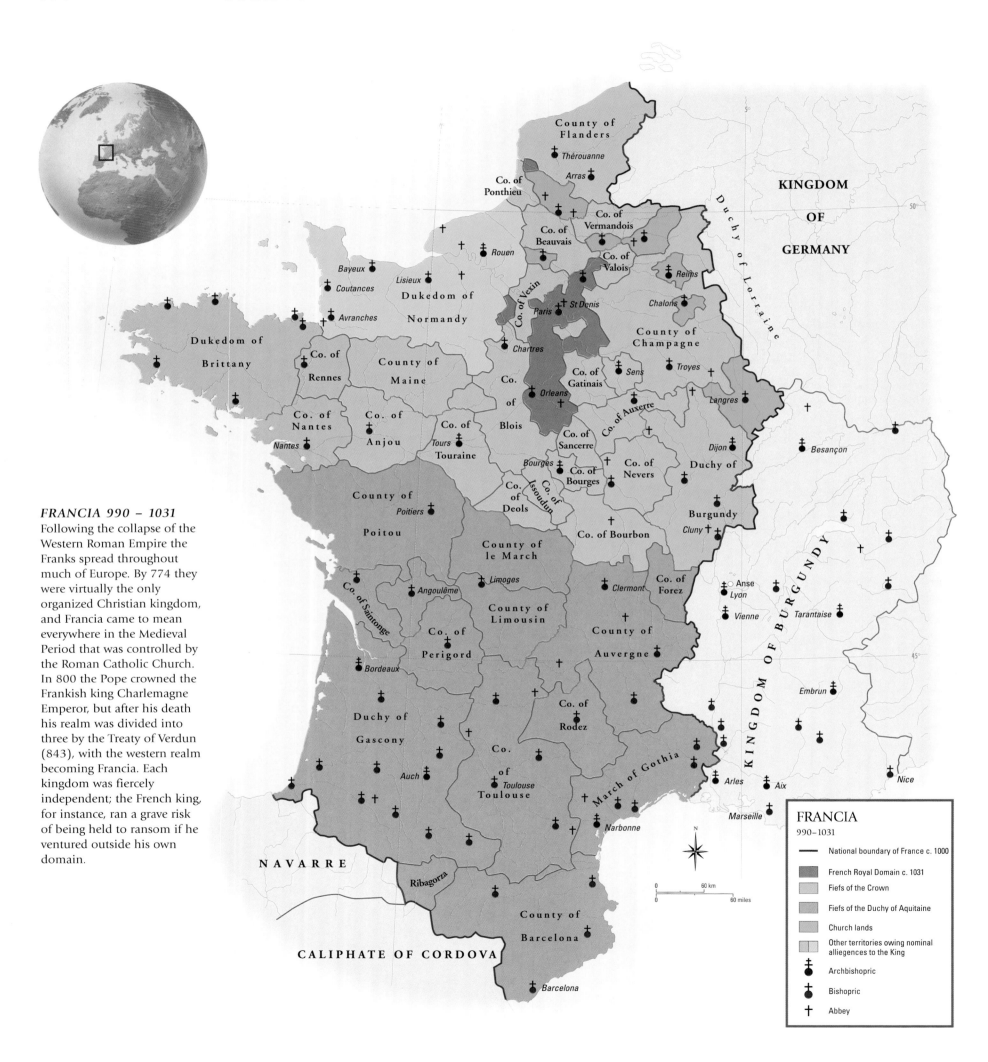

KINGDOM
OF
GERMANY

FRANCIA 990 – 1031
Following the collapse of the
Western Roman Empire the
Franks spread throughout
much of Europe. By 774 they
were virtually the only
organized Christian kingdom,
and Francia came to mean
everywhere in the Medieval
Period that was controlled by
the Roman Catholic Church.
In 800 the Pope crowned the
Frankish king Charlemagne
Emperor, but after his death
his realm was divided into
three by the Treaty of Verdun
(843), with the western realm
becoming Francia. Each
kingdom was fiercely
independent; the French king,
for instance, ran a grave risk
of being held to ransom if he
ventured outside his own
domain.

County of
Flanders
Thérouanne
Arras
Co. of
Ponthieu
Co. of
Vermandois
Co. of
Beauvais
Co. of
Valois
Reims
Rouen
Co. of Vexin
St Denis
Chalons
Bayeux
Lisieux
Paris
Coutances
Dukedom of
Avranches
Normandy
Chartres
County of
Champagne
Dukedom of
Brittany
Co. of
Rennes
County of
Maine
Co.
of
Blois
Co. of
Gatinais
Sens
Troyes
Orleans
Langres
Co. of
Nantes
Co. of
Anjou
Co. of
Touraine
Tours
Co. of Auxerre
Dijon
Besançon
Nantes
Bourges
Co. of
Sancerre
Co. of
Nevers
Duchy of
County of
Poitiers
Co.
of
Deols
Co. of
Isoudun
Co. of
Bourges
Burgundy
Poitou
Cluny
County of
le March
Co. of Bourbon
KINGDOM OF BURGUNDY
Limoges
Co. of
Saintonge
Angoulême
County of
Limousin
Clermont
Co. of
Forez
Anse
Lyon
Co. of
Perigord
Bordeaux
Vienne
Tarantaise
County of
Auvergne
Co. of
Rodez
Embrun
Duchy of
Gascony
Auch
Co.
of
Toulouse
Toulouse
March of Gothia
Arles
Aix
Nice
Marseille
Narbonne
NAVARRE
Ribagorza
County of
Barcelona
CALIPHATE OF CORDOVA
Barcelona

Duchy of Lorraine

FRANCIA
990–1031

— National boundary of France c. 1000

French Royal Domain c. 1031

Fiefs of the Crown

Fiefs of the Duchy of Aquitaine

Church lands

Other territories owing nominal
alliegences to the King

✝ Archbishopric

● Bishopric

✝ Abbey

0   60 km
0   60 miles

THE EMPIRE AND THE PAPACY

THE EMPIRE AND THE PAPACY

The Holy Roman Empire was a monarchy in Central Europe originally based on the Kingdom of Germany, but eventually consisting of a conglomeration of substates. The first Holy Roman Emperor was considered to be Charlemagne, who was crowned by the Pope on 25 December 800. The title Emperor carried with it the important role as protector of the Catholic Church and since emperors were ordained as subdeacons of the Catholic Church, women were ineligible. As the power of the papacy grew during the Middle Ages, popes and emperors came into conflict over church administration, leading ultimately to the growth of Protestantism.

THE EMPIRE AND THE PAPACY

- Empire border, 1152
- Kingdom of Germany
- Kingdom of Italy
- Kingdom of Burgundy
- Kingdom of Bohemia
- Imperial land in Italy
- Hohenstaufen demesne land
- Welf demesne land
- Ecclesiastical land
- • Archdiocese
- ○ Diocese
- ■ Lombard League town, 1167

EUROPE IN 1095

EUROPE 1095

The Holy Roman Empire was a group of states that formed the constituent part of Central Europe for around a thousand years, following the Pope's crowning of Charlemagne the Great as first Emperor on Christmas Day 800. The Empire consisted of hundreds of states and territories of various sizes, but effectively the Kingdom of Germany formed its major part. Although the Pope had always crowned the Emperor, this was in many ways an uneasy alliance.

In 1095 Pope Urban II preached a sermon in Clermont-Ferrand that led to the First Crusade to aid the Eastern Christians and to regain control of the Holy Land.

EUROPE 1095

— Holy Roman Empire
— Border
- - - Probable border

THE TIES OF TRADE 1300

THE TIES OF TRADE

The collapse of Rome in the west and the eventual decline of Byzantium in the east did not herald the end of classical traditions. Inheritors, in the form of new states, continued to be influenced by Roman political, military, technological, and economic innovations. Rome itself remained a key European city, in both trade and religious matters; stories of the city's glory spread far and wide along the trade routes from the Mediterranean to the Baltic, and Catholicism and Orthodox Christianity continued to be centered in the old Roman capitals of Rome and Constantinople. A number of conventions survived the demise of the Roman Empire, inspired as much by the romantic allure of Rome's glories as they were by practical considerations. For instance, in 962, Otto I, the first Holy Roman Emperor, styled himself "Kaiser," derived from the imperial title Caesar, a title borne by the rulers of the Holy Roman Empire until 1806. Similarly, in the east, Ivan III, Duke of Muscovy, married the niece of the last Byzantine emperor and used the title Tsar, which derived from the same Caesar origin. The title Tsar was formally adopted by Ivan IV (Ivan the Terrible) on his coronation in 1547, and subsequent Tsars considered themselves to be the successors of the Byzantine Empire.

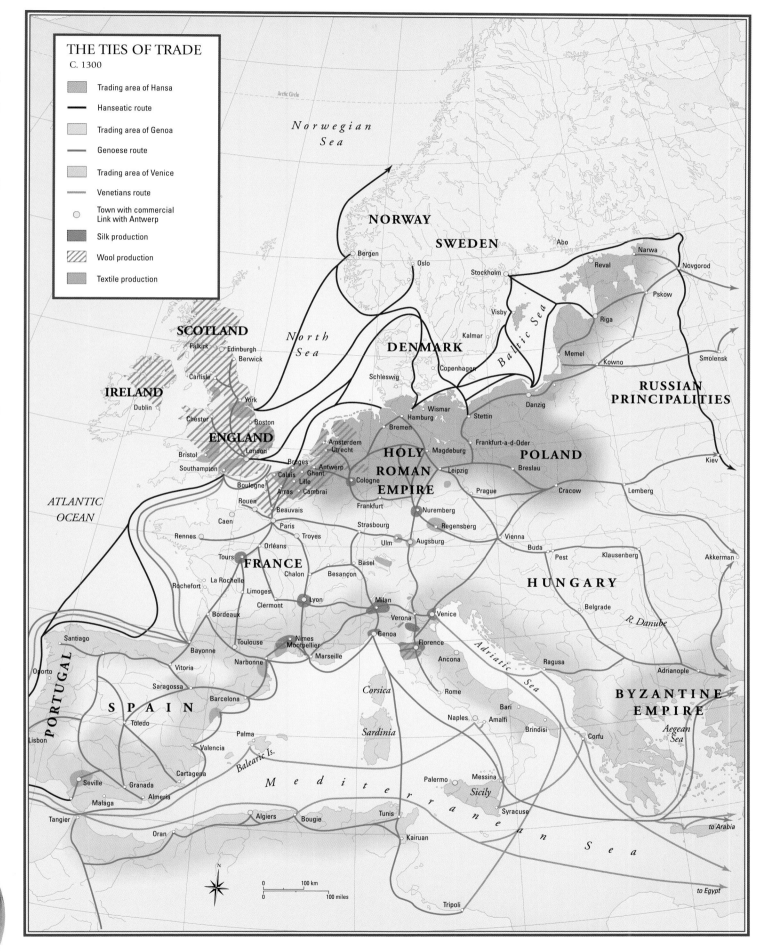

THE TIES OF TRADE
C. 1300

- Trading area of Hansa
- Hanseatic route
- Trading area of Genoa
- Genoese route
- Trading area of Venice
- Venetians route
- ○ Town with commercial Link with Antwerp
- Silk production
- Wool production
- Textile production

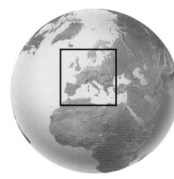

C.1000 – C.1500 CATHOLICISM AND ORTHODOXY

CATHOLICISM AND ORTHODOXY
During the time of the Roman Empire, Christianity was fairly widespread throughout Europe. After the Empire fell,

Christianity went into something of a decline, but the power of the Church in both Rome and Constantinople soon reestablished its influence.

By the Middle Ages, it had again spread throughout Europe, but had now been complicated by the Great Schism of 1054 that had split the church down the middle,

leaving the Catholic or Latin churches in the West and the Orthodox churches in the East. This was further complicated by Muslim expansion into much of the Iberian Peninsular.

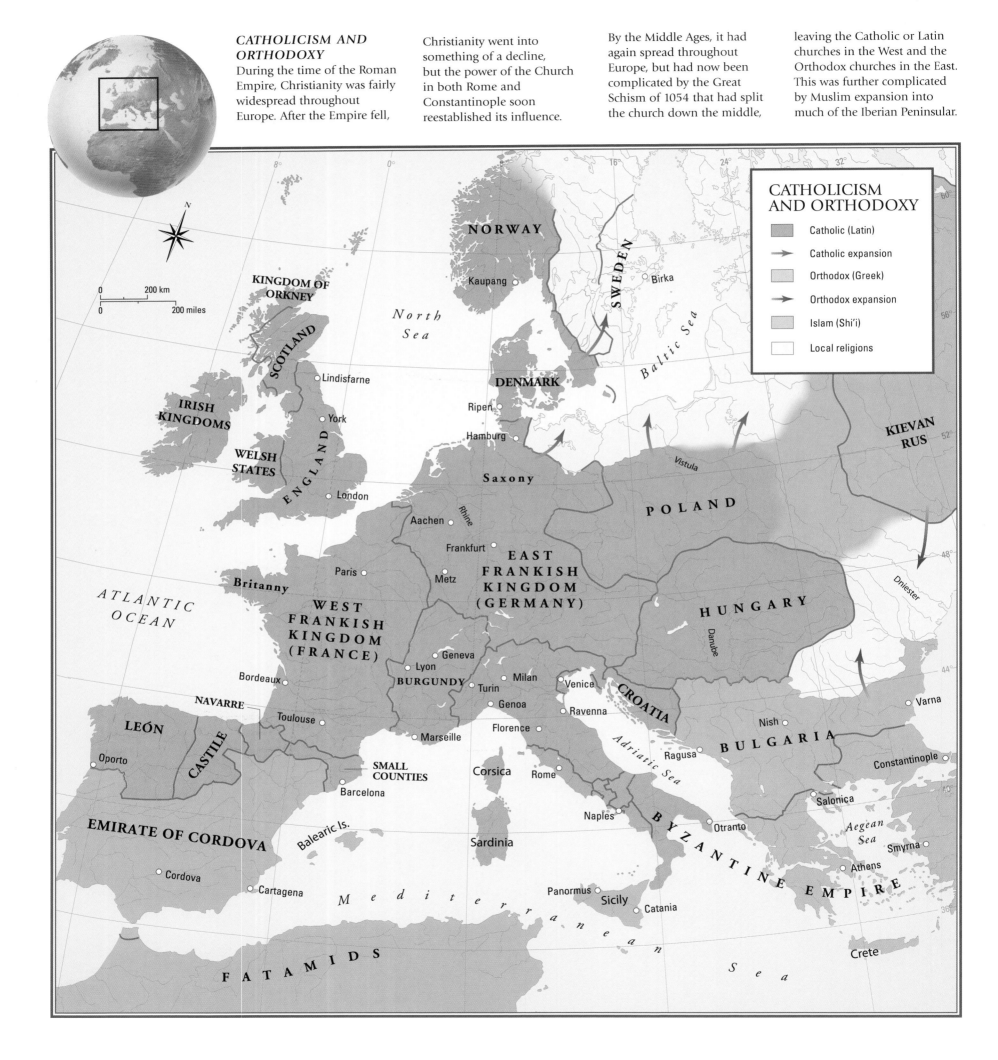

CATHOLICISM AND ORTHODOXY

- Catholic (Latin)
- → Catholic expansion
- Orthodox (Greek)
- → Orthodox expansion
- Islam (Shi'i)
- Local religions

NORWAY

SWEDEN

Kaupang

Birka

North Sea

Baltic Sea

KINGDOM OF ORKNEY

SCOTLAND

Lindisfarne

DENMARK

Ripen

KIEVAN RUS

IRISH KINGDOMS

York

Hamburg

Vistula

WELSH STATES

ENGLAND

Saxony

POLAND

London

Aachen

Rhine

Frankfurt

Paris

EAST FRANKISH KINGDOM (GERMANY)

HUNGARY

ATLANTIC OCEAN

Britanny

Metz

WEST FRANKISH KINGDOM (FRANCE)

Danube

Dniester

Lyon

Geneva

Milan

Venice

CROATIA

Bordeaux

BURGUNDY

Turin

Genoa

Ravenna

Varna

NAVARRE

Toulouse

Florence

Nish

LEÓN

CASTILE

SMALL COUNTIES

Rome

Adriatic Sea

Ragusa

BULGARIA

Constantinople

Oporto

Barcelona

Corsica

Salonica

EMIRATE OF CORDOVA

Balearic Is.

Sardinia

Naples

BYZANTINE EMPIRE

Otranto

Aegean Sea

Smyrna

Cordova

Athens

Cartagena

Mediterranean Sea

Panormus

Sicily

Catania

FATAMIDS

Crete

ITALY 1500

ITALY C.1500

By 1500, the glory that was Rome had long passed, and in the thousand or so years since the fall of the Empire Italy had fragmented. Although the Muslim Ottomans had moved into the Balkans, the various states that made up Italy were still staunchly Christian. The whole of southern Italy and Sicily were Spanish, although the French disputed this claim. Central Italy was made up of a collection of Papal States, while to the northwest a collection of Duchies and Republics all formed part of the Holy Roman Empire that stretched up as far as the Baltic. The Republic of Venice was to remain independent until 1797. Italy itself did not become a unified state until the nineteenth century.

ITALY C. 1500

- ☐ Italian states
- Ottoman Empire
- Italian/Christian territories
- ☐ Other states and territories
- — Border of the Holy Roman Empire

MAPS AND RECONSTRUCTIONS